Kathy
Best wishes
Sue Threefall
1996

ISBN: 1 85279009 -1

KINGDOM

GB-004

Published by Kingdom Books
P.O. Box 15
Waterlooville PO7 6BQ
England

Designed by Add Graphics
P.O. Box 15
Waterlooville PO7 6BQ
England

Printed in England

THE
World of Dogs
skye terrier

By

SINE

THRELFALL

FOREWORD

When anyone thinks of Skye Terriers the Isle of Skye immediately comes to mind.

Sine Threlfall has been involved with Skye Terriers since her childhood. Her beloved mother and mentor, Mary Macdonald, started Eilean Acheo kennels in 1959 - the only Skye Terrier kennel on the Isle of Skye at that time. Together they bred many nice dogs and started showing extensively, and their Acheo Skyes are now to be found in many countries around the world.

Following the death of her mother in 1976 Sine has maintained an active interest in breeding and showing, soon rising to the top and producing many champions. Her Acheo Skyes won great honour at Crufts 1995: Challenge Certificate (CC) in both sexes and Best of Breed (BOB). Her husband Allan and sons Colin and William have lent her great support.

My loving, long-time Skye friend has made "Skyedom" so worthwhile with her warmth, honesty and wonderful touch of humour. She has generously shared her friendship, wisdom and knowledge, ever ready to help and advise the sincere novice. She has written numerous articles on the breed and conducted a wide correspondence with Skye fanciers all over the world. She is adored for her tireless devotion to Skye Terriers and most highly respected as a breeder and judge in the United Kingdom today.

I truly believe that her book, Skye Terrier, is a great contribution to the Skye world. I know that I shall treasure this lovely book for ever.

Olga Smid
Olivia Skyes
(Established 1944 - Registered 1948)

CONTENTS

ACKNOWLEDGEMENTS

The author wishes to thank most sincerely all those who contributed photographs, information and encouragment for this book. In particular, special thanks are due to:

Miss Catherine Owen for feeding me with material from her own records;
Mr Clifford Boycott for sharing with me his treasured scrapbook and photographs;
Mrs Olga Smid for her help on the American Skye and on Eastern Europe and for her many photographs;
Mr Geoffrey Scott whose camera skills were put severely to the test;
Mrs Cathie McLeod who accompanied me on visits to Haddo House and the vast Warriston cemetery in Edinburgh to unearth information;
Huntly House Museum in Edinburgh for allowing me to use a photograph of Greyfriar's Bobby;
Mrs Iona Macdonald for supplying material on Allan Macdonald;
Dualchas for all their finds relating to the terriers of Skye;
Clan Donald Museum;
Donald John MacLennan MRCVS who advised on veterinary matters.

Finally, I should like to thank my family: Allan who encouraged me to stick to my task; Colin, without whom I could not have mastered that wizard of modern technology, the word processor; and Willie, whose efforts on the electric guitar served to keep me well out of his way thereby enabling me to complete my tome!

I have tried to present this book as accurately and truthfully as possible and believe that all the information contained therein is correct.

part **1**

*BRITISH
BACKGROUND*

*OWNERSHIP OF
THE*
**SKYE
TERRIER**

A unique Scottish ancestry

The Skye Terrier takes its name from the Island of Skye, which lies off the northwest coast of Scotland and is the largest of a group of islands known as the Inner Hebrides. The breed is known to be the oldest terrier breed of Scotland, going back to the fourteenth century at least. Terriers were needed wherever there were vermin and the best of these little dogs came from the far west coast in the Highlands of Scotland. It is almost impossible to trace the origin of the breed; to do so one has to piece together all the relevant information which has survived, mainly by oral tradition, for hundreds of years.

It is generally accepted that canine survivors of a wrecked man-of-war from the Spanish Armada bred with local terriers, producing a strain with a long, silky coat. Lady Macdonald of Armadale Castle certainly owned a kennel of terriers of this type. While this story is decidedly romantic there are a few discrepancies which ought to be considered. It is true that many ships from the Spanish Armada of 1588 found their way home blocked and had to sail round Britain, pursued by the English; several of these ships certainly came to grief on the hostile reefs around the coast of Scotland. The island of Raasay, just off Skye, is supposed to have been a haven for some of the survivors, who made their homes there, so it is not impossible to believe that a dog or two could have survived. How many would have been allowed aboard a man-of-war is debatable, however. In any case, the Macdonalds did not have a castle at Armadale until 1815, though the ruins of kennels remain from that time.

So, where did the Skye Terrier originate? It is unlikely that the tradition of the Armadale connection would have remained if it contained no truth whatsoever. However, the presence of terriers on the island is recorded prior to 1588, so we have to search further back in time. It is worth bearing in mind that the Western Highlands were first settled by the Picts from Ireland, followed by the Vikings. The Viking invasions were not all pillaging and raping as some stories suggest; the Vikings left their homes in Scandinavia to find a place in which to live, and many settled as far south as the Isle of Man.

Studies of the Vikings have shown that they took with them dogs which may also have had an influence on how the Skye Terrier developed. If one looks at the Drever, or Swedish Vallhund as it is better known in Britain, whose history goes back to Viking times, one can see that the body shape is similar to that of the Skye. Though the Vallhund is much more closely linked with the Corgi, the similarity to the Skye is one which must be considered. We may have something for which to thank the Vikings! Vallhund colouring is different, but brown Skyes are known to appear from time to time so we cannot dismiss the connection too hastily. Certainly Eilean A' Cheo, the Misty Isle, is well named, since the source of the Skye Terrier breed is hidden in the mists of time. In order to understand the geography of the island which gave its name to the breed it is also necessary to learn a little of its history.

Two Scottish clans dominate the story of Skye: the Macdonalds and the MacLeods. Over the years these clans fought a running war, their many bloody skirmishes furnishing material for still more legends of the Misty Isle. The chiefs of the clans were well educated men who led their clansmen in many famous battles. The clansmen, however, lived in poor conditions, barely managing to feed their families. When their chieftain wanted to put sheep on his land the people were turned out of their homes, some even being dispatched on ships to colonise Canada and America. Those who stayed behind settled on the coast, learning to fish in order to feed themselves. Despite their harsh treatment, the clansmen rallied when the call went out for troops, and fought till the bitter end.

The Macdonald chief lived in his castle at Duntulm, though earlier homes were found at Dunsgaith and Cnoc in the Sleat Peninsula. In 1670 the chief moved to Armadale in the

By kind permission of the Clan Donald Library.

Sir Alexander and Lady Alice Macdonald
of the Isles with Mr Connis

south of Skye, but in 1690 the house was burnt to the ground by troops of King William 111. This was an act of retribution against Donald, son of Sir Donald Macdonald, who had fought valiantly alongside Viscount Dundee (Bonnie Dundee) at the Battle of Killiecrankie in 1689. Although badly wounded, Donald had returned to Skye. After the fire the family returned to the castle of Duntulm, which was very damp and draughty by now, making frequent trips to a farmhouse in Armadale. Duntulm Castle was finally deserted in 1732, when the family was established at Monkstadt.

Sir Alexander Wentworth, 10th Baronet, 2nd Lord MacDonald and 17th Chief of Sleat, was born in 1773. In 1798 he built a new mansion in Armadale and made this his home. A family feud in 1799 resulted in a family split when

Godfrey, later to become 19th chief of the clan, eloped. When he died the titles fell to his second son, as his firstborn was alleged to be illegitimate according to English law. The family estates at Thorpe in Yorkshire were therefore given to the firstborn as compensation. Godfrey's grandson, Alexander Wentworth Bosville of Thorpe, married Alice Middleton in 1886, and when Alice investigated the case she found that the allegation of illegitimacy was quite false. Therefore, Alexander was reinstated as 21st Chief of Sleat in 1910 and known as Macdonald of the Isles. The clan now had two chiefs, the new one leasing 4000 acres of land in Duntulm and living in a house close to the ancient castle, which was excluded from the leasing agreement. The family home is nowadays better known as the Floddigarry Hotel. Sir Alexander and Lady Alice owned a Skye Terrier named Mr Connis. However, although she was a prolific writer, Lady Alice makes little mention of any dogs, so we are left not knowing his ancestry.

A Skye Terrier in his native landscape

Loyalties were obviously torn among the natives of Skye. An insight into the past comes to light in a letter Lady Alice wrote whilst on Skye in which she states: "We were constantly told of the extraordinary resemblance between Alex and the Chiefs of old, and our dog was a marvel to the people for never, they said, had such a dog been seen in Skye since the right people left." This statement is the only clue we have of similar dogs having been kept by the Macdonalds in days gone by.

In 1815 the castle at Armadale was built, becoming the home of the Clan Chief until 1934. Sadly very little of the castle remains today, but the Clan Donald Trust have made the grounds the Centre to which clan members from all over the world can come to trace their ancestry.

ORIGINS OF THE SKYE TERRIER

Research into the history of the Skye Terrier reveals the early existence of various types of terrier. Three examples of these are the Monkstadt, Drynochs and Camusunary, but these simply refer to the terriers kept on the estates belonging to the Macdonalds, Macleods and MacKinnons. The Macleods of Dunvegan were known to have owned terriers, but even Samuel Johnson, that most prolific of writers, who visited there in 1773, makes no mention of dogs, though he remarks on the abundance of otters, fox and weasel, which were no doubt dispatched by a pack of terriers. Captain Macleod of Drynoch also kept a pack of terriers, and Cairn Terriers are descended from these.

During the 17th century Farquhar Kelly of Drumfearn kept a strain of working terriers renowned for their hunting abilities, to which their scars bore witness. These were extremely game terriers who carried on their work regardless of losing an eye or a paw in battle. Farquhar Kelly always kept at least one white dog in his pack, despite the general opinion that this colour was of no use;

as white dogs were held to be unable to blend into the background they were usually put down at birth. These white terriers were just as efficient at their work, and were the progenitors of the most popular of the Scottish terrier breeds, the West Highland White Terrier. Another family of Kellys moved into Drumfearn from Borreraig in Dunvegan in the 1850s. They were the owners of another pack of terriers, known locally as the Kelly Terriers, but no description of these dogs has survived.

Photo: J Edwardss

Capt Allan Macdonald

The Waternish Terriers were the purest strain of terrier to be found on the island. The pictorial evidence of these terriers illustrates the typical working Skye, and a photograph of "Gleniffer" (1880) shows him very much a Skye, or he would be if he had a coat. That would have deprived him of his working ability, however. One must remember that the Waternish Terriers are behind the Cairn Terrier of today; Allan Macdonald of Waternish was an early president of the Cairn Terrier Club.

Allan Macdonald owned land in Arisaig on the mainland of Scotland opposite the Sleat Peninsula. In 1761 he married Jean MacKinnon of Corry in Skye, and their son, Allan, inherited the estate. Allan joined the army in 1799 and retired with the rank of Major in 1821, moving from Arisaig to Ostaig in Skye, which exhibitors today know as the venue for the Skye Terrier Championship Show every five years. With him he brought a pack of terriers. In 1832 he purchased the Waternish Estate where he took a great interest in building up the well known herd of Waternish Highland Cattle as well as working a pack of terriers for bolting otters from cairns under the sea cliffs of Skye, Harris and Uist. Major Allan had two sons, Patrick and Allan.

Allan obtained a commission in the 99th Regiment in 1848, joining his regiment in Tasmania and taking with him several terriers which are generally recognised as being the progenitors of the Australian Terrier. He returned to Britain in 1856 bringing back one terrier, which had sailed round the world, and which he left behind in Cork. Captain Allan Macdonald retired in 1857 and took up residence again at Waternish where he enjoyed the life of a gentleman on his estate which boasted an unusual variety of pets, including a tame deer and his fine pack of hunting terriers.

Patrick Macdonald emigrated to Canada in 1863. His son, Allan, was born there, but returned to live with his uncle at Waternish in 1880, eventually inheriting the estate. Allan continued to keep the terrier pack going as working dogs, but in 1909 this type of dog began to be exhibited at shows in the variety classes, with several Waternish dogs appearing at the Scottish Kennel Club show of 1912 as Cairn Terriers. There can be no doubt that this strain of terriers from Skye, the original Skye Terrier, is responsible for both the Cairn and the Australian Terrier we know today.

John Tolmie of Uignish (1793-1844) was a lover of animals and was known to have kept a kennel of Skye Terriers which were greatly sought after for their hunting abilities, and in particular for dispatching otters. Mention of Mr Tolmie is made by James Wilson in his book "A Voyage Round the Coasts of Scotland", published in 1842, in which he records receiving the gift of a black-faced sheep and a brace of Skye Terriers, which were named Uigish and Folliart. It is unfortunate that so little evidence of the breed known today as the Skye Terrier is to be found on the island of Skye, but we must be grateful for writers who have taken the time to describe their findings.

In the sixteenth century Caius wrote of "lap dogs which were brought out of the barbarous borders from the uttermost countryes northward, and they by reason of the length of their heare, make show neither face nor body, and yet these curres forsooth because they are so strange, are greatly set by, esteemed, taken up, and made of, in room of the spaniell gentle, or comforter". In the latter half of the sixteenth century the Bishop of Ross describes "a scenting dog, of low height, indeed, but of bulkier body, which when creeping into subterranean burrows, routs out foxes, badgers, martens and wild cats from their lurking places and dens".

Much later in 1860 Charles Richard Weld published a book of his travels in the Highlands, Orcadia and Skye in which he describes a journey from Sligachan to Kyleakin. He records that two miles from Broadford they realised that Captain Wood's Skye Terrier was missing. The dog is described as a charming little animal of the true breed, now very rare on the island. Despite the author's concern that the dog may be lost Captain Wood assured him that the dog was well known throughout Skye and frequently stayed behind waiting for the next mail car for a lift! As Captain Wood lived at Reraig near Balmacara the dog would have had to cross on the ferry and walk a further five miles before reaching home.

In 1878, the "Highlander" newspaper reported that a Mr Campbell of Portree had exported a number of Collies and Skye Terriers to a customer at the Zoological Gardens in Paris. There was a possibility of further orders.

Apart from written evidence the only other association with the island terriers comes from the celebrated Scottish landscape artist, Horatio McCulloch, who paid many visits to Skye to pursue his profession painting dramatic views of the Cuillins. During one of his trips to Skye he met his future wife, Marcella McLellan of Gillean, near the township of Tarskavaig. It is known that he had several Skye Terriers at his Edinburgh home and it is possible that he brought them from Skye with his wife.

A Skye Terrier found on the gravestone of Horatio McCulloch.

Horatio McCulloch's gravestone.

McCulloch had a number of paintings of his dogs, including one of Oscar by Macnee, Bessy by John Glass (which was exhibited at the Royal Scottish Academy in 1856), and a Skye Terrier by Thomas Duncan. After his death in 1856 Horatio McCulloch was laid to rest in Warriston cemetery in Edinburgh, and in 1873 a Celtic Cross was erected in is memory. At the base is a bas-relief of a palette, brushes and laurel wreath, while on the other side a Skye Terrier faithfully watches over his master.

THE EARLY DAYS OF THE SKYE TERRIER IN SCOTLAND

Although we have relatively little information from its native isle, the breed is fortunate to have had some extremely famous owners, so we have some information about their devoted dogs. The tragic Mary, Queen of Scots, after nineteen years of imprisonment by the English, was beheaded on the 8th February, 1587. While her clothes were being removed after the execution, the Queen's Skye Terrier crept out from under her skirts to position itself by the severed head of its mistress. The distressed dog was removed and bathed to remove any smell of the Queen's blood but, despite coaxing, refused to eat and died of a broken heart.

Greyfriars Bobby at the end of his life with Traill children.

Nearly three hundred years later, during the Indian Massacre of Cawnpore in 1857, an eye witness describes how sepoys stole guns, bags of rupees, gold watches and Skye Terriers. It seems almost incredible that Skye Terriers should have ventured as far as India until one realises that many soldiers and their families from Edinburgh were involved in the mutiny, and from the 1850s the Skye was the most popular dog to be found in both Edinburgh and Glasgow; no doubt some of them accompanied their families abroad.

The most famous Skye Terrier of all, Greyfriars Bobby, was born in 1856. Bobby was owned by John Gray, a police constable, and accompanied his master on duty as he patrolled the pens at the Cattle Market and Grassmarket to ensure that there were no thefts. The police were expected to patrol in pairs and to have a watchdog, which was bought for them by the constabulary. Bobby and his master had only had a short working life together when John Gray died of tuberculosis in 1858 and was buried in Greyfriars churchyard. For the next fourteen years Bobby kept a vigil by his master's grave, rejecting the Gray's home and preferring the shelter of a neighbouring gravestone.

Despite his lonely vigil Bobby had many friends who kept him well nourished. These included the Traill family, who owned a restaurant. In his later years, Bobby would stay overnight with the Traills. It was there that he died, by the Traills' fireside, when he was fifteen years old.

The story of Bobby's devotion caught the imagination of Scots from Inverness in the Highlands to the Scottish borders, and eventually his fame spread across the world. In 1912 Eleanor Atkinson wrote "Greyfriars Bobby", which became a best-seller, though her version is far removed from the actual story. In the 1960s Walt Disney made the film, "Greyfriars Bobby", based on Eleanor Atkinson's book. A Skye Terrier look-alike was cast in the leading part and became a celebrity in his own right. This canine film star was bought by the Chief Constable of Edinburgh, who later gave him to a children's home, where he lived until he was almost eighteen years old.

Today any visitor to Edinburgh should make time to go and see the statue erected in memory of Greyfriars Bobby in 1873 by Baroness Burdett-Coutts. It is situated at Candlemakers Row, close to Greyfriars churchyard, where John Gray is buried. A visit to Greyfriars churchyard should also be included; a memorial to Bobby, presented by the Dog Aid Society of Scotland, can be seen just inside the gates. The memorial was unveiled by the Duke of Gloucester in 1981. Friends of Bobby in America donated a gravestone which was erected in the

Robert Louis Stevenson and his father. c. 1850

churchyard in memory of John Gray. Huntly House Museum on the Royal Mile is also well worth visiting, as photographs of Bobby, his drinking bowl, collar, and other memorabilia kindly donated by the Traill family are on display.

Dr John Brown, a physician in Edinburgh, wrote several essays about his canine friends including one on Peter, his Skye Terrier. Dr Brown also campaigned for a Dogs Home to be set up for strays in Edinburgh. Unfortunately some Skyes were unwanted, for there was much poverty in the city in the mid 1850s. One stray found a welcome with Thomas Stevenson and was named Coolin. Thomas' son was just seven years old at the time but was to become one of the greatest adventure writers of all time, Robert Louis Stevenson.

Years later the eminent surgeon, Sir Walter Simpson, presented Louis and his wife Fanny with a black Skye Terrier. All his life Louis was plagued by ill health, having to spend winters "taking the air" in Switzerland. Naturally his dog, Wattie, went too, though he seemed none too impressed with hotels and lifted his leg wherever he fancied! Wattie was said to be much alarmed by his master's sledging activities, hiding his head in Fanny's shawl and occasionally peeping out to check that Louis was still in one piece.

Being a terrier, Wattie liked nothing better than a good scrap. This was rather one-sided in Davos, where the local dogs were obliged to wear muzzles at all times. In 1884, however, the Stevensons moved to Bournemouth, where Wattie continued his sporting activities, with many a serious injury testing the vet's skills; his opponents in England were not required to wear muzzles! His early death came about on the occasion when, still recovering from his latest hard battle, he launched into another offensive, which proved to be his last. His distraught owners were so heartbroken that they could never bring themselves to have another dog.

W H Naismith, founder of the Scottish Mountaineering Club, describes an expedition to Kingshouse in Glencoe in 1896. He and his companion cycled the one hundred and twenty miles from Edinburgh in two days, and on their arrival were greeted noisily by a Skye Terrier and two young Collies. They made their peace with the dogs by inviting them to share their dinner!

Charles St John in his book "Wild Sports and Natural History of the Highlands" writes of the Skye Terrier having a great deal of quiet intelligence, learning to watch his master's looks and understand his meaning in a wonderful manner. He goes on to describe the working Skye in great detail. The book is well worth reading, though modern conservationists will be horrified to learn of so many killings done in the name of sport.

THE DROP EAR SKYE TERRIER

Dog shows began in about 1860, and from then on it is possible to trace all the winners up to the present day through the official Stud Books. The earliest show dogs came from Scotland, some of them actually from Skye. Drop ears were in the majority until the turn of the century, when exhibitors favoured the prick eared variety. This is still the case today. Despite this preference the drop ear appears occasionally, though on the continent of Europe this seldom occurs because of the strict regulation which came into effect in 1934 forbidding the interbreeding of prick ear to drop ear dogs.

In most countries the drop ear is so unusual that it is treated as a novelty, but a great many Skyes have been drop eared, including the Countess of Aberdeen's Ch. Aberdeen Mike, Lassikin and Monarch of Haddo, Lady Marcia Miles' Ch Grey Dusk, Ch Merrymount Sundown, Sun Chariot and Sungleam, Lady Williamson's Elizabeth, Mrs L Austin's Ch Glenshiel Duchess, Mrs J

Bower's Ch Kirkleyditch Windflower and Miss N Bower's Ch Kirkleyditch Carbon Copy, Mrs L Hames' Ch Checkbar Dew Drop, Mr and Mrs Goose's Ch Coruisky Master Robbie, Evans' Ch Norwest Wandering Star and the American import Ch Skyecrest Lady of the Evening. In 1992 the sight of five drop ears at a British show caused quite a stir, and hopefully we shall see the original type return in numbers.

Some very fine drop ears have risen to the top in America, the outstanding Ch Milchrista's Doctor Pem having been a big winner in the sixties. He went on to sire several drops, many of which became champions, including Ch Malgrem's Missus and Ch Malgrem's Dr Pem 111. Ch Twin Town Sweet William, a cream drop, was the first of this colour to take his title in America, and Ch Teakwood's Dew Drop, Ch Dunvegan Cladich Brigadoon, Ch Skyecrest Rugby and Ch Skyecrest Lady Mona are all excellent specimens of the American drop ear.

In Sweden and Finland drop ears appear from time to time. Ch Floriando sired two drops, one of them being Silverprint Goodfellow at Esgia, who recently was imported into Britain. Ch Lollipops Good Locomotion and Ch Fairsky's Engel in My Heart gained their titles in Sweden, and Ch Suskey's Butterscotch and Ch Skyemoor Lucky Love in Finland.

In Australia the drop ear has become fairly common due to inbreeding as the available stock is limited. This has resulted in an above average number of drops, including Ch Danehill Gay Princess, Ch Skyeholm MacDougal, Ch Gardony Silver Melody, Raldoris Howdoee and Ch Skyeclan Bohemian Rhapsody. Those who have been lucky enough to own a drop ear will tell you that they are different from the prick eared variety. Having a Skye Terrier is a special experience, but having a drop ear defies description!

Choosing a
Puppy

Before you are tempted to view a litter of puppies, which you are sure to find irresistible, read as much as possible about the breed concerned. In the case of the Skye Terrier, however, very little material has been available in previous years. For further information it is advisable to contact a breeder through the Skye Terrier Club, the Kennel Club or the Scottish Kennel Club, who will direct you to breeders in your own area.

A typical puppy.

A visit to a breeder will give you an idea of what the breed looks like, and seeing some of the dogs should also give you an idea of the main characteristics of the breed so that you can go home and discuss among yourselves whether or not this is the breed for you. When you arrive home you may well think of several questions you wish you had asked, but do not be afraid to get in touch with the breeder again. You will find that good breeders welcome enquiries, as their main concern is to place puppies in suitable and reliable homes.

As the Skye Terrier comes in a variety of colours, some also having a different ear placement, how do you decide which to have? One way is visit a dog show where the breed is classified for exhibition. Details of forthcoming shows are published in the specialist weekly canine press, *Our Dogs* and *Dog World*, both of which are available from your newsagent. Information regarding shows may also be obtained from the above mentioned magazines.

On visiting a show a closer look at the breed will reveal that some Skye Terriers have prick ears and some have drop ears, though the latter are very scarce. Both ear placements are correct according to the official Kennel Club Standard of the Breed. There are also variations of colour and type. For example some dogs have ear

Time to play - Skye Terrier puppies come in a variety of colours, but they should all look alert and interested in their surroundings.

A Cream with pups.

fringes, and some do not, but all these things should be taken into consideration. You should also be prepared for some travelling as the type of Skye Terrier you want may be found at the other end of the country and you must be prepared to collect it.

A new owner should also be prepared to spend a great deal of time with the puppy and make sure it is not left alone for long spells; otherwise it may become destructive through boredom. In fact if all members of the household are out at work all day ask yourselves if you really want a dog at all. It is not fair to the animal, and many breeders will not sell a dog which is to be left alone for many hours, as this could eventually lead to many problems.

No doubt many of these things have already crossed your mind, and if you are still eager to own a Skye the next decision to make is whether it will be a pet or a show dog. Your pup may be bred from the very best bloodlines in the country, with a marvellous pedigree, and yet still be pet quality; not every puppy of top quality breeding is a future show dog. This does not indicate that there is anything wrong with the pup; simply that it just does not have that little bit extra which is needed to give it top show potential.

However, if you think that you would like to show your dog the breeder will advise you on the points to look for among the show quality puppies which are available. Unfortunately there can never be a guarantee that the puppy you buy at eight or nine weeks of age will develop into champion material. How a pup progresses through its growing stages is largely dependent on the owner.

Whether you are choosing a pet or a potential show puppy make sure you allow enough time to come to a unanimous decision on the one you want. If you have children look for one that is not overwhelmed by their antics. Some puppies in a litter may be quiet and slow in coming forward but this is not necessarily because they are nervous, rather that they are gentler in nature; these often become far more biddable dogs than the extroverts which are on a permanent high.

You must also make the decision whether to have a dog or a bitch. Many people believe a bitch to be quieter and more affectionate, and this may be so in other breeds, but the Skye Terrier male is extremely loyal, not a dog to wander away from his territory, and is less "bossy" than the female.

Many people who decide to have a bitch erroneously think that they should let her have a litter for the sake of her health. This is definitely not so. You should also take into account the fact that the Skye is a numerically small breed, still generally little known to the public, despite its long history. Selling puppies can therefore be quite difficult. Breeding a litter should not be looked on as a way of recouping the cost of the bitch and making a bit of profit.

What is the likely purchase price of your own puppy? Costs vary throughout the country but at the time of writing pups can be found for about £150 for a pet and up to £300 for a show prospect. Puppy prices, like all others, reflect the national economy and tend to increase rather than decrease.

When the pup has been chosen, check with the breeder that he, or she, has been wormed, as most puppies are infested. Worming is a simple procedure with tablets from a veterinary surgeon. You will also need to treat the puppy for worms as it grows older, and at regular intervals throughout its life. Your vet will advise you on this matter. If you live in the country where livestock is grazed it may be necessary to worm your dog more frequently than if you live in more urban surroundings.

Make sure that you are given a copy of your puppy's pedigree, and check that it is registered with the Kennel Club and that you have all the relevant papers. As puppy registrations sometimes take a few weeks the papers may have to be sent on to you, but when you receive the registration form you should transfer the puppy into your name; otherwise, in the eyes of the Kennel Club, it will still belong to the breeder. Transferring the puppy is particularly important if you intend to enter him at shows.

It is also important to check that your puppy is insured. Many breeders now insure their puppies for the first few weeks, and it is advisable to continue to do so by taking out an insurance policy of your own to cover future veterinary fees and other insurance risks. Also check whether your puppy has been vaccinated against distemper, hardpad, leptospirosis and parvovirus. Some veterinary surgeons recommend early vaccination and others prefer to wait until the puppy is twelve weeks of age.

If your pup has already been vaccinated you should receive a copy of the vaccination certificate. If he has not been vaccinated you must keep him away from other dogs, and do not take him outside your own property until he is fully covered. Your vet will advise you when it is safe for the pup to meet the big, wide world. In the meantime he will be quite happy in your own garden.

Three Finnsky pups: Tiffany, Teamwork and Tazzee.

care & Training

There are different methods of raising and caring for a Skye Terrier, and it is best for the owners to choose the way which fits in with their normal routines and life style.

HOUSE TRAINING

The Skye Terrier is a tough breed and is quite happy out of doors if you provide him with a dry kennel. However, you will probably prefer to have him in the house as a member of the family. You will often find your Skye prefers to lie against the door where he may find a slight draught, or he may try to lie under something such as a table. This habit can be traced back to the time when these earth dogs lay under stones or underground in a den which kept them safe and dry. Whatever the reason, the Skye feels safe under something, so don't think he feels rejected under a table - he prefers it!

Modern centrally heated houses can lead to dogs casting their undercoats as they have no need for them, so the house dog may have a thinner coat than those which are generally kept outdoors. A problem which arises with central heating is a proliferation of dust mites which can cause

The Skye is a tough breed, happy out of doors.

asthma in humans and skin problems in dogs. So there are several good reasons for having your dog out of doors, or perhaps just sleeping in an outside kennel at night.

In any case your puppy will need to become accustomed to the house and learn how to behave indoors so it is best to keep your newcomer inside or he will feel very lonely. When choosing a dog bed it is very useful to decide on a crate, which makes a comfortable bed and refuge for a puppy; once they get used to them dogs like them. Crates also allow the dog to be enclosed when necessary. They are actually indoor kennels, and well worth the investment.

Any new puppy may be fretful on the first night in his new home, whimpering or even howling the house down. Do not give in and take him to bed with you! Make sure he is warm (a hot water bottle under a blanket works wonders, but check that it is not so hot that it might burn him) and make sure he has emptied his bladder and his bowels before bedtime so that, hopefully, a good night's rest may be enjoyed by all. No animal likes to soil its own bed so he will soon learn not to dirty his bed or he will feel miserable.

Puppies like a selection of toys. The Nylabone range offers safe toys which are beneficial to the teeth and to the development of their jaws.

If you do not use a crate as a bed for your new puppy, barricade off an area, not too big, which he will soon recognise as his own territory. You may need to cover the floor with newspapers which the pup will soon learn to use. This is ideal for accidents which may happen overnight, but you will not want your puppy to become too adept at using newspapers or he will go out into the garden and come in to relieve himself on the papers.

Toilet training a puppy needs concentration on the part of the owner. You must be prepared to take him out first thing in the morning and last thing at night, regardless of the weather. He should be taken outside whenever he wakes from a nap, after eating and when he wanders into a corner or appears to be circling an area. Remember that puppies are babies and only gradually learn control; they are not born with it. You must be prepared to stay out with him until he has performed and praise him when he does, as this will greatly accelerate his progress. If you cannot be bothered to spend time outside with your puppy, training him will take much longer,

so work on it together. Be prepared for the occasional "accident", but before you scold your puppy stop and ask yourself if he is really to blame or were you in too much of a hurry to pay attention to him? Time spent in the early training days reaps rewards for ever.

Puppies like to play so a selection of toys should be available for him to chew. Take care to choose safe playthings which are not likely to be easily ripped apart or small enough to swallow. You will find suitable Nylabone toys in good pet shops, or at dog shows, and hopefully your pup will be happy to play with his own toys and will not chew up his master's favourite pair of slippers. If this happens the pup is not fully to blame, so don't be too hard on him. Of course you must teach your puppy right from wrong. This is very important or you will have a spoilt dog which is far worse than a spoilt child. If you have managed to raise children without them falling foul of the law you should find it easy to raise a puppy into a well behaved companion. If you haven't perhaps you should not have a dog.

The Skye needs to be taught from an early age what he may, and may not, be allowed to do. For example, if he barks every time the doorbell rings and you are quite happy with this behaviour, fair enough, but if you do not want him to you must reprimand him until he learns not to bark at the bell. Letting him do it as a

Teaching your puppy to walk on a lead can be quite simple if you start really early. Of course you should not take your pup out of your garden until his vaccination course is completed, but you can begin to get him used to his collar and lead during this time. A thin lightweight show lead and a cat collar are very useful for training

The Glenbrittle Heights "G" litter at the dining table.

puppy and then trying to change him when he is a year old will not work. Start as you mean to go on.

Never let your pup get away with any misdemeanour. Don't shout at him, but firmly let him know that what he is doing is wrong. When he does something right praise him with much fussing and reward him with a pat and kind words. He will soon learn what is right or wrong by the tone of your voice and every dog delights in pleasing his master or mistress.

puppies. Start by putting on his cat collar for a short time each day so he will get used to it. If he is distressed by this try to make a game of it, encouraging him until he is happy to comply.

When your pup is happy wearing his collar try adding the lead. "Walkies" round the garden are the next steps to take. Be patient, encouraging and praising, and don't forget to reward your pup for good behaviour. Sometimes it is better to ignore a small misdemeanour, but never, never forget to praise your puppy for something good....even if he is not a brilliant student!

The earlier you start lead training the easier it is. If for some reason you do not introduce a collar and lead until the pup is several months old you may find that at the first attempt he behaves like a rodeo horse. Should this happen try to calm him down or he may work himself into a panic, the memory of which will remain with him for many months to come. Take lead training and all new ventures slowly, and just for a short time each day, until your puppy gains confidence.

Dinner time.

FEEDING

Whichever method you choose to feed your puppy one thing is certain; he must be given plenty of food so that his bone development and growth rate are normal. Routine is very important in a dog's life so meals should be

Drop eared Dougie lunches with prick eared pot-bellied pigs.

offered at the same time each day. There are two excellent methods of feeding puppies and adult dogs well, but whichever method is chosen please remember that it is vital that your dog always has access to a bowl of clean drinking water.

The first feeding plan is the traditional one which has been followed for many years and which includes eggs, milk, cereals, fish and meat. For example:

Breakfast 9 a.m: Cereal (Farex or Weetabix) and milk, either goat's or cow's milk, or a little scrambled egg.

Lunch, 12 noon: Some Puppy meal (wholemeal biscuit) soaked with gravy, plus minced beef.

Dinner 6 p.m: As noon feed.

Supper: Repeat of morning feed.

To the above cereal foods some honey may be added, or fish (no bones, please) may be substituted for the meat at one meal. Extra vitamins should be added to the above diet, SA37, Canovel, or Stress being suitable products which may be obtained from your veterinary surgeon, pet shops or at dog shows.

How much does one give to an eight week old puppy? A litter of puppies feeding together clean up everything in sight! A single puppy which rapidly cleans his dish should be offered more. If a puppy does not finish his food perhaps you have offered him too much. Puppies vary a little so there is no hard and fast rule; use your own judgment.

At ten to twelve weeks of age the pup may start to go off his breakfast feed. Do not worry but increase his lunch-time meal according to his growth rate. Puppies should not be thin; neither should they be over fat. They are individuals and growth rates vary a little. Weigh your puppy weekly if you like to keep such records. Stand on your own scales with the pup and subtract your own weight from the total. That is much easier than trying to get him to sit on a scale!

By the time the pup is nine months old he may want only one main meal a day, usually in the early evening, and perhaps a snack or a drink of milk at breakfast time. Remember to increase his meals in content as they reduce in numbers. Not many people feed their dogs tripe or heart from the butcher these days. Generally people choose canned food for their dogs and most of these, but not all, need to have biscuit meal added to balance the diet. However, always read the labels on pet foods to check how they should be presented to your dog. One or two canned products are actually complete foods and recommend that you do not add extra biscuit or vitamin products to them. Over vitaminisation is as bad as lack of vitamins, so always check and if necessary ask your vet for advice.

There is also a more modern approach to feeding dogs. This method uses what are known as "complete dry foods." Dried dog foods are available nationwide and are a clean, convenient and excellent method of feeding as they really are complete and need no supplementation at all. They contain all the vitamins and minerals the dog needs so there are no extras to buy. Dry dog foods are available for puppies, or adult dogs, in pellet or flake form. The only extra necessity is that bowl of clean drinking water which must always be available for your dog. This is of particular importance if you use the dry feeding method.

Dry dog foods have no unpleasant smell to them, do not go stale if not eaten right away and the puppy varieties may be offered to pups at weaning time according to the directions on the boxes or sacks. Used as directed they are excellent products ensuring good growth and bone development. They are also very easy to use as they take the guesswork out of balancing your dog's diet.

Giving your pup scraps and treats is acceptable, but not while you are sitting at the table or you will be teaching your dog bad habits. Add them to the pup's meal. A nice big marrow bone is a treat your pup will relish, and it may help his teething not to mention keeping him quiet for an hour! Never give dogs chop or chicken bones as these can splinter and cause severe problems, or even death to the dog. Hide chews are readily available from pet shops and some dogs relish them, but they have their dangers too so do not leave your dog alone with one in case he chokes on it.

A dog which chews is generally trying to tell you that he is bored and has nothing to do. Despite the scolding he receives from you he prefers this to being left alone. If this is a problem

for you please take your dog into account. If you have to be away from him for a long period make sure you give him a good walk first and leave him some food and water. He may decide not to eat it until you get home, but at least he can think about it and maybe not chew up the house!

Willie Threlfall with Spit.

EXERCISE

Exercise is important but it is not necessary to take a young puppy for long walks; in fact it can be harmful to little legs. He will get plenty of exercise playing during the day. It has often been noticed that puppies who are over exercised when very young develop "Skye limp" between the age of five to twelve months. If this happens plenty of rest is advised until the limp disappears. When the pup is over a year old and has stopped growing walks may be resumed.

The adult Skye loves to walk and can go for many miles without tiring, chasing rabbits, paddling through streams, rolling in heather. If you make this a regular habit your dog will soon tell you that he is ready and raring to go, so you must be prepared to oblige. It will keep you fit as well.

Children and dogs have always had a special relationship though scaremongers would have us believe the two are incompatible. Parks are places where dogs love to run and kiddies love to play. We must make sure that our dogs are wormed regularly and remove any offending matter left by them when out exercising thereby

Cecil v Toswiesenhof enjoys jumping over obstacles as part of his obedience training.

When you return from a walk make sure you remove any twigs, heather or other detritus from your dog's coat to prevent tangles from forming. If your dog has got very muddy you will find that as he dries out you can simply brush the dust out of his coat. If you have been to the beach the same routine must be followed. Dogs should be allowed to swim if they wish. A rinse in fresh water afterwards and a touch of conditioner, such as you would use on your own hair, should restore the balance of the coat. The gentle use of a hair dryer helps, and if you get your dog used to this from an early age he will love having his coat groomed.

CHILDREN

Skye Terriers and children make great companions for each other. Despite the length of coat the Skye will take any amount of pulling from even a small child who knows no better. But nowadays the position of the dog in society is being threatened by anti-dog campaigners who are only too happy to bring the dog into disrepute. It is up to us to raise our dogs to be models of decorum and to be prepared at all times to make sure that they do not get a bad name.

preventing any possibility of a child becoming infected with Toxocara canis. If the eggs of the roundworm, Toxocara canis, are eaten by a human after they have matured for several days outside the body of a dog they can hatch inside that person's body. The resulting larvae will move through the body to various organs and can sometimes reach the eye. In very rare cases this can cause blindness, especially in children. Whilst this sad circumstance is rare, we as dog owners have a responsibility to ensure that it cannot happen, by keeping our pets clear of worms and by removing any mess they may make. Unfortunately, some uncaring owners let their dogs roam free and thus cause resentment against all dogs.

Children who are brought up in a house with a dog soon learn to be sensible with it. Tiny children will grab at anything and the Skye understands this and will rarely take issue. If it is too painful for the dog he is more likely to look so miserable that you will see his discomfort and rush to his aid. There is no point in separating the two as the Skye will quickly learn to keep out of the child's way if he or she is persistent. Very soon the two will be inseparable, especially at the child's meal time when the Skye will soon learn that a source of titbits is readily available! It is children who have no contact with animals who get excited and scream and thus alarm dogs which may react badly.

If you hope to show dogs, it is worth remembering that children are welcome at shows too. However, it can be a very long day for a child unless a supply of games, food and drink are packed and taken along to relieve boredom. You will not be bored, in fact the hours whizz past, but it can seem like forever to your child. Fortunately many children become interested in Junior Handling classes which are held at many shows and, in fact, the youngsters take it very seriously and are so accomplished they could teach their elders a few lessons about handling! The top junior handlers from all over the world come to compete in the finals at Crufts and some may go on to become the professional handlers of the future.

WORKING THE SKYE

The Skye Terrier is no longer a working dog in the true sense of the word. In fact he went out of fashion in the early years of the century, though one estate used Skyes much later on. The fall in popularity was due partly to their becoming a fashionable show dog, but mainly because the Skye had developed into a much bigger specimen by then and could no longer get into small cracks and crevices to flush away the quarry. The plucky little Jack Russell took over the job as the gamekeeper's favourite terrier particularly in the Highlands of Scotland.

More recently one Skye found a rewarding way of working as he became a PAT (Pets as Active Therapy) dog. Champion Coruisky Master Robbie, a top winning drop ear, used to accompany his owner when she visited the residents of the High Haven Home for the Elderly in Downham Market, Norfolk. Not only did the residents enjoy these visits and recall many happy times when they themselves had pets but Robbie, too, received much satisfaction in their company, not to mention enjoying all the titbits which came his way!

Skyes are very intelligent dogs and therefore thrive on doing things which exercise both mind and body. Several of the breed have excelled in obedience work and more people are taking up agility competition with their dogs. Agility is a fairly new canine interest, but one which has caught the fancy of huge numbers of exhibitors. It is also great fun with the dog learning to jump over and through various obstacles in as fast a time as possible. This sport has gained great popularity with small breeds and their enthusiasm is a joy to see. Dogs are not allowed to begin agility training until they are one year old, and may not compete before they are eighteen months. This is a sensible protection measure for growing puppies and allows time for the proper development of their bones.

Obedience work is very rewarding for both dog and owner. Teaching your dog basic commands such as SIT and STAY may seem quite simple but success is not always achieved without attendance at training classes. Learning how to give commands is important, and when it is done in the right manner you will have a dog which obeys you. As many of the larger breeds also go to obedience training it gives your dog the chance to mix with bigger dogs and learn that there is no need to start a scrap which some terriers find a novel way of entertainment! Perhaps if obedience classes had been around in the days of Robert Louis Stevenson his dog Wattie's early demise may have been averted! For details of all training classes in your area consult your local canine association. An enquiry to the Kennel Club will provide you with the name of the secretary.

Exercising your Skye should be beneficial to both you and your dog. There is nothing the Skye likes better than to go for a walk; whatever the weather he is ready. One Skye walked the West Highland Way, a journey of ninety-five miles, with her owners. The walk was spread over a week with no ill effects to the Skye, which is more than can be said for her mistress!

Snow brings out the kid in most people and Skyes just love it. Although it is great fun to watch the antics of the dog, and to see the state of his short legs as the snow turns them into huge snowballs which make movement difficult, care must be taken to remove all the snow from the coat after the game. This necessitates standing the dog in the bath and with a warm shower spray melting the snow off the affected parts otherwise the dog may suffer a nasty chill. Towel dry him and finish the job with an electric hairdryer and his hairbrush and comb. He will then be comfortable and look beautiful again.

Swimming is an excellent pastime and Skyes are generally good swimmers. Some breeders are horrified at the thought of their dogs swimming in salt water, but having lived near the sea all my life I can safely say that I have never seen it harm the coat if the dog is rinsed with fresh water afterwards.

Though the true working instinct has mostly disappeared from the breed the Skye, like all dogs, likes to chase rabbits, birds and even cats from the garden. This is quite acceptable when the dog is under control within the confines of your own property but owners should be very careful if the dog is allowed to roam free when in the country. For the dog brought up in the country the laws will have been strictly enforced from the start, but the town dog has no idea that the field full of sheep is not there for his amusement! On no account let your Skye loose without first checking the countryside for the presence of livestock. If a dog is caught in a field full of sheep, or other livestock, it could be shot. Unfortunately the countryside is a very dangerous place for dogs, so follow the code of practice to ensure that all is well.

In Britain today certain breeds of dog have received a very bad press, whether or not it is warranted. It is the responsibility of the owners of all dogs to keep them under control at all times, and never let a situation get out of hand. With care and good management your dog will gain more admirers than foes, and the work you have done in training him or her will have been a most rewarding experience.

Grooming
& Showing
your Skye

When you decided to have a Skye terrier you were obviously quite prepared to spend some time grooming or you would have bought a smooth coated breed. However, the Skye's coat should not be too much trouble if you follow a few simple rules and start to introduce your puppy to the brush and comb at an early age when he will take everything in his stride.

Grooming is easier if you stand your puppy on a table as he will not want to jump off from a height and you can reach every part of his

soft puppy coat will begin to disappear and the harder adult coat grow in. Extra careful attention to grooming is advisable during a coat change as this is always a danger period for knots and tangles.

As the puppy's adult coat comes in you may be able to make a parting down his back with a comb. A tail comb is useful for parting the coat, or you may use a knitting needle which is also a popular tool. Skyes normally have the correct hard coat which causes no problems, but occasionally a soft coated one turns up and the

Grooming: from wet dog to potential champion.

coat comfortably. If you put a rubber mat on the table it will stop the pup from slipping. Most exhibitors use a professional grooming table which can be purchased at shows, but most new owners manage with what they have already before deciding on that investment; a card table will do.

The puppy's breeder should have shown you what type of brush and comb is best for a Skye's coat. You need to groom through the hair thoroughly, not just gloss over the surface. It is better to prevent matts with correct grooming than to sort them out after they have developed. By the time your pup is five or six months old the

latter coat type will need constant attention to keep it tangle free. Provided your Skye is kept clean and dry his coat should need very little attention. The places to watch carefully are behind the ears where the hair is softer, and under the legs which are ideal places for twigs and heather to stick and cause matts to form. Always check your dog's coat when you come back from walks. It takes only a few minutes and can save a lot of grooming time.

There are no hard and fast rules about how often you should bath your dog. An old fashioned belief was that one should never bath a dog as it would permanently remove the natural oils present in the coat. Did those who shared that belief never wash their own hair? One does wonder! Of course you should bath your dog when necessary, and it is good idea to introduce a puppy to the bathing procedure at quite an early age so he will not fear it later on.

It is usually most convenient to bath the dog in your own bath, using a hand held shower spray. Please remember to put a rubber mat in the bath so that the puppy does not slip and slide on the shiny surface and choose a mild shampoo, either one which is specially prepared for pets or one you use yourself. Use lukewarm water, take great care not to get soap in the puppy's eyes and plug his ears with cotton wool to prevent water getting inside them.

You may have to lather him twice to cleanse his coat properly but be sure to rinse him thoroughly each time. It is also a good idea to use conditioner on his coat as this helps to stop tangling and is essential if you are going to use an electric hair dryer. When the bathing operation is complete, wrap him in a large towel to blot up most of the moisture and then take him somewhere so that he can have a really good shake! You will not want a wet puppy running all over your best carpet or jumping exuberantly on the furniture so this is a situation when a crate is very useful. Pups are always excited after their baths. When he calms down a little introduce him gently to the hair dryer.

Professional canine hair dryers are available, along with all other grooming equipment, at championship dog shows. They are also often advertised in the weekly dog press. Such equipment may seem quite expensive but it is also very efficient and long lasting as regular exhibitors and groomers will testify. However, your own hair dryer will suffice at first and the procedure of blow drying the coat is not difficult once you get used to it and the dog learns that it is a pleasant procedure for him. Brushing his coat as it dries creates the perfect finish.

Be prepared for your young puppy to find the bathing and blow drying procedure rather

alarming at first. Encourage him with kind words and gentle handling. If he does not like having his face dried don't persist; leave it till last when it will almost have dried by itself and may need only a few finishing touches. The adult dog needs to be groomed out completely after a bath with the parting down his back to finish the picture. Nothing looks nicer than a clean, shining coat perfectly groomed. Dogs which are bathed regularly soon become used to it and enjoy it. After all it is a time when they have your undivided attention, and all dogs love that!

How often should you bath your dog? Just as often as you feel the dog needs it. Show dogs are bathed before each show, which may be quite frequently. Others need bathing as soon as they look dirty. It depends on where you live, your

dog's lifestyle and the vagaries of the weather. Bathing is definitely not harmful and is part of all-over beauty treatment and general health care. For example, bath time is also the convenient time check for tartar on the dog's teeth. There should not be any on a puppy's teeth but an older dog may need to have it removed. After the bath check the length of the dog's nails; they will need to be cut if they are too long. Regular road exercise may help to keep his nails short, but they may need cutting sometimes. If you do not know how to do this ask a breeder, or your vet, to show you. It is not difficult, but you must be careful not to cut the quick which can be quite painful.

SHOWING YOUR DOG

The Kennel Club publishes an official Breed Standard for every breed of pedigree dog and this is the blueprint against which dogs are judged when they are exhibited in the show ring. All breeders and exhibitors need to be familiar with the Breed Standard which is reproduced here, by kind permission of the Kennel Club:

THE SKYE TERRIER BREED STANDARD

General Appearance: Long, low and profusely coated, twice as long as high. Moves with seemingly effortless gait. Strong in quarters, body and jaw.

Characteristics: Elegant and dignified.

Temperament: A "one-man" dog, distrustful of strangers, never vicious.

Head and Skull: Long and powerful, strength not sacrificed for extreme length. Moderate width at back of skull, tapering gradually with slight stop to strong muzzle. Nose black.

Eyes: Brown, preferably dark brown, medium in size, close set and full of expression.

Ears: Prick or drop. When prick, gracefully feathered, not large, erect at outer edges and slanting toward each other at inner edge, from peak to skull. When drop, larger, hanging straight, lying flat and close at front.

Mouth: Jaws strong and level with perfect, regular scissor bite, i.e. upper teeth closely over-lapping the lower teeth and set square to the jaws.

Neck: Long and slightly crested.

Forequarters: Shoulders broad, close to body, chest deep, legs short and muscular.

Body: Long and low, back level. Ribcage oval, deep and long. Short loin. Sides appear flattish due to straight falling coat.

Hindquarters: Strong, full, well developed and well angulated. Legs short, muscular and straight when viewed from behind. No dew claws.

Feet: Forefeet larger than hind, pointing truly forward. Pads thick, nails strong.

Tail: When hanging, upper part pendulous and lower half thrown back in a curve. When raised, a prolongation of incline of back, not rising higher nor curling up. Gracefully feathered.

Gait/Movement: Legs proceed straight forward when travelling. When approaching, forelegs form a continuation of straight line of front, feet being same distance apart as elbows. Principal propelling power is furnished by hind legs which travel straight forward. Forelegs moving well forward, without too much lift. Whole movement termed free, active and effortless and gives a more or less fluid picture.

Coat: Double. Undercoat short, close, soft and woolly. Outercoat long, hard, straight, flat and free from curl. Hair on head shorter, softer, veiling forehead and eyes. Mingling with side locks, surrounding ears like a fringe and allowing their shape to appear.

Colour: Black, dark or light grey, fawn, cream, all with black points. Any self colour allowing shading of same colour and lighter undercoat, so long as nose and ears are black. A small white spot on chest permissible.

Size: Ideal height 25-26 cms (10 ins), length from tip of nose to tip of tail 103 cms (41.5 ins). Bitches slightly smaller in same proportions.

Faults: Any departure from the foregoing points should be considered a fault and the seriousness with which the fault should be regarded should be in exact proportion to its degree.

Note: Males animals should have two apparently normal testicles fully descended into the scrotum.

The Kennel Club © March 1994

Most people show dogs as a hobby, but even so they are very serious about it. Be warned, it can be both addictive and quite expensive, and it is very easy to get hooked!

usually fit easily on the bench. In fact a purpose-made dog crate is an essential and excellent purchase, serving as bed, haven, and even dining room for your dog, at home or away.

Cladich The Laird at Wemoway, b 12/7/92 (Am Ch Candlewick Printers Devil ex Am Ch Candlewick Witch and Famous) at the Eastbourne Open Show 1994, handled by his owner, Mrs M Barraclough.

Photo: S M Zabawa

Apart from the price of a potential show quality puppy you need to be prepared to spend a con-siderable amount on petrol driving around the country to each show. You need a reliable car to do so, or a friend who is also interested in showing with whom you can travel and share the expenses. This cuts down travelling costs by at least half. Entries cost from approximately £12-£15 a time, with an average of two championship shows a month in the spring and summer and several other shows, including Crufts Dog Show, in the autumn and winter. Show entry fees, like all costs, rise regularly.

Equipment can set your bank balance back, too, should you decide to buy a dog crate, grooming table and trolley. If you have never exhibited before you may think this equipment is totally unnecessary. Of the above mentioned equipment the crate is the immediate necessity for the comfort and security of your dog, both during travel and at the show, where it will

A steady folding card table, with a rubber mat on top, can do temporary duty as a grooming table both at home and at shows, until you have decided whether you will be a regular exhibitor and have had the chance to look around at the equipment available. For example, some of the professional grooming tables do double duty, serving also as a trolley on which to transport your caged dog from the car into the show-ground and folding flat for easy storage when not in use. Many dog shows are very large affairs; the walk from the car park to the benches can be a long haul and seem like half a mile or even longer in bad weather, so a trolley to carry all your gear really helps. Browse around the trade stands at shows and compare prices, but be sure this is the hobby for you before you invest in expensive items.

RINGCRAFT

Where should you begin? In most parts of the country there are registered canine societies which run ringcraft classes and they are a wonderful way of introducing your dog to other dogs and making a new group of friends all of whom have the same interest. Such classes introduce the novice dog and owner to the ring procedure which is followed at all shows. It also gives the newcomers, both dogs and owners,

Ch Mariquita Flashback (Dog CC, BOB and Reserve Group) and Ch Mariquita Flashfleur (Bitch CC) with judge Marion Crook.

confidence which makes show outings enjoyable. Details of your area canine society may be obtained from The Kennel Club, 1 Clarges Street, Piccadilly, London W1Y 8AB.

At ringcraft classes show conditions are simulated and as different people act as "judge" for the occasion it gives a variety of experiences for the novice dog so that he will not be upset by real show conditions. Breeders of many years standing take their new pups out to these classes to introduce them to the show procedure: a good indication of the high value put on ringcraft training. Occasionally the ringcraft section may organise matches, which are very enjoyable com-

petitions. The idea is that everybody should have a good time and learn how to present their dogs to the best advantage. It certainly helps wash away nervous barriers.

Once you have attended a few sessions at ringcraft classes you become an addict, and you may feel that your dog completely fits the requirement of the Breed Standard and is a certain champion. You just can't wait to get him into the ring to take all the honours waiting out there.....but TAKE IT SLOWLY! When you think you are ready to enter competition you will find that all shows are advertised in the weekly dog press, *Our Dogs* and *Dog World*, and if you are already a member of your breed club you will be notified by the secretary of forthcoming club events.

It is best to start with a Limited or Open show. There may not be a class for Skye Terriers but you can enter in the variety classes. If you are lucky enough to find a breed class you will be able to compare your Skye with others. Always be critical of your own dog. The perfect specimen has not yet been bred and it is unlikely to be yours, so do not blame the judge if you are unplaced, or blame the dog for failing to win the first prize. Remember, it takes a dog and handler who complement each other. What one judge likes another may dislike. There is always another judge, another show, another day. Always take rejections with good grace and success with modesty. If you have done well at your first show it will be difficult to stop you wanting to enter others. If you have not done well, try again anyway. We all have our less successful show outings.

You may soon feel the time has come to try a Championship Show, and qualifying for Crufts, the Kennel Club's own show, will then become the target. Crufts is the only show for which entrants have to qualify by winning at another Championship Show, which gives it extra prestige. Every dog at Crufts has won his right to be there. Most Championship Shows have a good selection of classes, some of which will suit your requirements. Entries close several weeks before the event so make sure you watch the forthcoming show advertisements in the weekly dog press and apply for a schedule and entry forms in good time. Enter your dog in classes suited to his age and experience. When the big day comes both you and your dog will be caught up in the excitement of the event. People arrive at the show with trollies loaded with crates of dogs, breeds you may have never seen before, all doing the same as you and hoping to win. It has to be said, this is the big time, and the big guns will be out with first prizes in their sights. They have been around a lot longer than you and know all the ropes. As you struggle through the lower classes, grateful for a third place, you are no threat. If, however, you start to win firsts with a good dog you will soon find that, though there are well mannered people who are pleased to congratulate you on your good fortune, others may be rather jealous. Such is life! Never let other people's poor sportsmanship upset you.

A winner of another sort: Obedience Ch Princess Natasha Playmoor CDX.

Show days can be long and tiring as well as busy and rewarding in experience. Although refreshments may be bought at shows it is always a wise plan to pack some emergency rations for yourself and your dog. Above all remember your dog's drinking bowl and a bottle of water. There will be water points at shows, but probably not conveniently placed when your dog is desperate for a drink. Allow extra time for travelling, and plan to arrive early, as queues often build up at the entrance to the showground. Planning for your own, and your dog's, creature comforts will make show days more fun for both of you.

Finally, while not wanting to deter you from showing, I must point out that only those who have good dogs are likely to get anywhere. If you find you are always at the wrong end of the line when the winners' rosettes are handed out, think seriously about saving yourself a bit of money, or if you have space for another dog try and buy a better one. By now you will have a much better idea of what to look for, and will have been recognised as a serious exhibitor and future breeder. Genuine, caring breeders will recognise your plight and, as you will have gained some valuable experience, you should be able to find someone who is willing to part with a good show prospect.

The most important thing to remember is your dog. If he does not enjoy shows, however good he is, then let him stay at home for a while. You can always try showing again later and he may enjoy it after a break. Do not take yourself too seriously. After all, the breed has flourished for hundreds of years and will continue to do so, and dogs are remembered long after their show days are over by the appearance of their names in pedigrees.

ENTERING YOUR SKYE AT SHOWS

A visitor to his very first show may think he is watching the canine equivalent of a beauty contest. While it is true that a top class dog in full coat is indeed a beautiful picture, it wins on its breed type, construction and movement. Championship Shows are the most important events in the canine exhibition calendar.

Each breed has its own Breed Standard which describes the perfect dog, but as the perfect dog in any breed has never yet been born the exhibit most closely fitting the judge's interpretation of the ideal Skye will win the Challenge Certificate, the CC, at a Championship Show.

In Britain a dog needs three Challenge Certificates awarded by three different judges to qualify for the title of champion. In the course of a year the Kennel Club grants twenty sets of Challenge Certificates for Skye Terriers which are offered at Championship Shows throughout the country. This may give you the impression that it is easy to make up a champion, but believe me it is not. So how do you go about it?

Skyes are usually given about twelve classes at Championship Shows, six for dogs and six for bitches. The following classes could be scheduled:

Puppy: For dogs of six and not exceeding twelve calendar months of age on the day of the show.

Junior: For dogs of six and not exceeding eighteen calendar months of age on the day of the show.

Novice: For Dogs which have not won a Challenge Certificate or three or more first prizes at Championship Shows (Puppy, Special Puppy, Minor Puppy, and Special Minor Puppy Classes excepted, whether restricted or not.)

Post graduate: For dogs which have not won a Challenge Certificate or five or more First Prizes at a Championship Show in Post Graduate, Minor Limit, Mid Limit and Open Classes, whether restricted or not.

Limit: For Dogs which have not won three Challenge Certificates under three different judges or seven or more First Prizes in all at Championship Shows in Limit and Open Classes, confined to the breed, whether restricted or not, at shows where Challenge Certificates were offered for the breed.

Open: For all dogs of the Breeds or Varieties for which the class is provided and eligible for entry at the show.

Choose the appropriate class, or classes, for your dog from the show schedule, which should be obtained from the show secretary, and enter him, enclosing the appropriate fee. Entries for all types of shows, except Exemption Shows which are local events run in aid of charity and are good training grounds for the inexperienced, close several weeks before the show, so be careful not to miss the closing date. Dogs are always judged first, followed by bitches, so if you have a male arrive at the show venue in plenty of time to allow for parking, the long walk into the showground and, in the case of a benched show, finding your bench.

MAKING UP A CHAMPION

If your dog wins his class at a Championship Show and is not beaten in another class, he will be called in with the other first prize winners (unbeaten dogs) to compete for the Challenge Certificate. When the judge has awarded the CC the Reserve Challenge Certificate (RCC) winner is chosen. It is possible that a dog which has only been beaten by the CC winner may be called into the ring to compete for the RCC, so if you have won a second prize in your class stand by just in case your class winner becomes the eventual CC winner. The RCC does not count towards the Champion's title, but should the CC winner be disqualified for any reason the Kennel Club may award the CC to the Reserve Challenge Certificate holder.

When the bitches have been judged, and the CC and the RCC awarded, the two Challenge Certificate winners will be called into the ring so that the Best of Breed (BOB) can be chosen. The Best of Breed winner goes on to represent the breed in the Terrier Group. Should the Skye

Terrier win the Terrier Group, and only a few have done that in the past, it will have to compete against the other Group winners for the Best in Show (BIS) award. This may mean returning to the show on the following day, but if you have got this far the pleasure exceeds the inconvenience of rearranging your personal schedule!

The classes listed above are those generally scheduled at Championship Shows at which all breeds may compete. At the Skye Terrier Club Championship Show, which is for this breed only, there is a larger number of classes to suit all ages from Minor Puppy to Veteran. At local Open Shows you may find far fewer classes for Skyes, or perhaps none at all. In the latter case your dog could be eligible for entry classes scheduled for Any Variety Terrier or Any Variety Not Separately Classified, and of course in classes such as AV Minor Puppy, AV Puppy or AV Veteran, which is for dogs over seven years of age on the day of the show. Entering your young dog at some local shows should provide you both with valuable show ring experience before you become involved in the more expensive, and time consuming, outings to Championship Shows which also often involve long distance travel.

The Skye Terrier Club 40th Anniversary Show, 1986, judged by Mrs Liz Austin.
Best In Show: Ch Coruisky Master Robbie.
Reserve Best In Show: Ch Marjayn Mickey Mouse.
Best Puppy: Rhosneigr Shadow Fox.
Photo: Robert M Blunson.

JUDGING

Although it may take many years in a breed before you are invited to award Challenge Certificates in Britain, and are approved by the Kennel Club to do so, it is in fact easier to become a judge in this country than in many others. To become a good judge one has to be involved in the breed for many years, and have bred and shown a good number of quality dogs. It is also extremely valuable to attend Breed Club seminars on assessing and judging dogs, and to keep a record of such attendances, and of all judging appointments, as the Kennel Club will require this information when you are invited to judge at Championship level.

Even when they are involved in the breeding of dogs, the ability to choose a winner from an early age does not come easily to everybody, but some people have a natural talent for spotting a future star. If you have served your apprenticeship as a breeder/exhibitor, and the Breed Club agrees, you may be passed to have your name added to the Open Show Judges List. This list is forwarded to secretaries of Open Shows at which the breed is classified. However, you are not required to be on a club judges list to be invited to judge your breed or to accept such an invitation.

CHAPTER FIVE

Breeding

Unless you are breeding with a view to keeping the best of the litter for exhibition there is little point in letting your bitch have puppies. A long held belief that breeding at least one litter is beneficial to the bitch is unfounded. If a bitch has frequent false pregnancies the answer is not a litter, but spaying, which is the most effective and kindest remedy in such cases.

want, and using the same strain as your bitch will give you the same type of Skye. This is generally referred to as "line breeding."

Perhaps you have seen a wonderful dog in the show ring and would like to use him. Think before you do. For one thing his pedigree may have nothing in common with your bitch's blood

An alert litter of Skyes.

If you do not intend to show any of your bitch's puppies but still would prefer to breed a litter do not do so unless you have several confirmed bookings for puppies. This also applies to exhibitors, as it is far better to have some bookings for puppies before embarking on a breeding programme. Skyes are not the best known of terriers or the easiest to sell unless you are an established breeder of note, and there are far too many unwanted dogs around without adding to the number.

If, after careful consideration, you do decide to breed, several matters should be taken into account. Do you like what you already have? What points in your bitch would you like to see improved? You may find that the breeder from whom you purchased her has a suitable stud dog which should give you the improvements you

lines, and using him may result in puppies which take after neither parent and are a disappointment. The exception to this is when the stud dog you fancy is known to be a prepotent stud, which means that, regardless of the type of bitch brought to him, all his puppies resemble him. Using a non- related stud dog is known as "outcrossing".

Another breeding plan is to mate your bitch to one of his close male relatives, which is known as "inbreeding." The latter is practised in some kennels but generally it is not a good plan for the beginner breeder; it may be either an outstanding success or a dismal failure.

For the new breeder the safest plan is line breeding. For one reason it will retain, and hopefully improve, your original type; for

Litter of Barraglen pups in America, approximately 10 days old. Owners: Ann and Ross Bower.

another it opens the door to breeding plans for the next generation. It is important to keep at least one step ahead, in thought anyway, when planning a breeding programme, as you have not only your own future stock to consider but also the future of the breed.

Another point to remember is that, though you may have decided which dog you would like to use, his owner may refuse your request as she might not think your bitch suitable and will not want her dog blamed if the litter does not turn out as well as expected. The experienced breeder is more able to foresee what the result of a particular mating might be, and though you may be disappointed you may easily have reason later to thank her for her wisdom.

You perhaps may have seen several winning dogs which you admire. In this case you should check your show catalogues and note how they were bred and also what they themselves have sired. If you see that a dog has sired winning stock to a variety of bitches from different bloodlines it is worth using him, as he is an example of the prepotent stud. However, never blame the stud dog if you do not breed a litter of champions; the bitch plays her part too! Breeding dogs is easy, but breeding good dogs involves having an inbuilt ability to choose the correct combination of bloodlines, and a good eye when it comes to choosing puppies.

When you have decided on a stud dog, you should contact the owner to enquire if she will allow her dog to be used. If she is agreeable, well and good; if not you will have to consider alternative arrangements. So give yourself plenty of time; do not wait until your bitch comes into season or you may find yourself making a rushed decision.

The bitch usually comes in season (oestrus) for the first time at about eight months of age, though it may be somewhat later than this as individuals vary. After the first season she should come in again approximately every six months. As Skyes are a slow maturing breed it is better that she should not be bred from until she is over eighteen months old; better still if is she is over two years, and best if she is at least three.

When you decided to have a bitch the matter of her seasons should have been considered. You may be quite happy with a bitch having a six monthly cycle regularly throughout her lifetime, but many people find it difficult to cope with and worry about an unplanned litter as the result of the bitch in oestrus escaping, or a dog getting in during these times. However, if the garden is secure, and the family very careful, there should be no problems.

Some people like the idea of putting the bitch "on the pill" as a convenient way of avoiding this potential problem, but before birth control is prescribed the bitch should be allowed to have her first season naturally. An injection can be used to control the bitch's cycle but it is not advisable to use this method throughout her entire life. If you do not want puppies have your bitch spayed.

The oestrus cycle lasts for twenty-one days, during which time it is necessary to separate the bitch from any male dogs. During the first nine days she will probably "see off" any dog which shows an interest in her, but as bitches vary and you may not have noticed her condition for the first few days of the cycle do not rely on the figure nine. Male dogs become unsettled when they know a bitch is in season and tend to mark their territory by urinating in what humans consider unsuitable places, by refusing to eat and by generally making life difficult for the owner.

From approximately the tenth day of oestrus her previously red discharge will have changed to a slight colouration only, or be quite clear, and another dog or bitch will show interest in her. At this time she will accept the male. Her behaviour is a good indication of when she is ready to be mated as she will switch her tail well over to one side or "stand" ready to accept the male.

Matings are best carried out with the owner of the dog and the bitch both present. An experienced stud dog will perform almost imme-diately, though he may be guided by his owner. During the mating the owner should hold the bitch's head so there is no chance of her turning and attacking, or damaging, the dog. She may seem unsettled in strange surroundings, and even the most placid bitch can turn into a firebrand on these occasions. Some breeders prefer to see the bitch muzzled, but this could upset her even further so, unless all else fails, this is not recommended.

A successful mating is achieved with a "tie". At this time the dog cannot move away from the bitch and will lift one of his hind legs over her back so they are left standing tail to tail. The length of the tie does not decide the size of the litter and may last from one minute up to twenty, or even longer. Occasionally puppies may result without a tie.

When the mating is over keep the bitch quiet for a couple of hours. If the owner of the stud dog is satisfied that he has performed ade-quately there will be no need to bring the bitch back for a second mating. If you have travelled a long way which necessitated an overnight stay you may decide to stop over for another mating just in case, but such a decision will be made between the owners of the stud dog and the bitch.

After the mating you will pay the stud fee, which can vary from £75 for a novice dog up to £250 for a top winner. You should, of course, have enquired the price of the stud fee at the time of booking the bitch. Sometimes the dog's owner may prefer to have the pick of the litter instead of a stud fee, but this could mean you lose your best puppy. However, there are occasions when this may suit you, but think carefully before making such agreements.

If you wish to register your puppies with the Kennel Club, which is advisable particularly if you intend to show, do the paperwork now. You will need a copy of the stud dog's pedigree, and it is necessary for the dog's owner to sign the registration form as proof of mating. If for some reason the bitch does not produce pups do not automatically expect a free stud service next time she is in season. You are paying for the service, not for the result, and it is up to the owner of the dog whether or not to charge a second time.

THE PREGNANCY

The gestation period is sixty-three days, and during the first few weeks there will be little sign of change, though some bitches appear to quieten down and others may go off their food for a spell.

Normally the first obvious signs of pregnancy occur around five weeks when the nipples will redden and the bitch will begin to fill out. At this time you will need to increase her food to include milk and eggs in her diet. A good variety of vitamin and mineral supplements such as SA37 or Canovel are available, and many breeders swear by herbal supplements such as raspberry leaf tablets to ensure easy whelping. If her normal diet is one of the complete dry foods follow the directions on the container for feeding pregnant bitches, or ask your veterinary surgeon's opinion. Whatever suits her lifestyle, and yours, is the best advice.

Towards the end of the pregnancy the bitch may become uncomfortable if she is carrying a large litter. She may become quite restless and pant a great deal. These are the sure signs that she is nearing her time, and you should by now have arranged a quiet, draught-free spot where she is to have her puppies. A whelping box is very useful, but not essential as long as you have an enclosed area which she knows is hers.

The whelping area, or box, should be padded with newspapers. You will need a copious supply of newspapers during the whelping and puppy-rearing time, so you should have been saving yours, and possibly begging extra papers from friends and neighbours; you can never have too many! A vetbed or blanket on

The pup is usually born head first and will be enclosed in the membrane or sac which protects it in the womb. The sac often breaks as the puppy is born and the mother will immediately start to tear at the membrane and lick the pup until all the fluids have been removed. She will also break the umbilical cord by chewing through it, and will eat the afterbirth, which is quite normal. By this time the next puppy will be ready to make his entrance into the world, hopefully with no need for you to do anything more than admire her lovely pups.

An armful of five-week-old pups.

top of the newspapers gives added comfort, but you may remove it while she is actually whelping and she will tear up reams of paper before actually settling down to give birth.

On the whole Skyes are easy whelpers. They make very little fuss and give birth quietly without any need of assistance. Standing by, taking the bitch's temperature and whisking the new born pup away to be cleaned are unnecessary; get involved only if there are problems. For example, if there is still no sign of the pup after an hour of contractions call your vet for advice. It is as well to let him, or her, know when the bitch goes into labour in case help is needed.

Occasionally things can go wrong. For example a pup may be born in the breech position, that is hind legs first. If this is the case it is essential for you to help, gently but firmly by easing the puppy out and removing the membrane from its head before too much fluid from the sac is inhaled, or the pup might literally drown. Once this is done you may leave it to the bitch to clean up. You will know if the pup is healthy by the sound of its squeak! In some cases the bitch may show no inclination to cut the cord. This is where you step in with sterilised scissors, cutting the cord at least two inches from the pup. Always make sure that all the afterbirths are accounted for, otherwise the bitch could develop a serious infection.

It is hard to resist the temptation to examine the pup while it is still wet, providing the mother does not object, and usually she does not. It is a good idea to look closely at the pups in this state as the shape of things to come is there; many a champion has been picked at one minute old! This does need experience, however. Check, too, for any faults, a kink in the tail for example. Fortunately this fault has almost been bred out, but by running your finger and thumb down the length of the tail you will be able to detect whether there is a kink. If there is this pup should be sold as a pet. There is no point in hoping a judge will miss this fault, nor is it likely to disappear, and it is most likely to be passed on if the pup is bred from in the future.

Puppies are often born with a white spot on the chest. This is quite acceptable provided the patch is no more than two inches across. When all the pups are born the bitch will relax and have a good sleep. Before she does, make sure her bed is clean and dry, give her a well-earned drink of milk and leave her in peace.

All these things you can cope with by using your common sense. However, if the bitch has been having contractions for a long time and shows signs of distress, veterinary advice should be sought, as a caesarian may be necessary. Having a caesarian operation does not prevent the bitch from rearing her puppies in the normal fashion. Even though all has gone well you may feel that you would like to have your bitch and the litter checked by your vet to reassure you that all is well. Make sure that he can come out to your house as mother and puppies will be vulnerable to infection in his surgery.

CARE OF THE PUPPIES

You may like to keep a chart of the puppies' weights so that you can evaluate their progress. In this way you can tell if one of them is not gaining and contact your vet quickly. Puppies grow at such a rate it is almost possible to see them sprout in front of your eyes, and therefore many experienced breeders find no need to make notes of their progress.

Skye Terriers are usually born black but once they dry out you may well wonder what colour they are going to be. Creams are born with a black line running the entire length of their back, and in overall colouring they usually resemble a Siamese cat rather than immediately aspiring to the glamorous cream with black points which will be the end result. Creams themselves vary, and the pup which is much lighter, with a thin black line, may be lacking in pigmentation later on. Silvers can be born black, gradually turning a pale silver as the months go by. Others appear to be a creamy brindle which some mistake for cream, but they will finish up as silver. Greys appear as brindle; the lighter the brindle, the lighter the grey.

Blacks are difficult to breed unless you have a black strain. Many people think they have bred blacks only to find they turn much lighter in a few months time. A true black will have a very blue skin which will remain that colour throughout his life. Pay particular attention to the advice of the breeder of your bitch and the owner of the stud dog, as they will be able to tell you what colours their breeding produces. If there is a pup in your litter which appears to be black on top with cream legs and a cream underpart to the tail you have a parti-colour, which is a fault. Similarly, if there is a brown puppy, you will observe that the nose and points (ears) will also be brown; this is a fault too. Pet homes should be found for any puppies with colour faults.

At around two weeks of age the puppies' eyes will open. At three weeks you can begin to wean them by introducing them to milky cereal feeds and sloppy dishes of potatoes and gravy, which they will delve into, spreading it all over each other. Fortunately they quickly learn to feed themselves in a more tidy manner! You may decide to use a purpose-made puppy milk formula such as Lactol, and this may be obtained from a good pet shop or from your vet.

The manufacturers of complete dog foods also give instructions for weaning puppies, and the breeder of your bitch may have valuable advice to offer on this subject too. Dog breeders love to talk about rearing puppies! The important thing is to listen to advice and decide on the way you want to rear your puppies; use one method and stick to it. Chopping and changing will only result in puppies with upset tummies. Any changes in diet, for puppies or mature dogs, should always be made gradually.

By five weeks of age the puppies' meals should be divided into five small meals per day and, for example, may include a meat meal and one of soft scrambled egg as well as Lactol and cereal. The well-known manufacturers of canned dog foods all offer puppy grade meat products, which are excellent, but some breeders prefer fine-cut beef mince from the butcher to begin with. When the puppies are in the weaning stage you may notice that the bitch eats her own dinner and then appears to be desperate to see her puppies, whereupon she will regurgitate her food for them. They will launch into it with gusto! Although this may seem unpleasant to you it is a perfectly normal habit for a dog and nothing to worry about. For wild dogs, wolves and other animals in the wild, this is the natural way of carrying meat back to their young after the adults have hunted and killed other game. It simply shows dogs' ancestry and that some ancestral habits remain. However, if your bitch persists in regurgitating for her puppies you will need to feed her again to replace what she has given to them.

Another requirement at the age of five weeks is to treat the pups for roundworm. This should be repeated two weeks later. If the pups are sold at eight or nine weeks they should be clear of worms then, but you should recommend that new owners worm their puppy regularly, obtaining worming medicine and advice from their veterinary surgeon.

Hopefully you will have some clients for seven or eight week old puppies; once they are fully weaned they should be ready for their new homes. Unfortunately it is not always easy to place puppies, and occasionally clients may change their minds at the last minute. Sometimes one has orders for dog puppies and your bitch produces no male pups, or vice versa. In any case you should be prepared to "run on" puppies until they are sold, and of course you would want to run on your best pup, or puppies, if you intend to keep something to show or perhaps have an order from someone else who wants a potential show pup. This means that you will have to have accommodation for them.

Growing puppies are a delight! You can happily spend more time just looking at them than doing anything else. However they are also quite demanding as far as food is concerned, and rather messy before being house trained. They need a place of their own, and they need to be able to play outside too. The first consideration is an outdoor puppy run. This preferably should have a concrete base for easy cleaning and disinfecting, and puppy-proof fencing around it. They also need shelter and warmth. If there is no longer room in your house perhaps you have a suitable outhouse? Alternatively, if you are really hooked on breeding and exhibiting, an investment in a purpose built puppy house and attached run is wise.

If you have been attending championship shows you will have noticed various stands selling such equipment. If you regularly read either of the two weekly dog papers, *Our Dogs* and *Dog World*, you will have seen advertisements for puppy houses and kennels. These will give you some ideas of suitable buildings. If well maintained such structures will serve you well for many years. When you start to plan a litter you must be prepared for all eventualities, and as was mentioned earlier puppies are not always easy to sell. Therefore it is possible that you may have to accommodate them for much longer than their first seven or eight weeks. This is important for their health and development, and suitable quarters for them means easier work for you. Puppies are a pleasure of course, and to see them thrive and grow beautiful is reward in itself.

Health

Your Skye Terrier should spend most of his years with no major health problems, enjoying a healthy lifestyle with plenty of exercise and kind but firm handling. A yearly health check on your dog should be sufficient unless accidents of some sort occur.

A dog's normal temperature is 101.5 degrees Fahrenheit (38.5 degrees Centigrade). If your dog's temperature is raised he may have a warm nose and seem generally depressed. A rectal thermometer is necessary for taking a dog's temperature; if you do not have one it would be a good idea to purchase one from the chemist and keep it in your medicine chest. The chances are that you will rarely have to use it, but it will be there if needed.

Keep your dog's vaccination certificate safely and check with your veterinary surgeon regarding the appropriate time for "booster" shots. Also keep a record of his worming doses in puppyhood. As an adult dog he will need worming for roundworm and tapeworm twice a year. Fortunately dogs in Britain are not affected by heartworm, which can be a killer in other countries.

Inspect your dog's ears regularly; they may need a gentle cleaning occasionally, perhaps twice a year or perhaps more often. Careful application of a cotton bud may be all you need, but the accent is on "careful". If you notice any ear discharge, or find your dog holding his head on one side and scratching his ear without obvious relief, consult your veterinary surgeon.

A dog's teeth need to be tended, as tartar builds up, just as it would in humans, and needs to be removed. If it is not there is danger of gum disease, which may become a major problem. Buy your dog a toothbrush, but don't expect him to use it! You must brush his teeth for him at

intervals. If you start when his second teeth have all come through he will get used to this. Use any brand of toothpaste. If he gets a really heavy build-up of tartar the vet will have to scale your dog's teeth, but regular brushing at home will help keep the tartar down.

Dogs which live on soft foods are more prone to dental problems. For this reason your dog needs something hard to chew on, a marrow bone occasionally is a good idea, or changing his food to one of the complete dry foods in crunchy pellet form also helps to keep teeth in good condition.

Just as in humans, a high fibre diet is recommended for dogs, especially for the pet dog which perhaps does not take much exercise. This also applies to the older dog whose age is slowing him down. Adding bran to the diet may help, but again one of the complete dry foods which is rich in bran should suffice.

If your dog rubs his rear end along the ground, or appears to be trying to scoot along on his bottom, it is probable because his anal glands need emptying. Your vet will soon rectify this but seek treatment promptly to avoid infection of the glands.

Common illnesses which can occur throughout a dog's life include diarrhoea. This distressing complaint is sometimes caused by scavenging, a pastime some dogs appear to enjoy greatly regardless of the consequences! However, there may be some other reason, so if diarrhoea is a recurring problem seek veterinary advice.

Like people, dogs are susceptible to "bugs", so a bout of sickness may last only for one day. A dog which is "off colour" will want to eat grass, which will result in vomiting, and this sometimes effects a natural cure. If the bug seems to be persistent, seek veterinary advice, as there may be a more serious cause to the problem.

In summer, fleas, lice, mites and ticks may cause many problems if they are allowed to get out of hand. An infestation of fleas or lice will make the dog scratch incessantly, often tearing the skin and thus causing infection. Scratching can ruin the dog's coat in a matter of hours and it will take many months to grow in again. The need to keep your dog free of parasites at all times is paramount, and regular grooming helps by keeping you alert to the presence of unwanted visitors.

Fleas, which leave little black specks, can be seen moving in the coat. Lice and ticks cling to a particular spot, often around the head and ears. Ticks are a problem because their mouth parts become embedded in the dog's skin and trying to pull the tick off may result in the pincers being left behind. A dab of alcohol on the tick will sometimes cause it to release its grip. Sometimes pulling ticks away causes a nasty sore. If in doubt, a trip to the vet's surgery is indicated. Ticks are usually more common in farming areas.

Ticks, unfortunately, have taken on a more sinister role in recent times since the deer tick was identified as the cause of Lyme disease in North America. So far Lyme disease is rare in Britain, but people have been warned not to go barelegged in country areas, or deer parks or forests. It is reported that dogs infected with Lyme disease may not show any evidence of the disease for some weeks, though it may be heralded by the dog limping for no apparent reason. A blood test has to be taken to prove the presence of the disease, and if it is positive treatment can be given. As mentioned before, regular grooming of the dog's coat will reveal the presence of parasites.

If your dog has fleas he might have caught them from your cat, if you have one, or from long grass or other dogs. Fleas are very mobile and do not necessarily stay on the dog so it is necessary to treat the environment too. The dog's bedding will need to be thoroughly washed, and your carpets and soft furnishings should be sprayed. A suitable insecticidal spray may be obtained from your vet. Fleas are most bothersome in warm weather, and as they can live for many days off the dog infestation tends to recur unless the environment is resprayed at the recommended intervals.

Not only do parasites cause skin problems but pollen, dust mites, stress, change of diet or hormonal changes are all known to affect some dogs and may cause "hot spots". Fortunately these can quickly be rectified with a cortisone based cream. A change of diet can sometimes cause skin problems so dietary changes should always be made gradually. Sometimes changing to a lamb and rice diet may help, or perhaps one of the commercially prepared vegetarian diets for dogs. However, if you are one of the relatively few people whose Skye Terrier has skin problems it may take many months to solve the mystery of what is actually causing the trouble. Patience and careful detective work are needed, but once the cause is found the cure can be administered and hopefully the problem will not recur.

Cancers in dogs seem to be on the increase these days. Mammary tumours have long been known in the older bitch and if these develop on the mammary glands careful note should be taken of their size and growth rate. Fortunately many of them are benign and need not be removed, but if one appears to be rapidly increasing in size take advice from your vet, who will probably want to remove it before it spreads to other parts of the body.

"Puppy limp" is peculiar to the Skye Terrier, occurring between the age of five months and one year. It is simply a limp in one of the forelegs and is usually noticed after some boisterous play with another dog, or with children, and you may think the dog has been injured. It may disappear and return at a later date, causing worry to the owner, but it rarely causes much trouble to the pup, and with rest the limp will disappear as quickly as it arrived. In some cases in may last many months so an extended period of rest may be needed.

On no account let your puppy run up and down stairs or jump off chairs while he is growing. The Skye Terrier makes a lot of growth from five months of age, and one week he may look short backed while the following week he may be higher at the back end. He may look quite odd during these uneven growth periods and you may wonder if he will ever turn out like a Skye Terrier at all! At this stage his bones are soft, his body is long and therefore his front legs are taking a considerable strain, particularly if he is very active, so it is the body's way of saying, "Slow down, I'm growing." Too many owners, even those with the very best intentions, tend to over-exercise growing puppies. Take it easy. Once the pup is over a year old puppy limp will have disappeared and the dog will be as sound as a bell.

The premature closure of a growth plate is a more serious matter, and the first sign may be similar to puppy limp. However the condition may require surgery, as the ulnar growth plate nearest the paw may close at the age of five months instead of at the normal age of nine to ten months. When this happens the continuing growth of the radius causes the foot to turn outward and the elbow to be thrown out, giving the dog some discomfort. Surgery can correct this condition if it is diagnosed early, but as premature closure is an inherited condition affected dogs should not be part of a breeding programme.

Although the Skye has a long back it rarely has any trouble with back problems, unlike some other long-backed, short-legged breeds, though there are occasional exceptions. Generally it is not worth worrying about the prospect of it happening to your dog. If your vet categorises your long-bodied dog as a future sufferer from disc trouble, as some do, he clearly does not know a Skye Terrier, so change to one who has some experience of the breed.

A rather sinister new disease made its appearance in Skyes in recent years and is commonly known as "Liver Disease". Apart from the usual signs that something is wrong with the dog the most obvious symptom is abdominal swelling due to retention of fluid. Blood tests will show up any abnormalities, and a biopsy of the liver will give a complete diagosis. Serious cases may prove fatal, but others have recovered and may live for years before a recurrence.

The University of Liverpool is currently investigating Liver Disease to ascertain the cause and, hopefully, find the cure for this complaint. Naturally livers are needed to work on, and if you have the misfortune to lose your dog from this disease the University should be contacted, preferably by your vet, so that the liver may be used to assist in the eradication of this disease. Should anyone wish to contact the University please write to Dr S Haywood BVSc, PhD, MRCVS, University of Liverpool, Dept of Veterinary Pathology, PO Box 147, Liverpool L69 3BX. Telephone: 051 709 6022, Ext 3178.

ALPHABETICAL LIST OF COMMON DISEASES

Allergy: Pollen, fertilisers, chemical pesticides, various plants indoor and outside, central heating, diet and dust from carpets may all cause allergic reactions in dogs, the reactions ranging from runny eyes to skin disorders.

Arthritis: Painful inflammation of the joints, found more often in older dogs.

Cancer: Malignant new cell growth which may spread through the whole body if not treated in time. Surgery is sometimes successful provided there is early diagnosis.

Canine parvovirus infection: A highly virulent disease which has only been recognised in dogs since the late 1970s. The virus can be carried on clothing or footwear and particular care must be taken to disinfect anything which may be contaminated. The dog is affected by severe vomiting and profuse diarrhoea which is blood stained; a refusal to eat or drink may result in severe dehydration. In older dogs the strain on the heart muscles may prove fatal. If this disease is suspected contact your vet immediately but on no account take the dog to the surgery. Fortunately dogs can now be vaccinated against parvovirus in puppyhood.

Canker: One of the most common ailments with a wide variety of causes, including bacteria and yeasts, which result in a nasty, foul-smelling ear discharge. Daily cleansing of the ears with powder, ointment or drops as prescribed by your veterinary surgeon should rectify this condition.

Dermatitis: A skin disorder which is irritating and causes the dog to scratch. Dermatitis may be caused by an allergy, parasites, or infection; therefore it is important to determine the cause before the correct treatment can be prescribed. In some cases anti-histamines can be given to ease the condition systematically.

Diabetes: Older animals are susceptible to diabetes when the antidiuretic hormone produced by the pituitary gland fails to operate normally. Excessive thirst may be a sign of this disease and treatment may be in the form of injections which must be given for the rest of the dog's life.

Diabetes mellitus: Diabetes mellitus, or sugar diabetes, may present with similar signs of thirst and, in some case, loss of weight. Once the condition is diagnosed, diet and insulin injections will keep the disease controlled.

Distemper: Fortunately rarely seen these days, due to vaccination in puppyhood and regular "boosters" throughout the dog's life. Distemper is a highly infectious viral disease which is transmitted from one dog to another. The initial signs are a runny nose and eye discharge, accompanied by a high temperature and a cough. There will be loss of appetite, harsh breathing and possibly vomiting and diarrhoea. If treatment is not given the dog may show signs of chorea, fits or paralysis. If you suspect your dog may have distemper isolate him and contact your vet immediately. With early treatment the dog will stand a better chance of recovery. It is far better to see that your dog is fully protected by the appropriate vaccinations.

Dropsy: Usually found in older dogs, this condition occurs when an accumulation of fluid builds up in the tissues. In older dogs which may take less exercise, or have bad circulation, the fluid may be noticed in the region of the stomach (ascites). Treatment with diuretics will help keep the fluid under control.

Eclampsia: Found in pregnant or lactating bitches and caused by an imbalance of calcium in the blood. The bitch will be found panting, will have muscular pain, and may show unusual behaviour, anxiety and possibly collapse. Treatment by your vet, who should be called immediately, is usually successful. However, any delay in treatment could prove fatal.

Ectropion: A hereditary disease which causes the eyelids to turn outwards, leading to inflammation. Ectropion is not usually associated with the Skye Terrier.

Eczema: A skin irritation which can result in skin sores sometimes referred to as "hot spots", or it may be seen as dry, scaly flakes in some cases. The cause may be a change of diet, hormone imbalance or allergy, but it could take some time to determine. In the meantime creams or medicated baths as prescribed by your vet may alleviate the condition temporarily.

Enteritis: An inflammation of the intestines resulting in diarrhoea, which may be bloody, and/or vomiting. Withhold food for twelve hours but make sure a controlled amount of water is available at all times. If the animal is at all off colour, or the condition persists, contact your vet.

Entropion: The turning in of the eyelid which results in the eyelashes rubbing against the eyeball, causing irritation and a discharge. This condition is hereditary in certain breeds but is not usually associated with the Skye Terrier.

Hardpad: A form of canine distemper.

Hepatitis: This inflammation of the liver is caused by the dog swallowing matter contaminated by an infected dog. A certain form of chronic hepatitis has been found in Skye Terriers. In these cases the dog will show signs of lethargy, loss of appetite, increased thirst and urination, but more importantly abdominal swelling due to fluid accumulation. Some forms of the illness are more extreme than others. In all cases veterinary help should be sought.

Leptospirosis: This is a bacterial disease. The dog contracts the infection from a place where rats have been. He does not have to come in contact with a rat but may pick up the disease from rat urine on the ground. The dog will develop a high temperature, thirst, pain in the region of the abdomen, diarrhoea with blood and vomiting. Treatment should be carried out urgently by a vet. Leptospira canicola is a similar disease contracted by dogs sniffing at urine deposits on lampposts etc., and should be treated similarly.

Kennel cough: A virus infection readily transmitted from one dog to another, in a kennel for example or at a dog show. The affected dog will sound as though an object is stuck in its throat and, although the condition sounds serious, the adult dog usually continues to eat and act normally. However, in puppies care must be taken that the cough does not turn into pneumonia, which can result in death. If your dog or puppy has kennel cough, isolation is imperative. On no account take him among other dogs, which includes visits to the vet's surgery. Fortunately there is now a vaccine available which will assure protection for six to nine months.

Pyometra: An infection found in the bitch in which pus builds up in her uterus four to six weeks following her season. There are two versions of this condition; in the open case an dark, evil-smelling discharge is obvious, whereas in the closed condition the bitch will show tenderness around the abdomen, excessive thirst, frequent urination and a high temperature. Pyometra usually occurs in older bitches which have not had puppies, but exceptions may occur.

Quick action must be taken, as an emergency operation to remove the uterus and ovaries may be necessary to save the animal.

Rabies: (Hydrophobia). British quarantine regulations have kept the country free from rabies in our wildlife for many years, and at the time of writing a few other island nations which have quarantine regulations, notably Australia, New Zealand and Hawaii, are also rabies-free. Rabies is the most feared disease known to humans, as once the disease has developed there is no known cure. In continental European countries this disease is known to be carried by foxes, but it can be carried in the saliva of any warm-blooded animal and is transmitted by the bite of the infected animal, or by its saliva infecting a wound already present. The virus then travels via the nervous system to the brain, which becomes inflamed, causing spasms.

If an animal is infected it may take several months before signs of the disease appear, hence our six months quarantine detention regulation. Some continental European countries now claim that modern vaccines have freed them from rabies in their wildlife, and pressure has been put upon Britain to relax our quarantine system, which has proved successful over many years, in favour of vaccination, which is claimed to have been effective in recent years. So far this pressure has been resisted. It must be remembered that domestic animals, dogs and cats, are imported into Britain from countries other than Europe; in many third world countries rabies is endemic.

In an animal affected by rabies early signs are indicated by personality changes. Facial expression also changes, the affected animal spending long periods staring and drooling. A fear of light which results in the animal being extremely dangerous to approach is also indicative of the progression of the disease. The only solution is to euthanise the affected animal. After its death the brain will be examined to confirm the presence of the disease.

Toxocariasis: A type of roundworm which lives in the intestine. The importance of regular worming of pups and adult dogs cannot be emphasised too strongly. The responsible dog owner should also be prepared to remove faeces which their dog leaves in the garden, the park or the street as there is a risk to humans, and to children in particular. In a few severe cases blindness has developed in infected children and much publicity has been given in the national press to these sad occurrences. Dogs which are regularly treated for worms are not any danger to the public, but in all cases dog faeces should be removed from your own garden and public places for reasons of hygiene.

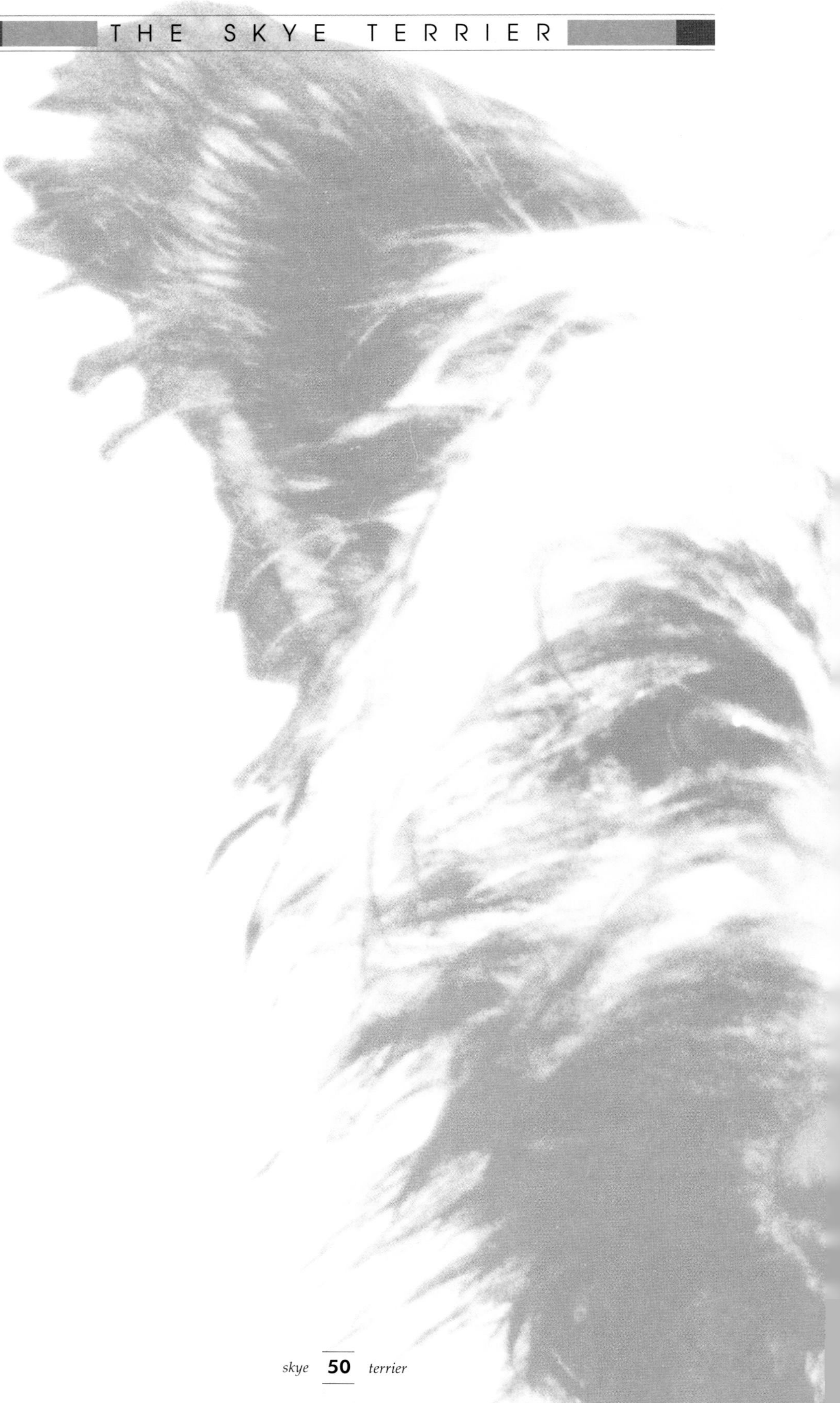

part **2**

SHOW DOGS
OF
GREAT BRITAIN

&

THE
UNITED STATES
SKYE
TERRIER

During the latter half of the nineteenth century, dog shows in Glasgow and Edinburgh attracted many entries of Skye Terriers. After years of working to control vermin the dogs were now required to be able to win prizes for their beauty, and some early exhibitors to fare well in the show ring included Mr W Wilson of Glasgow, whose Flora I, Flora II, and Flora III and Spunkie I and II were noted prize winners.

Mr H Martin showed several dogs successfully and, according to the Scottish Kennel Club catalogue of 1882, he also owned a successful business, selling first class Skye, Dandie Dinmont, Black and Tan and Fox Terriers. However, according to remarks left on the pages of a stud book, one of his Skyes, Staffa, a drop ear which took first prize at the Crystal Palace in London in 1872, was observed by an onlooker to be "A cur"!

Mr James Kidd was a notable breeder and exhibitor in 1882 whose prick eared Rob Roy (North ex Nellie) won well. Rob Roy was bred by John Munro who was to sell Skyes to Mrs Adams of Talisker fame in Canada. Duncan Cunningham, another great breeder of the time, won well with Venus, a prick ear noted for her outstanding conformation, and Warlock (Charlie ex Perkie). Perkie was a drop ear bitch. It was in Edinburgh towards the end of the 1880s that the young

Countess of Aberdeen's Skye Terriers, Monarch and Feuriach.

Rosslyn Bruce whilst staying with his uncle, William Skene, first came across the Skye Terrier. They were very popular in the capital city, and also in Glasgow with, according to the famous author Sir Compton MacKenzie, "Hardly a doorstep not graced by a Skye stretched out on it."

In 1888 Rosslyn Bruce provided his Aunt Fifi with a Skye from Edinburgh, called Tatters. For himself he purchased Rona (Ch Old Burgundy ex Brown Sherry), then just five weeks old, for the sum of thirty five-shillings. Ch Old Burgundy was the big winner of his day and in later years his daughter, Rona, gave birth to Rona II owned by Queen Victoria. During his short stay in Scotland Rosslyn Bruce enjoyed showing and would enlist the help of the Boys Brigade Company, of which he was Captain, to assist him on his trips to the dog shows.

At the Scottish Kennel Club Show of 1893 the breed specialist, John King, judged an entry of forty Skyes which were competing for the various cups and medals offered by the Skye Terrier Club of England and the Skye Terrier Club of Scotland, the latter club offering gold and silver medals. The President's Gold Medal was presented by the Right Honourable Viscount Melville. Mrs Hughes of Wolverley fame showed Laird Duncan (Stanley III ex Venus II) bred by D Cunningham, and Wolverley Fitz (Prince George ex Metty). Mr William Cummings of Edinburgh exhibited Burgundy (Prince ex Wasp), Medoc (Red Hock ex Nan), Madeira (Old Burgundy ex Jenny) and Lady Teak (Burgundy ex Lassie).

Two daughters of Hector
Munro of Auchindoun
with pet Skye.

Another great enthusiast, Mr William Miller, bred the above mentioned Medoc and Lady Teak. He exhibited Kate Dalrymple (Old Port ex Lady Mathieson) and Sparkling Hock (Medoc ex Nip) and owned the outstanding Ch Old Burgundy (Albany ex Nellie II). Mr Miller would buy promising Skyes in poor condition off the street, smarten them up and either sell them or show them, such was the abundance of the breed at this time!

Elphinstone (Falkirk ex Daisy) was entered by John Shiells, unplaced on the day, but later exported to America where he became one of the earliest champions in the breed in 1894. Also exhibiting at the SKC Show of 1893 was the Rev David Dobbie of Kelso in the Borders, an early secretary of the Skye Terrier Club of Scotland who had presented Queen Victoria with Diana of Aldivalloch in the 1870s. Here he exhibited Roy of Aldivalloch (Lord Lennox ex Queen Bess 11) and Her Majesty (Roy of Aldivalloch ex Roy's Wife). Most of the dogs on exhibition were advertised for sale, the asking price ranging from £5 to £1000 for Roy of Aldivalloch! The winner of the day was Tackley Roy (Davock ex Kingston Yum Yum), owned by the Rev Thomas Nolan.

By the turn of the century several new fanciers had emerged, including the Countess of Aberdeen, who had an impressive kennel of both prick and drop ears at her home, Haddo House, in Aberdeenshire. Noted winners from the kennel included Ch Gillie Glas (Ch Bodach ex Millie), Ch Buchan Meg (Wolverley Duncan ex Royal Princess), Ch Buchan Baillie (Angus Grey ex Kelpie), Ch Aberdeen Mike (Ch Buchan Baillie ex Wee Wifie) and Ch Aberdeen Jock (Aberdeen Loon ex Coulaig).

Family favourites, Monarch and Feuriach, lived in the house, enjoying great hunting expeditions together. All their lives they were inseparable until at the age of fourteen Feuriach died as the result of injuries received in one of their forays. Monarch was devastated and sadly died of a broken heart. Haddo House belongs now to the National Trust for Scotland and is open to the public. Inside the silver replicas of Monarch and Fleuriach decorate the dining room table, whilst outside a life size bronze of the pair overlook the grounds where they had such fun.

Mr Miller's "Scott" kennel was one of the most successful, producing some wonderful prick eared dogs, among them Ch Walter Scott (Jonnie ex Florrie), Young Wattie Scott and Liz

Seonaird Nicholson Kilpatrick
photographed with a Skye, 1894.

Scott (both by Ch Walter Scott ex Mary Queen of Scots) and Rosie Scott (Young Sandy Scott ex Grey Lady). Mr A White entered Hector Monarch (Wallace ex Talisker) at the 1903 Show in Scotland. This dog was bred by Mr MacDougall who sent Oban Jock to Mrs Adams of the Talisker Kennels in Canada the following year. Mr Thomas Brash of Edinburgh was a keen exhibitor, registering his Skyes under the Marchiston affix. His son, too, always shared a love of the breed owning Acheo Bla Bheinn (Olivia Radovan ex Acheo Kalgoorlie Kate) for a short time in the 1970s.

Skyes continued to support shows in reasonable numbers until the first world war when showing activities were curtailed. By the 1920s classes were no longer separate for prick and drop ears, the latter sadly having gone out of fashion. Miss Murdoch and her O'Craighmhor Kennels were very successful in Stirlingshire. Although she seldom showed south of the border her exhibits were rarely beaten by those who came north to the championship shows. Para Handy (Lucky Jim ex Lucky Ann) and Jenny Nettles (Donachadh Liath ex The Vindictive) were two well known winners in the 1920s. Later, with her O'Craighmor affix, the kennel produced many champions, including Ch Catriona (Para Handy ex Kilmeny), Ch Bonnie Jean O'Craighmhor and Int Ch Phoebe O'Craighmhor, the latter two becoming a great influence on the de la Chamardiere Skyes in France.

Mr Alex Duthie from Aberdeenshire exhibited some good dogs in the 1920s, the family having kept Skyes since 1820. Captain Duthie, grandfather of

Alex, established the Duthie Shipyard in Aberdeen in 1816 and always took his Skyes to sea with him on the tea clippers, introducing them to Australia between 1850 and 1870, though he felt the climate did not suit them too well because of their heavy coats. Alex Duthie's Netherby White Heather (Searchlight ex Smokecloud) was a CC winner at the 1925 Scottish Kennel Club Show, and homebred Netherby Roberty (Netherby Nipper ex Netherby White Heather) was a consistent prizewinner. Alex Duthie's daughter, Miss Gladys Duthie, who was born on board ship (it was not only the dogs who went to sea!), was always a dedicated lover of the breed and kept at least two throughout her life.

John Millar of Paisley bred many good Skyes and several made their names under the Merrymount affix, though he did not use an affix himself. He owned Rip of Merrymount (Ch Chummie of Merrymount ex Holmesdale Tilda) who was also a consistent winner and sired the lovely Ch Silver Lass of Merrymount and Ch Murdie (ex Silver Merrymount). These both went on to France to establish the Luchar Kennel after successful careers in England.

By the end of the 1930s, which brought the start of the Second World War, breeders of Skyes in Scotland had almost disappeared. During the war years all

Ch Gillie Glass, an early drop ear Skye.

dog shows were suspended, and by 1945 when the war ended very few enthusiasts remained north of the border, although on the Isle of Skye Mrs Mary Macdonald of the Acheo affix had purchased her first Skye Terrier, Darkie Dene (Rip of Merrymount ex Grianach Spark) from Mr Millar in 1944. Fortunately interest in the breed revived in the late 1950s and early 1960s, ending the darkest period in the history of the breed in its native country.

Until the mid 1800s the Skye Terrier was best known as a working terrier with a remarkable talent for doing the job correctly. The first dog shows in Britain started around 1860 with Skyes first appearing at the Birmingham Dog Show, which scheduled classes for "Scotch Terriers". At that time any terrier native to Scotland could be exhibited in such classes, and ten Skyes were accordingly entered.

James Pratt with Piper (Toddy ex Mist), by kind permission of Miss Catherine Owen.

In 1861 Manchester Dog show scheduled classes for Skye Terriers, and at a show in Leeds that year Mr H Smeeton's Doormat, "imported from the Isle of Skye", was placed third in his class, the class winner being Mr E Tiffany's Punch (Doormat ex Gypsy). Mr Smeeton also showed Tyro, bred by Mr Gascoyne on the Isle of Skye, which was placed first at the Islington, London, Dog Show the following year.

The Rev J C Macdona was one of the earliest breeder/exhibitors to show his dogs successfully. Rook (Billy ex Vic) and Rook II (Rook ex Kelpie) were early winners and well respected Skye Terriers. The Rev Macdona, who was also instrumental in introducing the St Bernard to Britain, took a lively interest in all dog matters.

Mr J Bowman of Darlington was equally enthusiastic with his Skyes. Mona (Billy ex Vic) won firsts at shows in Birmingham, Edinburgh and Glasgow in 1872, and in Birmingham, Nottingham and at the Crystal Palace in 1873. His drop ear Tartan (Fearig ex Sinfie), Sweep (Tartan ex Jessie) and Dandy (Toddy ex Sinfie) were also prize-winners.

The most famous Skyes in London were owned by a butler, James Pratt. Mr Pratt's Dunvegan (Donald ex Ness), a blue bitch, was bred from the strains of dogs owned by the Duke of Argyle, MacKinnon of Corry, MacLeod of Dunvegan, Lord Macdonald and Malcolm of Poltalloch. Mr Pratt's Skyes included Mist, litter sister of Dunvegan and described as white, as was Donald. Piper (Toddy ex Mist) and Boddach also belonged to James Pratt.

James Pratt's Piper and Sandy Grant from 1886

Mr Pratt's dogs were exercised daily in Hyde Park where they became local celebrities. Boddach was trained to take letters to the postbox, which of course was too high for him to reach, so he used to wait there patiently until some kind person put the letters into the box, only then returning to his master. Boddach's other duties included shopping. He would carry a shilling in his mouth and bring home a bag of eggs without cracking one of them; that is, unless he spied a cat, whereupon all thoughts of duty flew out of his head! In the home he would collect the newspaper and carry various items to help his master with his chores, for example he could carry wine glasses one at a time by the stem.

On one occasion James Pratt loaned Donald and Boddach to a Bazaar to raise funds for the "Temporary Home for Lost and Starving Dogs". The dogs were instructed to sit and stay on a table until eight o' clock at night. A notice above their heads read, "Skye Terriers. Donald and Boddach are perfectly quiet and will gladly receive donations on behalf of their needy friends, the starving dogs of London. Lent by J.P." The princely sum of £7, a lot of money in those days, was realised.

Queen Victoria on horseback by Landseer.
By kind permission of her Majesty the Queen.

Queen Victoria was known to have owned a Skye as early as 1842, which coincides with her first visit to Scotland with Prince Albert and the beginning of her long love of all things Scottish. The monarch's visit to Scotland opened up the country to Victorian travellers, who ventured north to explore the mountains and lochs. During their travels they discovered the native terriers, which were taken south in considerable numbers. Queen Victoria owned several Skyes during her long life. The Duke of Argyll was known to have given her two from his stock, and her most famous dog, Rona 11, was given to her by the Rev Rosslyn Bruce. She was also known to have cast her eye favourably over the beautiful Wolverley Skyes. A few portraits by the famous royal painter, Landseer, depict Queen Victoria with Skye Terriers.

During the 1880s HRH The Princess of Wales (later Queen Alexandra) exhibited Dandy and Fancy, bred by the Prince of Wales. However, the noted Skye fanciers of that era were breeders/exhibitors such as Mr A Boulton of the Flying Dutchman Inn at Accrington and Mr Mark Gretton of the Cross Keys Hotel at Hull. Mr Boulton owned the famous Accrington Wonder, bought as a ten-year-old by Lady Alexander and made up to champion status after a hitherto unremarkable show career; Mr Gretton owned Sam, who was subsequently exported to Belgium, becoming the first recorded Skye in that country.

The aforementioned Rev Rosslyn Bruce, lover of all God's creatures since infancy, was introduced to the Skye Terrier while staying with his uncle in Edinburgh in 1887. This great man went on from Edinburgh to study at Oxford, taking with him his beloved Rona (Ch Old Burgundy ex Brown Sherry), and he acquired many more animals during his years of study. Officially this was forbidden, but he managed to persuade the dons to let him keep his pets. He housed the smaller ones in cupboards and wardrobes, and the larger ones in a disused piggery. One of his pets was an elephant! To pay for the animals' food Bruce would buy stale bread and buns from the bakery and sell them to the public and students to feed to the animals.

In 1891 Rona produced a litter under his bed. One of these puppies, Rona II, was owned by Queen Victoria. Rosslyn Bruce not only loved Skyes but was also a great Smooth Fox Terrier man, and a noted and much respected judge of both breeds. His daughter, Rhalou, inherited his love of Skyes, and accompanied her father to America on a judging engagement as soon as she left school. Another of his daughters, Verily Anderson, wrote his biography, which is thoroughly recommended to dog lovers and is an insight into a very special man.

Sir Claud Alexander's first Skye, Ghillie, a son of James Pratt's dog, was a drop ear who was never shown or registered and sadly died young. However, Ghillie sired one litter which produced Ch Cuthulin, and also Panda, who was to become the foundation bitch of the respected Ballochmyle kennel. Sir Claud and Lady Alexander, owners of this kennel, were both great admirers of the breed and were noted for their outstanding Skyes and Clydesdale Terriers. The Alexander's Clydesdales were some of the last dogs of that breed. Dogs were not the only interest of the Alexanders. On their estate in rural Sussex they had a private zoo with a variety of animals ranging from owls to bison. Cattle also played an important part for many years and their British White Cattle were eagerly sought, as were their lovely horses.

Some of their outstanding Skyes included the previously mentioned Ch Accrington Wonder, who was bought at the age of ten and gained his title shortly afterwards, and Ch Young Roseberry, an outstanding dog which was never used at stud because of his horrendous tail which curled over his back. Being so well trained he never raised it in the show ring and nobody guessed the truth! Other prominent dogs in the Alexander's kennel were Ch Wee Mac of Adel (Ch Wolverley Chummie ex Little Molly) who won the Terrier Group at Crufts Dog Show in 1907, Ch Sally Scott, Ch Ballochmyle Abbess, Ballochmyle Brilliant who was previously named Young Wattie, Ch The Laird of Ballochmyle, Ch Ballochmyle Bashful, Ch Ballochmyle Lightning who was a big winner in the 1920s as were Ballochmyle Whisky and Ch Ballochmyle Stella.

The Ballochmyle Kennel was famed for both prick and drop ear Skyes and Sir Claud purchased many of his top Skyes from Mr William Miller who would pick up promising Skyes in poor condition from the streets of Glasgow and Edinburgh, where they were extremely common, tidy them up and sell them to his clients, one of whom was Sir Claud. The Alexander's daughter, Mina, inherited their love of animals, and in her later years she also established a successful kennel.

Ch Wolverley Chummie (Ch Wolverley Jock ex Wolverley Rosie) an outstanding dog fom the Wolverley Kennel.

The famous Wolverley Kennel belonging to Mrs Hughes was established in 1892. Mrs Hughes and her two sisters, the Misses Greenwood, kept the dogs in luxurious kennels built to Mrs Hughes' specifications; the tiled floors were covered with linen carpeting to prevent any breakage of coat. Three persons were employed solely to look after the dogs, and a fourth was employed just to wash the linen used on the dogs' beds and floors. The dogs' diets were most important. The dog kitchen was stocked with joints of meat from the butcher, rabbits and chickens, and the cupboards contained ample supplies of wheat flour to bake bread daily for the dogs. There were also stocks of rice, oatmeal, peas and other vegetables to provide nourishing meals for her top winning Skyes.

The Wolverley Skyes were well known for their outstanding coats and greatly admired by all who saw them. One young girl, whose name was Marcia, was to fall for their charms and vow that one day she too would have Skyes to match the Wolverleys. Her dreams were realised: that young lady was none other than Lady Marcia Miles of the famous Merrymount strain.

One of Mrs Hughes's earliest Skyes, Wolverley Cronie (Ch Iron Duke ex Jenny Nettles), when bred to Ch Laird Duncan (Stanley III ex Venus II) produced the lovely Wolverley Jock, who in turn sired Ch Wolverley Roy (ex Wolverley Rosie). Roy measured a total length of forty-seven and a half inches from nose to tail. The elegant Ch Wolverley Duchess (Wolverley Fitz ex Wolverley Bogie) was a consistent winner, though she had the occasional off day when she would show her dislike of the judge. The most famous dog from the kennel, Ch Wolverley Chummie (Ch Wolverley Jock ex Wolverley Rosie) holds the breed record of twenty-seven Challenge Certificates, though not from a different judge every time. Born in 1899 Ch Wolverley Chummie was, and still is, recognised by many as the ideal Skye Terrier. During his show career he was never beaten, and his outstanding record has not yet been equalled. After his death in 1910 his body was donated to the National History Museum in London and can still be seen today at the Zoological Museum in Tring Hertfordshire.

Miss McCheane's Adel kennel included the top winning Skyes Ch Adel Monk (Iron Token ex Dowager Duchess) born in 1898, Ch Adel Bridget (Ch Wolverley Chummie ex Ch Wolverley Nanette) born in 1906 and Ch Wee Mac of Adel (Ch Wolverley Chummie ex Little Molly) who won the Terrier Group at Crufts in 1907, the first Skye to do so. Ch Wolverley Chummie was owned by Miss McCheane from 1907, winning ten Challenge Certificates for her before his death.

In this era also the Hon Mrs Jocelyn owned a large kennel of quality Skyes which included the beautiful drop ear Ch Prince Donard (Ch Walter Scott ex Silver Doris) and the love of Skyes was passed down to her daughter, Lady Marcia Miles, who made such a big impact on the breed in later years.

At the beginning of the twentieth century a great many fanciers bred some outstanding stock and each of them has a special place in the history of the breed. Mrs Hugh Ripley's Markington kennel was responsible for the lovely drop ears Markington Queen and Markington Sunshine, Ch Perfection and Unique. Among her prick ears was the well known winner Wick (Ch Wolverley Chummie ex Wolverley Mrs Hughes).

Mrs V F Bosanquet's Piper Grey (Winsome Boy ex Ch Ballochmyle Bashful) was also a well known drop ear as were Fairfield Fancy (Duncan Grey ex Ch Ballochmyle Bashful) and Fairfield Famous (Duncan Grey ex Grey Mopsey). Another drop ear, the Challenge Certificate winner Elizabeth, owned by Lady Alison Williamson, was shown in full coat right up until her death at eleven years of age.

Miss Alice Katherine Snow Clifton won Challenge Certificates with Weybourne Jack, Jock of Weybourne, and Weybourne Rebecca. The Weybourne Cup won by the Crufts Best of Breed (BOB) winner each year was presented to the show by Miss Snow Clifton and is the most sought after cup in all the Skye Terrier calendar.

Towards the end of the first decade of the twentieth century the popularity of the Skye waned somewhat while its cousins, The West Highland White and the Cairn Terrier, rapidly gained recognition and popularity. Then came the First World War and the suspension of canine activities for the duration. However, in the early 1920s a new wave of breeders and exhibitors emerged.

Miss Alice Wishaw bred the wonderful drop ear Ch Grey Dusk (Moonlight ex Ch War Cloud) who, along with Ch Grey Cloud, Grey Dawn and Ch Grey Light, came from an outstanding litter. Miss Wishaw and Miss Tatham registered their Skyes under the successful Southernhills affix. Ch Southernhills

Moonglow, Ch Southernhills Smoke Cloud, and Ch Southernhills Shining Light are just some of the famous names of Skyes bred at Miss Wishaw's kennels.

Lady Marcia Miles had grown up with Skyes. Her mother, the Hon Mrs Jocelyn, had a large kennel of good dogs, but it was while attending a show at the tender age of eight years that the youngster saw a team of Wolverley Skyes, all in full coat and most beautifully groomed, and vowed that one day she too would own a kennel of dogs to match the famous Wolverleys. As we all know she did this, and more, owning the most successful kennel in her day. Even today none can claim to equal the total of champions which Lady Marcia bred and owned at home or which were exported to other countries.

Int Ch Royalist of Merrymount (Challenger of Meerend ex Rebecca of Merrymount).

The Merrymount Kennels were established in 1906, though it was not until the early 1920s that Lady Marcia, as she was affectionately known, began to gain fame with some outstanding dogs. She was to own or breed over a hundred champions in her lifetime. Among her early successes were Ch Grey Dusk, bought by Lady Marcia after judging him and awarding him his title in 1924, Ch Southernhills Smoke Cloud, Ch Chummie of Merrymount (Ch Silver Boy ex Myosotis), the winner of five Challenge Certificates and the sire of fourteen champions, who can be found behind almost all of the Merrymount champions. Ch Murdie and his sister Ch Silver Lass of Merrymount bred by Mr Millar of Paisley, plus Int Ch Goldmine of Merrymount, were later exported to France in the 1930s where they helped establish the famous Luchar Kennel belonging to Mme Williamson.

Later outstanding dogs from the Merrymount kennel include a plethora of stars in the 1950s, among them Int Ch Royalist of Merrymount, who was exported to the Iradell kennel in America. Others were Ch Merrymount Sunset, an outstanding brood bitch with several drop ears among her progeny, Int Ch Merrymount You'll Do who made a big name for himself in the Iradell kennels, Ch Merrymount Sun Chariot and Int Ch Merrymount Sungleam, two wonderful drop ears, as was Ch Merrymount Sundown, and the prick ears Ch Merrymount Wot No Sun and Ch Merrymount Mid Day Sun. The 1960s saw Ch Merrymount Mid River, Ch Merrymount His Grace and Ch Merrymount His Majesty, the last champion from this amazing breeder who did so much for the breed and whose name is so revered around the world. With the death of Lady Marcia Miles in 1972 the breed lost one of its greatest and most knowledgeable characters.

Miss Rosabel Watson came into the breed as a result of the death of a friend, Mrs Dearmer, who owned several Skyes. During World War 1 Mrs Dearmer joined the Red Cross and set off for Serbia, leaving her dogs with Miss Watson. Sadly Mrs Dearmer died of typhoid fever in 1915 and Mr Dearmer gave Miss Watson the dogs which were to bring her much success after the war. Miss Watson caused quite a stir when she bought Luckie Jim, formerly known as Prince Rufus, from Mrs Connell in Scotland, as Jim was a red Skye with a dudley nose.

Despite his colour Jim was a handsome dog and had he carried the correct pigment the general opinion was that he would have been hard to beat. Jim was entered at shows "Not for Competition" and was admired by many. He sired a great many puppies, including champions, not one of them inheriting his colour, though some breeders of the time thoroughly disapproved of this! Miss Watson also bred Ch Dusk, Ch Luckie Faith and Ch Luckie Cronie. As a judge she was well respected, the only lady judge to be invited to the first World Show in Frankfurt in 1935, and she judged in Vienna in 1937.

The Peacehaven kennel belonging to Mrs Morgan produced some fine Skyes, including Ch Roland, Evan and Boadicea of Peacehaven (Luckie Jim ex Priscilla), the last two from a later litter. Mrs Corbould enjoyed some good wins with Ch Grey Boy, Rona, and Ch Dusk who won a total of twelve Challenge Certificates. Mrs Sandwith's Holmesdale kennel owned the lovely bitch Ch Pamela Grey, but is chiefly remembered for breeding the famous Int Ch Holmesdale Fergus who was exported to France.

The Meerend affix, established in the early 1920s, belonged to Mrs Cuthbert, who was ably assisted by her daughter, Miss Manville. The Meerend Skyes were noted for their healthy appearance, no doubt due to the ample amount of fresh meat on which the dogs were fed. Mrs Cuthbert had an arrangement with local farmers that when their beasts died she bought the carcase. Miss Manville then personally butchered the cow, whereupon it was put into the dogs' boiler to provide a wonderful tasty stew. I wonder how many people would be prepared to undertake a job like that these days? It is far easier to open a can of dog food!

Notable champions from the Meerend kennel include Ch Becky of Meerend, Ch Sheila of Meerend, Ch Janet of Meerend, Int Ch Phoenix of Meerend, Am Ch Portia of Meerend, Ch Laurie of Meerend, Ch Crown Prince Charles of Meerend who took the first World title at the World show in Frankfurt in 1935, Ch Challenger of Meerend, Am Ch Tilly of Meerend and Ivor of Meerend who figures in the pedigrees of many of today's winning Skyes.

Mrs Eaden's kennel "of the Mynd" bred and owned some outstanding bitches which include Ch Ann of the Mynd, who was bred by Mrs Crook better known for her Rhosneigr affix, Ch Ida of the Mynd, Ch Alison of the Mynd, who was exported to Mrs Adams' Talisker kennel in Canada in the 1950s, and Int Ch Bettine of the Mynd, owned by Lady Miles who made her a champion, bred from her and then sold her in whelp to Mrs Sylvia May of Switzerland, where she gained her International title.

The Bracadale kennel belonging to Mrs B and Miss V Axtell bred that great winner in America Ch Bracadale Henry (Holmesdale Bonnie Charlie ex Bracadale Berenice). Henry was a Terrier Group winner and was placed second in the group at the 1942 Westminster show, the highest award for a Skye at that time. Ch Bracadale Nanette and Ch Bracadale Marguerite gained their titles in 1938 and 1939.

Miss J Craig's Skyhigh kennel bred and owned a number of well known winners in the 1930s, the most famous of which, Skyhigh Lady Fay of Talisker, went on to become a champion at the Talisker kennel in Canada. Mrs Mowbray's Ch Prince of Quarrydale and his son Ch Corin were very well known in the show ring and were immortalised by Maud Earl's famous painting of the two.

Lady Miles' daughter, Miss V Black, bred a few litters in the mid 1930s by Ch Chummie of Merrymount ex Bright Lass for her Fanling affix. By the end of the 1930s the leading kennels were Merrymount, Mynd, Meerend, Peacehaven, Bracadale and Skyhigh.

THE BRITISH SKYE TERRIER 1946-1970

A great change took place after the Second World War. The present Skye Terrier Club was established in 1946 with the amalgamation of the Skye Terrier Association and the Skye and Clydesdale Terrier Club. In 1976, for the benefit of the Scottish members north of the border a Scottish Branch, which supports classes and holds fund raising activities for the benefit of the breed, was approved.

From 1946 onwards breeders slowly recovered their former position in the world by producing once again the quality which overseas buyers expected, though it took about five years to regain the standard which critical breeders expected from their own stock, and one of the first stars was to emerge from the Merrymount kennel, Ch Merrymount You'll Do. The Meerend and Mynd kennels continued to breed good stock and new kennels which were to create their own place in the history of the breed sprang up, including the famous Rhosneigr Kennel belonging to Marion Crook who is known throughout the world.

Marion von Feldmahr was born in Vienna, Austria. When she was just eleven years old her father died and a few years later, while on a holiday trip to Venice with her mother, she met a handsome oil engineer, Bob Crook. It was love at first sight for them both. Bob proposed the next day and they rushed to the British Consul to make arrangements for the wedding. Meanwhile Marion's mother was most alarmed, thinking her daughter was about to be whisked away by a white slave trader!

At the end of their holiday Marion returned home with her mother, and Bob followed a short time later for the marriage, which took place at the Town Hall in Vienna. For the next six months the Crooks lived in Venice, as required by Bob's business contract, returning to England in 1936 and bringing with them Marion's Maltese Terrier, a breed she has kept all her life. At the outbreak of war they moved to Anglesey, to a place called Rhosneigr, which is now better known for Skye Terriers than for anything else, though the inhabitants of Rhosneigr would doubtless disagree!

Rhosneigr Raffles (Bracadale Silver Laird ex Anna of Peacehaven), Marion's first Skye, came from Bristol and cost £5. Raffles was joined shortly after by Rhosneigr Ragamuffin and by Rhosneigr Roundabout, a younger brother of Raffles. In 1943 Raffles produced the first Rhosneigr litter to Christopher of Meerend. There were four pups in the litter and a dog, Rhosneigr Retrobate, was kept. Retrobate was bred to Bracadale Janette in August 1944 producing Rhosneigr Rumplstilzchen, the first big winner for the kennel. He went on to take two Challenge Certificates and twelve Reserve CCs and was extremely unlucky not to gain his title, though Marion is the first to admit that it was difficult to break through the Merrymount barrier which was then at its height.

From then on the Rhosneigr kennel made its presence felt in the ring with many outstanding champions including Ch Rhosneigr Redoubtable, Ch Rhosneigr Rightaway, NL Ch Rhosneigr Raoul, Am Ch Rhosneigr Sir Roger, Ch Rhosneigr Ravioli, Ch Rhosneigr Reef Knot, Ch Rhosneigr Radar, Ch Rhosneigr Rippling Foam, Ch Rhosneigr Rolling Pin, Ch Rhosneigr Right Fionn, and Ch Rhosneigr River Toy who gained his title in America. The beautiful Ch Rhosneigr Red Shoes (Ch Rhosneigr Rightaway ex Rhosneigr Real Platinum) went Best of Breed at Crufts in 1959 and 1960 before crossing the Atlantic to join the Merrybrac kennels. Ch Rhosneigr Risingstar, a big winner in England, then joined the famous Iradell kennel where he was campaigned to his American title.

During the 1960s the Rhosneigr kennel bred several champions including the Crufts Best of Breed winner in 1961 and 1962, Ch Rhosneigr Blonde Bit (Ch Rhosneigr Rightaway ex Rhosneigr Real Platinum); Ch Rhosneigr Recamier; Ch Rhosneigr Rise Again; Ch Rhosneigr Rarest Do; and Australian Ch Rhosneigr Blonde Ever. In addition to these, Int Ch Rhosneigr Recovery and Int Ch Rhosneigr Silver Flash both gained their titles in Finland for the Skyeline kennel.

In 1968 Mrs Crook astounded the Skye fraternity by announcing the sale of her dogs as she and her husband were moving to Spain. Several of her prize Rhosneigrs went to breeders and exhibitors. One, Ch Rhosneigr Clever Dusty, gained her title by winning the Challenge Certificate at Crufts in 1970 for owners Mr and Mrs Bevan Jones. Fortunately for us Spain did not work out for them and they returned after a couple of years. Marion resumed breeding with Rhosneigr stock, producing the champion brother and sister, Ch Rhosneigr Silver Ravissant and Ch Rhosneigr Cream Ravish of Drewsteignton, who gained their titles in 1973/74. Ch Rhosneigr Blonde Flora took her title in 1976, followed by Chappell and Stephenson's Ch Rhosneigr Cream Raging Moon and Rhosneigr Silver Solo Quest in 1979. During the 1980s Ch Rhosneigr Right Cream Tops took her title for Messrs Chappell and Stephenson's Mariquita kennel. Ch Rhosneigr Blonde Revenge and Ch Rhosneigr Blonde Returning to Mallysmar and Ch Rhosneigr Blond Reviver at Mallysmar also gained their titles.

The 1990s saw Rhosneigr Cream Flashpoint taking the Challenge Certificate at the South Wales Championship Show in 1990. Though the colourful figure of Marion Crook, who has been a Championship Show judge of Skyes and Maltese for many years and is a past President of the Skye Terrier Club, is seen less often at shows nowadays the Rhosneigr kennel is still fully operational with Rhosneigr Duncan's Dream (Rhosneigr Shadow Fox ex Rhosneigr Blonde Rebel) carrying on the kennel tradition by winning the large Puppy Stakes Class at the Southern Counties Canine Society Championship Show at nine months of age.

In the late 1940s Mr and Mrs Haddrell enjoyed great success with their Ch Atom of Brackenville. Then in the 1950s Mr and Mrs Wattsford bought the Skye, Rhosneigr Ravioli, and were encouraged to show her, which they did most successfully, and she became their first champion. She was later bred to Ch Atom of Brackenville producing the famous Ch Gavin of Culsh, a dog who figures in many top winners' pedigrees.

Miss Mina Alexander, daughter of Sir Claud and Lady Alexander of Ballochmyle fame, had grown up among a wide assortment of animals. This great character, loved by all who knew her, judged her first little dog show at the age of eight years. During the war years her brothers, who did not share the family interest in animals, took up arms, so it was left to Mina to continue the upkeep of the farm and zoo with her father. Many of the larger animals had to go in those difficult times, but when Miss Freda Cheeseman arrived to work with the Alexanders in 1941 there were still wolves, silver and Arctic foxes, a bison, zebra, many varieties of deer, owls, tame rats and mice, sixteen Skyes and nineteen show cats, plus horses, Park Cattle and British Old Cattle. Fortunately Freda was not put off by the hard work involved in looking after so many animals, and she remained at Faygate until Miss Alexander's death in 1986. Freda is now retired and lives in one of the farm cottages with her Faygate dogs.

In 1949 Miss Alexander bought Katrine of Peacecot who won at least one Challenge Certificate. From the Merrymount kennels she bought Ch Merrymount the Baron who gained his title, as did the beautiful drop ear Ch Merrymount Sundown. Miss Alexander's first Faygate litter, affixed after the village of the same name, produced Faygate Dawn, Faygate Wise Girl and Faygate Guy Fawkes, all excellent dogs who did a fair amount of winning, with Guy Fawkes later joining Mrs Adams' Talisker kennel in Canada.

Ch Faygate Dusk gained his title in 1968, followed by his daughter Ch Faygate Miss Spiv (ex Merrymount Mid Day Cloud). Faygate Daybreak was the winner of one Challenge Certificate while her litter brother, Faygate Rowland, was the particular favourite of his owner and shared the house with some of the equally famous Faygate Australian Terriers. Ch Faygate Twilight and Faygate Nijinsky, winner of two CCs, continued to bring top honours to the kennel. The Faygate kennel was also home to CC winner Merrymount Wot Airs, Jebusa Titania (a lovely cream owned owned by Miss Cheeseman), Glenshiel Arkle, Merrymount Mid Day Cloud and Cantor Apollo.

Yet another great name in Skyes is that of Mrs Rhalou Kirkby Peace, of the Kirkby affix, who grew up among Skyes and animals of all shapes and sizes. Mrs Kirkby Peace, daughter of the Rev Rosslyn Bruce, accompanied her father to many shows as a child and, on leaving school, went with him to America on a trip which combined preaching sermons and judging dog shows. After her marriage to Kirkby Peace in 1935 she rekindled her interest in Skyes with Southernhills Dawn (Ch Bill Merrymount ex Southernhills Moonshine) born in 1937. Dawn produced a litter to Fergusson in 1940. Two of the puppies, Finella and Fullerton, were owned by Rev Rosslyn Bruce, while Mrs Peace kept Kirkby Dusk. Kirkby Dusk was mated with Minor of Meerend in 1943, producing a litter which included Kirkby Yonnie who produced Int Ch Kirkby Longago (by Kirkby Kelpie) in 1945.

Though the Kirkby kennel did not produce as many champions as some, possibly due to the fact that there were six sons to raise, the kennel was famous for such names as Am Ch Kirkby Silver Tip, Am Ch Kirkby King, Kirkby Queen (the winner of two Challenge Certificates) and Am Ch Kirkby Hailstorm of Talisker. In addition to her Skyes Mrs Kirkby Peace bred some very good Manchester Terriers which achieved championship status.

Mrs Jarvis' Applecross affix was well known, particularly for Drummer Boy of Applecross (Bracadale Laddie ex Bracadale Wild Rose) born in 1945. Mrs Weber had a great run in the late 1950s winning several Challenge Certificates with her Ch Merrymount Happy Jack (Ch Gavin of Culsh ex Merrymount Desire).

Miss Joyce Braham had been a kennel maid at the famous Merrymount kennels and fell for the breed, successfully establishing her own kennel based on

Merrymount stock. The Happyhill kennel made up some lovely champions including Ch Merrymount Mary Jane (Int Ch Merrymount You'll Do ex Sheena of Meerend) who was the foundation bitch of the kennel. Mary Jane was first bred to Merrymount Wise Guy producing Ch Happyhill Gay Gordon, and later to Ch Merrymount Mid Day Sun producing Ch Happyhill Minnehaha. In the 1960s the top winners from this small quality kennel included Ch Happyhill Hokey Cokey and Ch Happyhill Minette. Not gaining their titles but always among the top prize-winners were Happyhill Anna Maria and Happyhill Eliza Jane.

Mrs Julia Gibbons' first Skye, Merrymount Belle, enjoyed some success in the ring. After the death of Mrs Weber Mrs Gibbons acquired Ch Merrymount Happy Jack and in 1958 she bred her first litter, from which came Jebusa Much Ado and Jebusa Tempest, both well known in the show ring. The cream bitch, Rhosneigr Ever Ready, was a consistent winner at shows, and when subsequently mated with Merrymount Wot Airs she produced a lovely cream winner, Jebusa Titania, with littermates Jebusa Plain Kate and Jebusa MacBeth also well placed at shows. Vanghapara Something Special, bought in 1978, was another winner in the ring, though the big green card eluded her.

Always a lover of drop ears, Mrs Gibbons, with Messrs Chappell and Stephenson, imported the black drop ear Am Ch Skyecrest Lady of the Evening (Rusalka's Ebony ex Skyecrest Lady Bridget) in 1986. After spending the compulsory six months in quarantine the bitch was campaigned to her British title and bred a litter for the Mariquita kennel. She then went to Mrs Gibbons, who bred her to Ch Mariquita Flashback, producing the outstanding Ch Jebusa Miranda at Mariquita, already the winner of three Terrier Groups, including Crufts 1992, and one Terrier Group Reserve at the tender age of two years. From this same litter Mrs Gibbons kept Jebusa Othello who won a Challenge Certificate in 1991, while her litter brother, Jebusa Mustardseed, took his title in 1992.

Mrs Gibbons can be a shining example to all those who are impatient to own a champion. She may have had to wait a long time but look what can happen when you do! Patience is its own reward. Not many people can boast about breeding the Crufts Terrier Group winner as Mrs Gibbons is perfectly entitled to do, and neither does living on the Channel Island of Alderney prevent her from following her hobby. Despite the inconvenience of travelling by cargo ship with her dogs Mrs Gibbons manages to support a great many championship shows.

Mr and Mrs G H Bailey came into the breed in the early 1950s through buying a Skye in an auction! The dog, Ch Rhosneigr Rolling Pin, went on to be joint Skye of the Year 1955. Soon the whole family were interested in Skyes, with Miss Muriel Bailey's Ch Rhosneigr Right Fionn the next big winner, followed by Mr and Mrs Bailey's famous Ch Rhosneigr Risingstar who was to go on to gain more honours for the Iradell kennels in America.

The Bailey's bred their first Marjayn litter in 1960 by Ch Merrymount Mid Day Sun out of Happyhill Maid of Perth producing three champions. They were Ch Marjayn Maxwell (who was handled so perfectly by Miss Bailey at Crufts to win the Challenge Certificate in 1962 and was later exported to Switzerland), Ch Marjayn Mink, and the lovely Ch Marjayn Meta, a big winner in the ring. Ch Rhosneigr Rarest Do (Rhosneigr Right Laddie ex Rhosneigr Ravishing Rita) joined this successful kennel in 1961, followed by Ch Merrymount the Rock (Ch Merrymount Mid-day Sun ex Merrymount Rockette). A litter by The Rock out of Ch Marjayn Meta produced two dogs, Ch Marjayn Fairy Wonder and Int Ch Marjayn Dougal, a big winner in Finland. A repeat mating in 1967 produced Ch Marjayn Dirk.

Ch Marjayn Coruisk Fancy (Ch Acheo Sea Sprite ex Kirby Harmony) became the next title holder for the kennel. Bred to Ch Marjayn Dirk she produced Ch Marjayn Melita, a Terrier Group winner, Ch Marjayn Marengo and Ch Marjayn Manfred, who had collected a staggering eighty-nine Best in Show awards at open shows before he ever stepped into a championship show ring. Ch Marjayn Coruisk Fancy then left these shores for Finland where she took her international title.

After the death of her parents Miss Bailey continued to breed and show the Marjayns and has kept the flag flying with yet more champions. Ch Marjayn Mona and Ch Marcus (Ch Glenshiel Stroller ex Ch Marjayn Melita) are both reserve Group winners, Ch Marjayn Merry Xmas, Ch Marjayn Midge Modge, Ch Marjayn Mickey Mouse, Ch Muffy of Marjayn, Ch Marjayn Moser (winner of the Terrier Group at the Driffield Show in 1989) and his litter sister, Ch Marjayn Mischief, bring us to date with this small but very select kennel.

The Burmar kennels belonging to Mrs Marshall and Miss Burton were perhaps better known as a Smooth Fox Terrier kennel but some fine Skyes were bred here with several champions abroad. The kennel owned Kirkby Queen, the winner of two Challenge Certificates, and Merrymount Sunspot, the winner of one CC. These two produced the drop ear, Burmar McGuffie, who figures in a lot of pedigrees to this day. McGuffie sired some excellent stock including Am Ch Burmar Alexandra of Iradell, Am Ch Burmar Sandman of Iradell and Am Ch Burmar Drummer of Iradell. The cream bitch, Burmar Cream Bun, who was bought by the Tarskavaig kennels, is behind many of the top winners in this kennel.

Miss Salter established the Douce kennel with stock from Meerend, Rhosneigr and the dog Athluain Chummie. The first Douce litter, by Ch Athluain Chummie out of Phillipa of Meerend, was registered in 1950 and contained seven dogs! One, Douce Blaven, was kept and he accompanied Miss Salter on a trip to Skye in 1951. *The Clarion of Skye* reported the visit saying Douce Blaven had walked sixteen miles with his kennel mates to be photographed beside the mountain after which he was named. Miss Salter was known to keep all excess hair which was groomed out of the Skyes, spun it into yarn and knitted waistcoats, hats and socks for her friends.

Mrs P Gamble of Renfrewshire in Scotland owned Douce Suency, the winner of one Challenge Certificate. A litter by Rhosneigr Rare Do and Suency produced Genteel Silver Sail and helped to establish the breed again on its native Isle.

Mrs Khan, a native of Skye, owned Jebusa Tempest and Rhosneigr Rising Tide and when they were bred together the first litter of Coruisk Skyes were registered - a popular name for an affix. One of this litter went to Mr and Mrs John McGarva of the Speywood affix.

In 1944 Mrs Mary Macdonald bought Darkie Dene (Ch Rip of Merrymount ex Grianach Spark) from Mr John Millar of Paisley. Having married a Skyeman and been introduced to the breed by her brother-in-law, who owned one, it seemed only right that she should have a Skye Terrier too. During the war, while her husband was at sea, she lived in Liverpool. After the war they moved up to Skye and built their home on the Isle. Mrs Macdonald was dismayed to find only one other Skye on the island, an old Merrymount, and was determined to reintroduce the breed to its original home. This was no easy task as Skyes were scarce. Meanwhile daughter Sine was born, and while looking after her and two dogs (the Skye and a Cairn) Mrs Macdonald put the idea on hold. Darkie died at twelve years of age in 1951 and it was to be another six years before the dream could be realised.

Genteel Silver Sail and Genteel Misty Maid came to Skye from Renfrewshire in 1957, Misty Maid going to another member of the Macdonald family. It was three years before a suitable dog, Douce Granite (Douce Horizon ex Douce Sieglinda), was found, and he was followed shortly after by Merrymount Mid Ship (Ch Merrymount Mid-Day Sun ex Merrymount Gala Queen) in 1961. With these three the kennel slowly took shape. The number was doubled in 1962 with the arrival of Merrymount Mary Ellen (Ch Merrymount Mid Night ex Ch Merrymount Mary Jane), Kirkby Harmony (Douce Horizon ex Serene of Meerend) and the dog Marjayn Jock of Dornoch (Int Ch Rhosneigr Risingstar ex Merrymount Sundry). All were registered in Sine's name with Mrs Mary Macdonald and Miss Sine Macdonald taking the Acheo affix for the Eilean Acheo kennels. Two litters were bred in 1962 with Sine Acheo (Douce Granite ex Genteel Silver Sail) going to Mrs Margaret MacDonald who was also in the process of establishing a Skye kennel at her home in Tarskavaig.

The first exports from the kennels took place in 1962 with Eilidh and Ros Mhairi Acheo going to America, the latter to Gordon Jackson of The Rocks Skyes. In another early litter Darrach Acheo (Douce Granite ex Kirkby Harmony) was sold to Mr James Philp of Uig in Skye, who had been the only other owner of a Skye when Mary first moved to the island.

A visit to the kennels in 1964 by Madame Williamson of the famous Luchar affix led to an exchange of ideas, the Macdonalds deciding to import a dog from the Olivia kennel in Czechoslovakia. Negotiations were started and Olivia Whist (Int Ch Olivia Jatagan ex Ch Eike v Seehaus) entered the country in 1965. Having been released from quarantine in September of the same year, Ch Acheo Olivia Whist went on to take his title in 1967. Several of his offspring went abroad to take their titles in later years, Ch Acheo Olga Olivova in Australia, Ch Acheo Good King Wenceslas in America and Ch Acheo Scottish Nationalist in New Zealand. In 1968 the kennel imported Olivia Laska (Int Ch Jack v Bary ex Ch Olivia Zinien) who won several Reserve Challenge Certificates.

Ch Acheo Olivia Whist (Int Ch Olivia Jatagan ex Ch Eike v Seehaus).
Photo: D Whyte's Studio.

Acheo Angus of Armadale (Ch Olivia Whist ex Merrymount Midship) won Best of Breed at Crufts Show in 1970 under breed specialist Mr H Bailey, then went on to be among the last five in the Terrier Group under the noted terrier judge, Walter Bradshaw. Angus was later exported to Belgium. The first Acheo champion to take his title in Britain was made up by Mrs Sue Atkinson with Ch Acheo Sea Sprite (Darrach Acheo ex Sorcha Acheo) in 1970 and Ch Acheo McPherson's Rant, a son of Sea Sprite (ex Rhosneigr Right Rippy), gained his title in 1971.

At the end of 1970 Sine went to Australia where she married Allan Threlfall. While there they bought two Skyes, Aust Ch Danehill Gay Princess (Ch Rhosneigr Blond Ever ex Ch Danehill Frigga) a cream drop ear, and the silver prick ear Ch Danehill Silver Sail (Danehill Oliver ex Danehill Greyhen). Both were shown with moderate success in Western Australia, the first Skyes to reach that state. Gay Princess took Best in Show at a parade, which was another first for a Skye. Both gained their titles in Australia, and when the Threlfalls returned to Skye in 1972 the dogs followed after their six months quarantine in Britain.

Just as the Threlfalls had arrived back with a son so, too, did the Skyes arrive with offspring; Acheo Kalgoorlie Kate was born in quarantine. During the time which Sine spent in Australia Mary carried on with the Skyes at home, enjoying considerable success with Maid of the Loch of Acheo (Tarskavaig Deerstalker ex Methilhaven Queen Sheba) who took two Reserve Challenge Certificates. In 1975 Aust Ch Danehill Gay Princess was sold to drop ear enthusiast Mrs Alice Smith of the Dunvegan affix in America, and she gained her title there, producing the occasional drop ear for her American owner.

In 1976 Mary Macdonald died and it was left to Sine to carry on breeding and showing the Skyes. That year Acheo Kalgoorlie Kate produced a litter to Dracula's Luxy of Kirkleyditch, in partnership with Mrs Peggy Heap, from which came Ch Pendlebrook Lady Stair and Hungarian Ch Pendlebrook Prince

Willie Threlfall with Acheo Am Basteir (Acheo Bla Bheinn ex Acheo Inverie).

Fergus. Together Sine and Mrs Heap imported Olivia Radovan (Am Ch Talisker's Fearless ex Olivia Novela) who won several RCCs and sired the lovely Ch Drewsteignton Avesta in Australia, Ch Drewsteignton Electra in America and Ch Drewsteignton Arlanda in Finland (ex Int Ch Larrikin's Iris of Drewsteignton), Ch Buchan Boy from Whodeanie (ex Coruisk Kilmandy) and the Challenge Certificate winners Acheo Maighdean Bhan and her brother Acheo Bla Bheinn (ex Acheo Kalgoorlie Kate), the latter winning the Terrier Group at Driffield Championship Show in 1981.

Int Ch Acheo Alice Springs (Acheo Bla Bheinn ex Acheo Inverie) was bitch of the year in 1984 before going to Sweden where she gained her international title. Younger brother Ch Acheo Somerled won three Challenge Certificates before his export to France, where he too became an International Champion. Ch Checkbar Jennifer Eccles (Ch Vanghapara Wild Highlander ex Ch Kirkleyditch Jenny Geddes) joined the kennel in 1983, going Best of Breed at Crufts in 1985, to complete a total of seven Challenge Certificates, with a Reserve Best Terrier in Group at Driffield Championship Show in 1980.

In addition to those already mentioned the Acheo kennel has produced the following champions: Ch Acheo Bonnie Jean, who won Best of Breed at Crufts 1972, and Ch Acheo Linsey Macdonald, who did likewise at Crufts in 1983. Abroad, Am Ch Acheo Eilean Dhu took her American championship in

1967, the first champion for that kennel; Int Ch Acheo Prince Charlie, Am Ch Acheo Mhairi Bhan, Nor Ch Acheo Gavin Hastings, SF Ch Acheo Local Hero, Aust Ch Acheo Robbie's Pride, and Dk Ch Acheo Donald Angus have all gained their titles, with SF Ch Acheo Roy Laidlaw the most recent in 1992. The latest British champions bred by the kennel are Ch Acheo Capercaillie at Joyscavey and Ch Acheo Glittertind Morag at Skykim who also gained their titles in 1992.

Int Ch Acheo Alice Springs
(Acheo Bla Bheinn ex Acheo Inverie).

Int Ch Acheo Alice Springs.

Mrs Margaret MacDonald of the Tarskavaig kennels, which she started on the Isle of Skye shortly after her marriage in the early 1960s, first met Mary Macdonald and her three Skyes soon after her arrival in Skye and decided that she, too, would like to become involved with the breed. Her first Skye, Merrymount Gay Countess sadly died young, but her second, Rhosneigr Rushing Dame, went on to win one Challenge Certificate and proved her worth as an excellent brood bitch.

Sine Acheo joined the Tarskavaig kennel as did Merrymount Gay Chummie, with Chummie going on to become the kennel's first champion in 1965. In 1963 Chummie and Rushing Dame had a litter which included the outstanding dog, Tarskavaig Great Scot, the winner of two Challenge Certificates in this country before his export to the famous Iradell kennel in America where he was quickly campaigned to his American title. His litter sister gained her crown in 1965. Adding Burmar Cream Bun (Burmar McGuffie ex Burmar Elspeth) to the Tarskavaig kennel was an excellent move as she proved to be a great brood bitch, producing Ch Tarskavaig Highland Fling, Ch Tarskavaig Scots Grey and Int Ch Tarskavaig Royal Scot in Finland, all by Tarskavaig Great Scot in one litter. Ch Tarskavaig Mary Morrison also won her title in Britain before going to Finland where she, too, gained her international championship.

Ch Tarskavaig Glorious Twelfth, a beautiful bitch, easily achieved her British title before being exported with Tarskavaig Lord of the Isles to the Cherry Lane kennels in America, where they were both campaigned to their American championships. Gloria's dam, Silver Birch, also made her way across the Atlantic to gain her crown. Eastneuk Rory Mohr (Ch Tarskavaig Scots Grey ex Tarskavaig Silver Dew) was shown under Olga Smid in 1968, taking the Challenge Certificate, and he, too, was later exported to America.

Merrymount Thou Swell, the winner of two Challenge Certificates, had joined the Tarskavaig kennel, Margaret piloting him to his title in 1969. His daughter, Tarskavaig Bonnie Scotland, gained her title in 1971, followed by the lovely Ch Tarskavaig Esmeralda in 1973. The last Tarskavaig champion born on the Isle of Skye in 1973, Ch Tarskavaig Bonar Law, gained his crown in 1977. Mrs MacDonald later left Skye and remarried. Now known as Mrs MacDonald Cross, she continues to show most successfully with her husband, Bob.

Ch Wismar Silver Sword, co-owned with John Burrows, was campaigned to his title in 1978 and Ch Tarskavaig Passion Flower gained hers in 1982, Ch Speywood Rowantree, owned by Bob Cross, taking his title in 1983. Other title holders to have graced the kennels include Ch Wismar Cream Delight, Ch Tarskavaig Poinsettia and Ch Tarskavaig Northern Lights, the latest, Ch Wellknowe Wordsworth (Tarskavaig Ben Nevis ex Wismar Weeping Wilow), gaining his crown at Crufts in

Ch Tarskavaig Glorious Twelth (Merrymount the Rip ex Ch Tarskavaig Silver Birch) at nine months of age.

1992. The newest star to emerge from the Tarskavaig kennels is his daughter, Tarskavaig The Glory Road, who has already made her presence felt by winning two Challenge Certificates.

In addition Ch Tarskavaig Clansman, Ch Tarskavaig Hallmark, Ch Tarskavaig Sugar and Spice, Ch Tarskavaig Wee Geordie, Ch Tarskavaig King's Royal of Glenshiel, and Ch Tarskavaig Illicit Still have all gained their titles in other ownership. It can be seen that the Tarskavaig kennel is behind many of the current top winning kennels in both England and Scotland.

Mr and Mrs John McGarva have owned Skyes since 1958, beginning with a Coruisk Skye bred by Mrs Khan. In 1967 they bought Tarskavaig Highland Dancer and caught the "show bug". After a modest start in the show ring Dancer was bred to Ch Merrymount Gay Chummie and a bitch, Speywood Rhona, was retained and shown with some success. Her daughter by Glenshiel Arkle, Speywood Bonnie, a lovely cream, became the first champion for the kennel in 1981. Bonnie produced two litters and from the first, to Ch Wismar Silver Sword, Speywood Gigha was retained and went on to win two Reserve Challenge Certificates. Her second litter, to Ch Tarskavaig Bonar Law, produced two champions, Speywood Rowantree (owned by the Tarskavaig kennels) and Speywood Luckenbooth Lucy, who was kept by her breeders. The latest addition, Orasaidh Dallas Dhu at Speywood, is a grandson of Rowantree and has begun his show career most successfully by attracting much attention for his extrovert behaviour.

Liz and George Austin went to see Walt Disney's film *Greyfriars Bobby* and ended up with a highly successful kennel of Skyes! In 1962 they bought Burmar Elsa, who sadly died young. She was followed by a Tarskavaig Skye out of Burmar Cream Bun, litter sister to Elsa, and Ch Tarskavaig Highland Fling as she was known went on to win Best of Breed at Crufts in 1967 and gained a total of five Challenge Certificates.

Merrymount Mid-Day Cloud, who was bought in whelp to Merrymount Wot Airs from Miss Alexander, produced the first Glenshiel litter, with Ch Glenshiel Miss Muffet, a beautiful cream, winning Bitch of the Year in 1968. The next title holder for the kennel, Ch Glenshiel Duchess, an outstanding drop ear, gained her title in 1970 and for many years was the only drop ear to be exhibited in the British Isles. Ch Glenshiel Scots Borderer took his first Challenge Certificate in 1971 when he was also Reserve in the Terrier Group at Three Counties Championship Show. He gained his crown in 1973, beating his sire, Ch Glenshiel Stroller , who won his title in 1974.

Since then rather than breeding Skyes the Austins have bought in dogs to show and have been most successful. Ch Whodeanie Lizzie Dripping of Glenshiel gained her title in 1979, Ch Pollyanna of Glenshiel took her title in 1983 and Ch Tarskavaig King's Royal of Glenshiel won his crown in 1986. He then came out in the veteran class at Crufts in 1991 to win the Challenge Certificate and Best of Breed, a fine achievement! This kennel has not been home to as many Skyes as some during the last thirty years, but all the Austin's dogs, except their first, have lived exceedingly long lives thanks to the loving care of their devoted owners.

Mrs Kaye McDonald's first Skye, Ch Merrymount Anna, gained her title in 1966. Her Tarskavaig Pipe Major was a consistently well placed winner who was unfortunate not to gain his title though he and Anna were very well matched and won many brace classes together. The pride of Kaye McDonald's kennel, Ch Kirkleyditch Polomint, was a big winner who went Best in Show at the National Terrier Show in 1977. Later Mrs McDonald enjoyed considerable success with Whodeanie Imperial Mint who was, of course, out of Ch Kirkleyditch Polomint.

Ch Kirkleyditch Maiden of Rona with her son Pensford Lord of Arran.

Mr and Mrs Tom Tasker established their Eastneuk kennel with Skyes of Mrs Margaret Macdonald Cross' Tarskavaig breeding and their Ch Tarskavaig Scots Grey gained his title in 1970. His son, Eastneuk Rory Mohr who was out of Tarskavaig Silver Dew, was awarded one Challenge Certificate before his export to America. Eastneuk Cream Cracker, who was from a repeat mating of Scots Grey and Silver Dew, and the Tasker's Tarskavaig St Nicholas both enjoyed some good wins, Nicholas winning a Reserve Challenge Certificate before his export to Italy where he gained his crown.

Jill and John Bower returned from a holiday on the Isle of Skye with a Skye Terrier by the name of Tarskavaig Clansman and were later persuaded to show him. Like so many before and since, they caught the show bug! Clansman became the first champion for the Kirkleyditch kennel. Happyhill Jemma joined the Bowers, producing their first home bred big winner, Kirkleyditch Tiggy Winkle, by Clansman of course. Tiggy Winkle won one Challenge Certificate, two Reserve CCs and was Bitch of the Year in 1970. She was then sold to Ireland and therefore did not complete her campaign for a title.

In 1970 the Bowers imported Dracula's Luxy of Kirkleyditch from the Netherlands. He was a controversial dog who was considered small by British standards at that time, but he justified his owners' faith in him by winning two CCs and seven RCCs, and was unlucky not to gain his title. His strength as a stud dog firmly established the Kirkleyditch kennel as the top name in Skyes in the 1970s and 1980s. His matings to Happyhill Jemma produced the lovely elegant black, Ch Kirkleyditch Petrel, Ch Kirkleyditch Dalesman, the winner of fourteen Challenge Certificates and himself an outstanding sire, Italian Ch Kirkleyditch Destiny and NL Ch Kirkleyditch Diamond. In addition to Jemma's litters, Dracula's Luxy of Kirkleyditch sired many champions to different Skye bitches and he has champion progeny in many countries as well as the British Isles, being a wonderful example of a prepotent sire.

Ch Kirkleyditch Maxamillion (Ch Kirkleyditch Marksman ex Kirkleyditch Annabelle).

During the 1980s Miss Nicola Bower began to campaign Balquhatston Silver Magic most successfully, piloting her to her crown in 1982. Nicki bred Magic with Ch Spaceman of Skye Devils Inn, producing Ch Kirkleyditch Arran. In 1986 Nicki bred a litter by Kirkleyditch Ace of Clubs ex Arizona Pie of Kirkleyditch which produced the top winning drop ear, Ch Kirkleyditch Carbon Copy, who has a total of nine CCs and many Best of Breed awards, including Crufts 1990. Many Skye champions have emerged from this famous kennel, including the lovely Ch Kirkleyditch Silvery Star who went Best in Show at the first Skye Terrier Club Open Show to be held on the Isle of Skye under judge Walter Goodman in 1980. Other notables include: Ch Kirkleyditch Seanab of Whodeanie, Ch Kirkleyditch Border Queen and SF Ch Kirkleyditch Border King (Ch Kirkleyditch Dalesman ex Hornblower Hoola-La); Ch Kirkleyditch Maiden of Rona (Ch Spaceman of Skye Devils Inn ex Kirkleyditch Annabelle); Ch Kirkleyditch Rosetta (Ch Kirkleyditch Marksman ex Kirkleyditch Annabelle); Ch Kirkleyditch Benzina (Mariquita Flashlightning of Kirkleyditch ex Kirkleyditch Snowpoppy); and the latest star, Kirkleyditch Rebecca (Kirkleyditch Viking ex Ch Kirkleyditch Rosetta). Now Jill and daughter Nicki continue to maintain the high standard which is associated with the Kirkleyditch kennels.

Mr and Mrs J Newsham of Lancashire bought their first Skye from its native island in 1965. She was Tarskavaig Sunday Ferry, (Ch Merrymount Gay Chummie ex Happyhill Minuet) who did a fair amount of winning and was the foundation bitch on which this small but successful kennel was built. Their first homebred litter, by Ch Merrymount the Rock, produced Ch Drewsteignton Jane who was kept along with Drewsteignton Donna. Donna was bred to Ch Rhosneigr Silver Ravissant to produce Ch Drewsteignton Be Fair in 1975. Another bitch to gain her title was Ch Rhosneigr Cream Ravish of Drewsteignton who was made up in 1973, and Ch Fereymount Cassiopeia of Drewsteignton achieved her title in 1977. During that year the Newshams also imported the beautiful Int Ch Larrikins Iris of Drewsteignton from the Netherlands, who quickly added her British title to an already impressive list of honours.

Homebred Ch Drewsteignton Kingmaker gained his third Challenge Certificate in 1979 and the Newshams next litter produced three pups and three champions, Ch Drewsteignton Avesta in Australia, Int Ch Drewsteignton Arlanda in Finland and Ch Drewsteignton Electra in America, who were by the imported Olivia Radovan ex Int Ch Larrikin's Iris of Drewsteignton. Drewsteignton Christmas Star of Skyeline was imported from Finland and won one Challenge Certificate here, while homebred Drewsteignton Emma gained two before the Newshams gave up exhibiting their Skyes though both still judge the breed.

Mr and Mrs Fish were introduced to the breed in the mid-1960s and enjoyed considerable success with Happyhill Mini Major. In the 1970s their Ch Moonraker gained her title, while litter sister, Silver Sweep of Hogscross, also did some winning. Unfortunately illness prevented the Fish's from showing Kirkleyditch Jill in the 1980s.

Mr Abe Harkness, whose Senkrah Staffordshire Bull Terriers are very well known, became interested in Skyes in the 1960s and has owned and bred them since 1969. Senkrah Bandsman and Senkrah Birthday Girl (Ch Tarskavaig Scots Grey ex Mo-cridhe Acheo) were early winners for the kennel, followed by Blairside Highland Queen. Tarskavaig Clydesider joined the kennel in 1977 and was consistently placed at shows. In the 1980s Senkrah Flora Macdonald won a Reserve Challenge Certificate at Manchester Championship Show. Though the Senkrahs have always been shown sparingly their owner is a popular choice as a judge and has officiated in the breed both at home and abroad.

Mrs Ann Sim is best remembered for breeding Int Ch Marjayn Coruisk Fancy (Ch Acheo Sea Sprite ex Kirkby Harmony) in the 1960s. Mrs Sim's mother hails from Elgol on the Isle of Skye, close to Loch Coruisk, so it was appropriate for her to choose the affix Coruisk for her kennel. Establishing her kennel with stock from the Acheo kennel, Mrs Sim enjoyed a great deal of success with Acheo Angus Og, and producing the aforementioned Fancy from Kirkby Harmony who was bought in whelp.

Ch Coruisk Gleamour was sold to Mrs Sue Atkinson of the Silhill kennel and gained his title in 1970. Coruisk Imp, a delightful bitch, won a Reserve

Challenge Certificate for her breeder in 1969, with Sine Macdonald's Coruisk Kilmandy winning two Reserve Challenge Certificates in the early 1970s. Shortly after this Mrs Sim had to give up her Skyes due to ill health but her sister, Mrs Taggart, keeps up the family's interest in the breed with her Skyes, although they are unshown.

The famous Silhill kennel was established in 1968 with Ch Coruisk Gleamour becoming the first big winner for Mrs Sue Atkinson. Shortly after Ch Acheo Sea Sprite joined the kennel, just achieving his championship before Gleamour, and was followed by his son Ch Silhill Acheo MacPherson's Rant. In 1971 the spectacular Ch Silhill Silver Secret made his debut in the show ring, quickly taking his title in 1972 and going on to win the Terrier Group at Crufts in 1974. Ch Hornblower Tora Tora, Ch Silhill Sea Breeze, who later became an International Champion in Finland, Ch Silhill Sparky of Zapangu and Ch Silhill

Ch Silhill Silver Secret (Tarskavaig Canny Scot ex Kirkleyditch Moonlight) winner of the Terrier Group at Crufts 1974.

Silver Shadow, who both also went to Finland to win top honours over there, all did a great deal of winning in the 1970s. By the end of the 1970s the Silhill kennel was well known worldwide, and it came as a great blow to hear of Mrs Atkinson's decision to retire from breeding and showing for personal reasons.

In 1988 Mrs McCourt, as she is now known, returned to the dog scene and has revived the Silhill affix. First she handled Ch Acheo Somerled to his qualifying Challenge Certificate for owner Mrs Judy Averis, then handled her own Ch Balquhatston Crimebuster of Silhill to his title in 1990. Now living in France, Crimebuster is already well on his way to gaining his international title. In 1991 Mrs McCourt handled Tear and Green's Ch Balquhatston Sunburst to his title.

The first Silhill litter to be bred for many years produced the dual CC winner, Silhill Bee Mine at Glorfindal in 1990. The latest Stars are Sundance Kid of Silhill, already the winner of two Challenge Certificates, with Silver Legacy of Silhill, the winner of many Best Puppy awards during 1992.

Mr James Falconer's first winning Skye, Tarskavaig Deerstalker, was a Reserve Challenge Certificate winner. However it was his son, Ch Scarista Fighting Scot who brought top honours to the kennel in 1972. A repeat litter produced Mackenzie's Scarista Huntsman, who won a Terrier Group at just over one year old. Ronang Araminta was campaigned to two CCs before the Scarista kennels changed breeds to Scottish Terriers with even greater success.

John Burrows began exhibiting Wild Rose of Merrymount in 1969. However, it was not until Ch Wismar Silver Sword gained his title in 1978 that this affix became well known. Since then the kennel has won with Acheo Maighdean Bhan (winner of one Challenge Cerificate), Ch Wismar Cream Delight, Ch Wismar Sweet William (a very big winner and Dog of the Year in 1989), and Ch Williamina of Wismar, who won her third Challenge Certificate at Crufts in 1991.

In the 1960s Miss Catherine Osborne of the famous Osmart Bearded Collie kennels spent many of her holidays at the Tarskavaig kennels on the Isle of Skye. Her first Skyes, Tarskavaig King Wenceslas and Tarskavaig Tinker Lass, were both well known in the show ring, and Osmart Kiss me Kate, a lovely cream daughter of this pair, won two CCs. Though absent from the show ring for a number of years Mrs Parker, as she is now, hopes to make a return in the near future.

After many years in Afghan Hounds Mrs Linda Lancashire bought her first Skye, Acheo Yule Star, as something easier to show. Unfortunately Yule Star hated shows. However she was bred to Glenshiel Harvester to produce one of the most outstanding dogs in Skyes for many years, namely Ch Vanghapara Wild Highlander. At his first show this remarkable dog stood alone in his class, and might have been expected to win, but received the second prize card because of his bad behaviour. Fortunately both judge and owner saw the potential in the dog, so his owner worked hard on teaching him better ring manners and the same judge awarded him a Challenge Certificate in later years. The moral of this story is that one should never give up!

The Vanghapara kennel is also noted for producing Vanghapara Gay Duchess, the winner of two CCs including Best of breed at Crufts in 1977. Vanghapara Dolly Varden, a Yule Star daughter, also won two CCs and her daughter, Ch Vanghapara Penny Black, gained her title in 1984. Other notable successes of this kennel include Ch Vanghapara Ladybird, a daughter of Penny Black, and Australian Ch Vanghapara Scot of Raldoris, who came from a litter of thirteen by Dracula's Luxy of Kirkleyditch ex Vanghapara Gay Duchess.

The Bevan-Jones, of the Meurig affix, owned Ch Rhosneigr Clever Dusty who won her third Challenge Certificate at Crufts in 1970. Mr T Logie's kennel produced Metilhaven Queen Sheba who did some winning in America; her daughter, Maid of the Loch of Acheo, won two Reserve Challenge Certificates for owner Mrs Mary Macdonald. Dr and Mrs Hamer's Lady Grace of Merrymount was campaigned to one CC, and the Hamer's homebred Klinta King of the Mountain was a well known class winner.

Mrs Rene Sanderson of the famous Spenmoss Australian Terrier kennels also bred some notable Skyes including the Challenge Certificate winner Spenmoss Sweet Sally, and litter brothers Ch Hingjake Serica and Ch Spenmoss Fancy Pants, who were by Ch Marjayyn Dirk ex Kirkleyditch Mimosa.

THE SEVENTIES TO THE PRESENT DAY

During the 1970s yet more fanciers were attracted to the Skye Terrier breed and enjoyed much success.

Mr and Mrs Alan Bishop's first Skye, Ch Acheo Bonnie Jean, became a champion in 1975 as did their second, Ch HingJake Serica, who won three Terrier Groups, at the City of Birmingham Championship Show 1978, The West of England Ladies Kennel Society Championship Show 1980 and Birmingham National Championship Show 1980, an honour rarely bestowed on a Skye in this country.

The Littlecreek kennel belonging to Mr and Mrs Frank Cassidy is famous for its Newfoundlands, and though their association with Skyes goes back a long way they did not begin exhibiting them until the 1970s, which they then did with much success. Dimple Marsay of Littlecreek won one CC and Jill Bower's Ch/Ir Ch Littlecreek's Randy of Kirkleyditch was a big winner and was Skye of the Year in 1976.

In 1977 the Cassidy's imported Skyeark Glamour Girl of Littlecreek and Skyeark Sir Walter Scott of Littlecreek from America. Breeding with these imports produced Ch Littlecreek Glengarry and Ch Littlecreek Elgin. Elgin then departed for the USA where he won his American title and also many group placings.

Ch Littlecreek Chad was campaigned to his title in 1985 and his litter sister, Littlecreek Bridie at Whodeanie, owned by the McCann's, emigrated with them to South Africa where she won her title. In Canada Ch Littlecreek Lisa and Ch Littlecreek Maree were both big winners with many group awards, while in Europe Littlecreek Reay and Littlecreek Argyle Lad have been very influential in the breeding programmes of the Isle of Skye and Grimsby kennels.

Messrs Chappell and Stephenson's Mariquita kennel is undoubtedly the top kennel at the time of writing. Their quest for stardom began with Ch Rhosneigr Cream Raging Moon, who was born in 1972 and gained his title in 1979. From then on this small kennel has never been out of the spotlight, with such champions as Ch Rhosneigr Silver Solo Quest, Ch Tarskavaig Wee Geordie, Ch Rhosneigr Right Cream Tops and Ch Mariquita Flashlight.

In 1985 the Mariquita kennel imported Am Ch Fleur of Morningsky, a German bred bitch, from America. In the same year homebred Ch Mariquita Flashback gained his third Challenge Certificate and Best in Show at the Skye Terrier Club Championship Show on the Isle of Skye under breed specialist Olga Smid. This outstanding dog went on to win 23 CCs under 23 different judges, surpassing the record set by Ch Wolverley Chummie, who won several of his under the same judge so long ago.

Ch Mariquita Flashback, winner of 23 CCs.
Photo: John Hartley

Am Ch Mariquita Bonnie Isle returned to the home kennel from America and won her British title in 1985, and the great Ch Mariquita Flashfleur gained her crown in 1987 along with Best in Show at the Skye Terrier Club's Championship Show under judge Kari Jarvinnen of Finland. Flashfleur became Skye Terrier of the Year in 1987 and 1988 and in all she amassed a total of 25 CCs.

Ch Mariquita Flashfleur

The next title holder for the kennel was the lovely drop ear, Am Ch Skyecrest Lady of the Evening, who was imported in 1987 and co-owned with Mrs Julia Gibbons. Her drop ear son, Mariquita Flashpoint, won one CC in 1988. Champions Mariquita Highlight at Pyon, and Twilight of Betsett, both gained their crowns in the 1980s as did older sister Ch Ceri Cream Delight. Ch Pollyanna of Glenshiel, bred at the Mariquita kennels, took her title in 1983.

In 1990 Elissa's Alexander, co-owned with Mr and Mrs D Hadleigh, was imported from America, coming out of quarantine two days before the Skye Terrier Club's Championship Show on the Isle of Skye and winning his puppy class. Making her show debut on the same day, and winning Best Puppy in Show, was his kennel mate, the famous Ch Jebusa Miranda at Mariquita. Alexander took his first Challenge Certificate in 1992 at the Scottish Breeds Championship Show, and won his second at Bath Championship Show, going Best of Breed over Miranda on that occasion. Alexander's qualifying CC came at Leeds Championship Show, making him the latest title holder for the Mariquita kennel. Ch Jebusa Miranda at Mariquita took her title, and also the Terrier Group at the Border Union Championship Show in 1991, while still a junior, and was Reserve in the Terrier Group at the Three Counties Championship Show in the same year.

The year 1992 saw Miranda win the Challenge Certificate and Best of Breed at Crufts and then go on to win the Terrier Group on this great day, her second birthday! At the Scottish Breeds show she took her thirteenth CC and went Best of Breed over her kennel mate, Alexander. At Manchester she was again awarded Best of Breed and once more took the Terrier Group. There can be no doubt that this stylish youngster could well be the top winner of all time for this kennel. The Mariquita kennel has taken the double, that is both the dog and bitch CCs, on ten occasions, a remarkable achievement. International Champions Mariquita Flashdance and Mariquita New Moon, and Italian Champion Mariquita Double Luck have all made excellent impressions abroad.

Miss Megan Rees, President of the Skye Terrier club, spent many years as the manager of the Talisker kennels in Canada, and returned to her native Wales following the death of Mrs Adams, the kennel owner. She brought with her from Canada her old favourite, Ch Talisker's Peter Piper and his half sister, the young bitch Talisker's Ciboulette, who was campaigned to her British title. Sadly Ciboulette died leaving no offspring. In 1984 Miss Rees imported Skyecrest Lady Lisa from America, who enjoys helping her mistress in the garden much more than winning top awards at shows!

Long time enthusiasts Brian and Angela Harris have been involved with Skyes since 1968 when visits to Skye introduced them to the breed at the Tarskavaig kennels. Though at first not interested in showing the Harris' began to exhibit Tarskavaig Harris Tweed in 1981. Tragedy struck when Angela and her son, returning from a show with Harris Tweed and Tarskavaig Mountain Ash, were involved in a road accident. Unfortunately their bitch was killed while Harris Tweed, though injured, kept close to his mistress, keeping her head clear so that she could breathe until rescue arrived. Despite his devotion he died from his injuries five months later. Mrs Harris, though now confined to a wheel chair, is still a great enthusiast and accompanies her husband to shows with Tarskavaig Illicit Still, and had the delight of seeing him win his first Challenge Certificate in 1991 and gain his title to become their first champion in 1992.

Mrs Doreen Hill, whose Suncharm kennel of Miniature Pinschers is very well known, made quite an impact on the Skye Terrier scene with her exhibits, Suncharm Highlander and Suncharm Tartan Lad, who won one Challenge Certificate each. Ch Suncharm Dominator (Dracula's Luxy of Kirkleyditch ex Davesfame Kilty), a lovely cream, went Best Dog under Walter Goodman at the first Skye Terrier show held on the Isle of Skye in 1980. Suncharm Silver Lady, by Dominator ex Kilty, and Ivory Miss of Suncharm, by Dominator ex Parlour

Blonde Bombshell, won one and two CCs respectively. It was a great loss to the breed when Mrs Hill retired from Skyes.

Mr and Mrs Dalrymple first met Skyes while working on Eilean Shuna off the west coast of Scotland where Archie was a gamekeeper and the dogs were used for work. Later, while living in Slamannan near Falkirk, they renewed their interest in the breed. Their first Skye, Ch Blairside Highland King, gained his title in 1978, with Tarskavaig Kate Dalrymple a frequent prize-winner too.

Ch Pendlebrook Lady Stair, by Dracula's Luxy of Kirkleyditch ex Acheo Kalgoorlie Kate, gained her crown in 1979 and was bred to Ch Kirkleyditch Dalesman producing an outstanding litter containing Ch Balquhatston Blockbuster, twice reserve in the Terrier Group, who was exported to

(above) Sine Threlfall with her Crufts CC winners in 1983: Ch Balquhatston Blockbuster and Ch Acheo Linsey Macdonald.

(below) Balquhatston Challenger and Balquhatston Star Choice keeping dry.

Ch Kirleyditch Arran (Ch Spaceman of Skye Devils Inn and Kirkleyditch ex Ch Balquhatston Silver Magic) bred by Miss Nickki Bower and owned by Mrs Julie Viles.

America and won his title there. His littermates were Ch Balquhatston Trailblazer of Azrakhan, Ch Balquhatston Silver Magic and Balquhatston Wee Dram, who was rarely shown but was a sure champion had he been campaigned. Also in this amazing litter was Balquhatston Victoriana who has been an excellent brood bitch for the kennel. A repeat mating produced Ch Balquhatston Daredevil of Mallysmar, winner of eight Challenge Certificates.

Balquhatston Star Choice (Acheo Bla Bheinn ex Ch Pendlebrook Lady Stair) won two Challenge Certificates and the next litter produced Ch Balquhatston Skyjack (Ch Aelfric the Predictor ex Balquhatston Victoriana) whose wins include Best of Breed at Crufts 1988. Ch Balquhatston Ghostbuster at Arym and litter sister, Ch Balquhatston Ferry Girl (Ch Aelfric the Predictor ex Ch Pendlebrook Lady Stair) continued to keep the kennel to the fore.

Mr Dalrymle died in 1985 and illness prevented Mrs Dalrymple from showing seriously in 1990. However, she had the pleasure of seeing Ch Balquhatston Crimebuster take his title that year with his brother, Ch Balquhatston Equaliser (Ch Balquhatston Skyjack ex Balquhatston Queen Bee) gaining his crown in 1992. In 1990 Mrs Dalrymple returned to her native Germany to care for her aged mother taking her Skyes with her.

The late Mr Bill Hall and his daughter, Lorraine Hutchison, were already well known in Scottish Terriers before they became involved in Skyes. Ch Tarskavaig Hallmark, their first title holder in 1976, became Skye of the Year, giving them a splendid start in this breed. Hallmark produced the top winning cream Ch Perlor Sgianach and his sister Ch Perlor Sound of Raasay by Ch Wismar Silver Sword, and Perlor Peighinn Roghail by Tarskavaig Pipes and Drums, who was the winner of two Challenge Certificates.

Ch Tarskavaig Sugar and Spice gained her title for the Hall and Hutchison partnership in 1986 and holds the distinction of being the best bitch under judge Olga Smid at the Skye Terrier Club Championship Show held on the Isle of Skye in 1985. Perlor Sugar Almond (Ch Perlor Sgianach ex Tarskavaig Sugar and Spice) won her first Challenge Certificate at the Scottish Breeds Show in 1988. The littermates Perlor Silver Fox, who has one CC and Perlor Moaning Minnie (Ch Perlor Sgianach ex Perlor Peighinn Roghail) has two. Perlor Silver Lining, (Tarskavaig Gordon for Me ex Ch Tarskavaig Sugar and Spice) also has two CCs. Mrs Hutchison, who now has a young family of her own to keep her occupied, has not been able to attend many shows in recent years, but the Perlor flag will surely fly again in the not too distant future.

Mrs Peggy Heap won one Challenge Certificate with her first Skye, Spenmoss Sweet Sally, and in 1976 became the co-owner with Sine Threlfall of Acheo Kalgoorlie Kate, who produced Ch Pendlebrook Lady Stair and Hungarian Ch Pendlebrook Prince Fergus. In 1977 Mrs Heap and Mrs Threlfall imported Olivia Radovan and Ch Buchan Boy from Whodeanie (Olivia Radovan ex Coruisk Kilmandy), bred by Mrs Heap, gained his title for owner Mr McCann in 1980. Pendlebrook Toom Tabard and his daughter, Pendlebrook Anna Duff, were both frequently shown with success. After a spell away from dogs Mrs Heap, now Mrs Smith, returned to the ring with Arym Call My Bluff (Ch Balquhatston Ghostbuster of Arym ex Acheo Flower of Scots at Arym).

Dave and Pat McCann's Whodeanie kennel enjoyed a great deal of success with some great Skyes, their first ones coming from the Silhill kennel. Silhill Dinah Do won one Challenge Certificate and Ch Silhill Silver Shadow was the winner of ten CCs and also achieved a Terrier Group win and one Group Reserve. This splendid dog was exported to Finland, where he became an International Champion. Ch Kirkleyditch Seanab of Whodeanie, Ch Buchan Boy of Whodeanie and Champions Whodeanie Hopscotch and Sea Wolf were all worthy title holders for the kennel.

Dave McCann co-owned several top winning Skyes which he handled, including Ch Littlecreek Glengarry, Ch Littlecreek Elgin and Ch Littlecreek Chad for the Cassidys; Ch Skyeline Glimmer in Shadow from Whodeanie for Mrs Westerholm, and Champions Whodeanie Sea Wolf and Hopscotch for Mrs Kaye McDonald. The McCanns now live in South Africa where Sea Wolf and Littlecreek Bridie have both been campaigned to their South African titles.

Miss Lesley Taylor and her mother, Jean, owners of the small but very successful Checkbar West Highland White Terrier kennels, who won Best in Show at Bath Championship Show in 1971 with Ch Checkbar Tommy Quite Right, branched out to include Skyes in 1974 when Lesley bought Acheo Bluebell of Scotland (NZ Ch Acheo Scottish Nationalist ex Tarskavaig Jeannie McColl) winning a Reserve Challenge Certificate at an early age, but sadly Bluebell died as the result of an accident. Her next Skye, Kirkleyditch Jenny Geddes, gained her title in 1978. Her daughter, by Ch Vanghapara Wild Highlander, the homebred Ch Checkbar Jennifer Eccles, enjoyed a very successful show career, winning seven CCs and a Reserve Best Terrier in Group at Driffield Championship Show in 1980, and became the top Skye bitch for that year. Another of her many successes was winning Best of Breed at Crufts in 1985.

For her second litter Ch Kirkleyditch Jenny Geddes was bred to Ch Balquhatston Blockbuster producing a lovely litter which included the delightful drop ear Ch Checkbar Dew Drop and Checkbar Justa Jiffy at Mallysmar. Jiffy began her show career most successfully but is best remembered as an excellent brood. Tragedy dealt the Taylor family a devastating blow when Jean died from cancer in 1981 and Lesley died of the same disease in 1983. Ch Jennifer Eccles was given to Sine Threlfall and continued to shine at shows and Ch Checkbar Dew Drop lives with Lesley's father and enjoys an occasional outing in veteran classes.

Mr and Mrs Alec Watson own the well known Ramlacin kennels in Yorkshire and have had considerable success with their Skyes which include Ch Tarskavaig Ben Loyal of Ramlacin and Mariquita Dynamic Dixie of Ramlacin and the homebred Lord Edward of The Isles who have both won Reserve Challenge Certificates.

Mr and Mrs Ralph Valerio of Wishaw own the well known Varla Dobermanns. From the 1970s to the mid-1980s they exhibited Skyes with considerable good fortune. Tarskavaig Claret and Amber (Ch Tarskavaig Bonar Law ex Tarskavaig Sweet and Low) gained a Reserve Challenge Certificate and Varla Scots Mede (Tarskavaig Son of Scotland ex Cantor Andromeda) was Best Puppy in Show at the Skye Terrier Club Open Show in 1978 under judge Megan Rees.

Ms Wendy Legg made up her lovely cream, Ch Kirkleyditch Border Queen (Ch Kirkleyditch Dalesman ex Hornblower Hoola-la) in 1980 and

Kirkleyditch the Wizard of Drumfearn was frequently placed at shows. She is best remembered for producing the popular Ch Drumfearn the Conjurer owned by the Thomas family.

Miss Gillian Nicolson, who later became Mrs Johnnie Dalrymple, showed a number of Skyes in the late 1970s, but was most successful with Ch Aelfric the Predictor who went Best Puppy in Show at the National Terrier Show in 1983 under Stanley Dangerfield, and completed his title by winning Best in Show at the Skye Terrier Club Championship Show under Jill Bower in 1984. He sired three champions, Ch Balquhatston Skyjack, Ch Balquhatston Ghostbuster of Arym and Ch Balquhatston Ferry Girl of Gallondean. Beaufort of Balquhatston, owned by Gillian, was Best of Breed at the Scottish Kennel Club Show in 1985.

Mr and Mrs Priestley of the Skyecrest kennel in Yorkshire spent a short but successful time in Skyes with their gorgeous bitch, Ch Kirkleyditch Silvery Star (Ch Tarskavaig Bonar Law ex Hornblower Hoola-la), who gained her title in 1981 with some excellent wins behind her. These included Reserve Best in Show at the Skye Terrier Club Open Show in 1979 under Finnish judge, Mrs Westerholm, and Best in Show at the Skye Terrier Club Open Show the following year on the Isle of Skye under Walter Goodman, and she finished her career with four Challenge Certificates and six Reserves. Ch Spenmoss Fancy Pants (Ch Marjayn Dirk ex Kirkleyditch Mimosa) won his title in 1982, taking four CCs and several Reserves.

Mrs Jackie Brown's Pyon kennel is noted for Pyon Mhairie Rose and Pyon Ailsa Craig (Ch Hingjake Serica ex Kirkleyditch Florence) who were both well known winners. Ch Mariquita Highlight at Pyon (Ch Tarskavaig Wee Geordie ex Kirkleyditch Skybound) gained her crown in 1986 with three Challenge Certificates and eight Reserve CCs, winning the Bitch of the Year award in 1986. The drop ear, Pyon Flaming Tarka, has had some excellent wins at Open shows, with a Best in Show awarded in 1992 when Tarka was being handled by Mrs Brown's daughter, Ros. During 1992 she was awarded her first Challenge Certificate and two Reserve CCs. As well as breeding and exhibiting her Skyes Mrs Brown has done a great deal of sterling work for Skye Terrier rescue.

Mr and Mrs David Goose of Norfolk own the Coruisky affix. It was really their daughter who got them involved in Skyes as she dearly wanted to own one. After studying dog books on the breed, and after a lot of thought, they bought her Fenbeach Venus (Ch Kirkleyditch Dalesman ex Suncharm Sheer Elegance) for her sixteenth birthday. Venus was bred to Ch Spenmoss Fancy Pants in 1981 producing a litter of four, three prick ears and a drop, Coruisky Silver Sam. He was a lovely drop with, unfortunately, a terrible tail and was therefore unshown.

Speywood Deacon Brodie, by Ch Speywood Rowantree ex Speywood Gigha, joined the family and was bred with Fenbeach Venus, who again produced three prick ear and one drop ear, Ch Coruisky Master Robbie, who gained his title in 1987. During his show career he won a total of ten Challenge Certificates and two Reserve CCs, with Best in Show at the Skye Terrier Club Championship show in 1986 under Mrs Austin (Glenshiel), Best in Show at the Skye Terrier Club Open Show in 1987, and at the Border Union Championship Show in Scotland in the same year he was Reserve in the Terrier Group under well known and highly respected all rounder, the late Mr Tom Horner. When not at shows, Robbie, who at a year old was the first Skye Terrier to become a PAT (Pets as Therapy) dog, was a regular visitor to the residents at the High Haven Home for the Elderly in Downham Market, where he was much loved by everybody.

Ch Wismar Wild Rose joined the kennel in 1987 and gained her third Challenge Certificate in 1990, ending with a total collection of four CCs and four Reserves. In 1991 she produced a litter of four pups to Tarskavaig Ben Nevis, including Coruisky Fresh Cream, Coruisky Silver Dollar and Coruisky Briar Rose, who will all be making their debut in the show ring in due course.

Ch Wismar Wild Rose (Tarskavaig Doodle Dandy ex Tarskavaig Blancheflower),1989.

Mr Andy Hamilton of Lanarkshire has been involved with Staffordshire Bull Terriers for many years, and with Skyes since 1978. For a long time he showed his Skyes only sparingly, but with encouraging results. Shawrigg Swordsman (Senkrah Explorer ex Acheo Silver Lady) was always well placed as was Shawrigg Saracen (Tarskavaig Pipes and Drums ex Acheo Silver Lady) who won a Reserve Challenge Certificate. Shawrigg Better Canna Be went Best Puppy in Show at the Skye Terrier Club Championship Show in 1989 and is currently being shown most expertly by granddaughter, Tracey, who handled him to Reserve Best in Show at the Skye Terrier Club Open show in 1992. Shawrigg Bonnie Meg is currently being campaigned, and this lovely bitch has one CC and three Reserves to date.

Mr and Mrs Blake of Manchester campaigned their Ch Ceri Cream Delight (Ch Tarskavaig Wee Geordie ex Kirkleyditch Skybound) to her title in 1984 when she went Reserve Best in Show at the Skye Terrier Club Championship show under judge Jill Bower. Home bred Hazelfield Sky Diver (Kirkleyditch Royal Destiny ex Spenmoss Highland Queen) was well placed in breed classes.

Mr and Mrs Jarvis of Bolton in Lancashire had a great run of success during 1988 with Mallysmar Cream Dream (Ch Balquhatston Daredevil of Mallysmar ex Checkbar Just a Jiffy at Mallysmar) who took one Challenge Certificate and three Reserves.

Mrs Jenny Kendrick worked in the Silhill kennels so naturally decided this was the breed for her! Early successes in the show ring were recorded with

Jeraro Sonny Boy, Jeraro Georgie Boy the winner of three Reserve Challenge Certificates. Jeraro Magical Mystery, a Junior Warrant winner and the Skye Terrier Pup of the Year 1986, was outshone by his famous brother, Ch Jeraro He's Magic, who gained his title in 1990 and is always a consistent winner of Terrier Groups and Best in Show awards on the Open Show circuit. The latest winner for the Jeraro kennel is Selena Simply Special of Jeraro (Jeraro Saintly Simon ex Salena Drambuie Cream) who won her first Challenge Certificate during 1992. Jenny Kendrick's sister, Mrs Sue Breeze, has also enjoyed some pleasing wins. Her Jeraro Georgie Boy's successes have already been mentioned, and Mrs Breeze is the breeder of Salena Drambuie Cream, who has one Challenge Certificate with litter brother, Salena Cheavers Regal, a Reserve CC winner, and the latest certificate winner for the Jeraro kennel, Salena Simply Special of Jeraro.

Mariquita Flashman at Esgia (Ch Mariquita Flashlight ex Am Ch Fleur of Morningsky).

Mr and Mrs George McLeod of Kintore in Aberdeenshire own the Esgia affix. Cathie grew up in Skye and spent all her spare time at the Acheo kennels and has therefore been with Skyes for at least twenty-five years! Her first Skye, Acheo Sea Shanty (Darrach Acheo ex Sorcha Acheo), was bought with her pocket money in 1968 and was exhibited by her young owner at several

Jeraro Gypsy Dancer (Humphrey from Whodeanie ex Silhill Tartan Kilt) with litter containing Ch Jeraro He's Magic.

shows. In 1970 she acquired Acheo Jamie Stuart (NZ Ch Acheo Scottish Nationalist ex Acheo Rosiebelle). Around this time Cathie's parents moved to the Isle of Rum, and the dogs moved too while Cathie remained on Skye to complete her education. Despite attempts to breed the pair nothing was forthcoming until Sea Shanty produced a surprise litter of three pups in 1973 at the rather advanced age of eight years. One of the litter, Rhum Surprise, was exported to France.

In 1980 Cathie married George McLeod and they have established a successful kennel which includes Ch Orasaidh Leezie Lindsay (Acheo Bla Bheinn ex Acheo Can Seo at Orasaidh) who gained her title in 1987. Checkbar Desdemona won several Best of Breeds awards at Open Shows and is the dam of Challenge Certificate winner Esgia A'Mhaighdean by Mariquita Flashman at Esgia, who is also owned by the McLeods and has numerous Open Show wins to his credit.

Esgia Beinn Eighe got off to a very promising start by winning puppy classes before some collapsing benching at a show frightened him so badly that his show career came to a premature end. In 1991 the McLeods imported the drop ear Silverprint Goodfellow at Esgia from Sweden, who was awarded two Reserve Challenge Certificates in 1992.

Mr and Mrs McLeod were briefly involved in Italian Spinones and bred a litter which produced three show winners. In addition to the dogs three Vietnamese Pot Bellied Pigs complete the animal picture at the Esgia home, where all live in perfect harmony. The McLeod children, David and Stuart, frequently attend shows and compete in the Junior Handling competitions. making this truly a family interest.

Mr C MacLean of West Lothian has had three Skyes over the past eleven years. His first, Kirkleyditch Highland Wind, unfortunately died young as a result of an accident. His

Sweet Georgie Boy (Ch Balquhatston Blockbuster ex Rhosneigr Blond Dream) owned and bred by Mr and Mrs Colin Dann.

second, Balquhatston Challenger, won one Reserve Challenge Certificate, but the star of the family, Ch Balquhatston Equaliser (Ch Balquhatston Skyjack ex Balquhatston Lianora) is one of the most eye catching dogs around. He won his third CC and was also Reserve in the Terrier Group at the South Wales Championship Show in July 1992, and also is the winner of several Green Stars, and a Group, during his visits to the Irish Show Circuit in 1992.

Mr and Mrs Colin Dann already had Afghan Hounds when they bought their first Skye, Rhosneigr Blonde Dream, in 1979. In 1982 she was bred to Ch Balquhatston Blockbuster, producing Sweet Georgie Boy, the winner of one Challenge Certificate, and Ebony and Ivory, who has proved to be a useful brood bitch. Brassia Masculata, (Ch Whodeanie Sea Wolf ex Ebony and Ivory) won his Junior Warrant and three Reserve Certificates, with litter sister Cymbidium Mimi also winning a Reserve CC.

Skynoustie Shaggy Parasol, an Ebony and Ivory daughter by Whodeanie Imperial Mint, is also a Reserve CC winner. The latest winner bred by the Danns, Skynoustie Magnum, (Brassia Masculata ex Skynoustie Mini Ha Ha) won Best of Breed at an Open Show from the puppy class. Skynoustie's Kay's Delight, litter sister to Magnum, is a drop ear. The Danns' daughter, Debbie, is a competent handler and won her way through to the Junior Handling finals with her Afghan Hound in 1987, finishing fourth. She also handles Skyes; yet another family affair!

Mrs Coralie Fowler moved to Oronsay, just off the Isle of Skye, with her husband, family and three Wolfhounds in 1980. While husband, Richard, was away on holiday in the Faroe Islands later that year Coralie decided to surprise him on his return with a Skye Terrier pup. Acheo Can Seo at Orasaidh (Checkbar Joe Louis ex Acheo Inverie) was duly chosen and met her new master on the platform of Inverness railway station. Fortunately they liked each other! Ch Orasaidh Leezie Lindsay, Orasaidh Tibbie Dunbar (winner of one Challenge Certificate) and Orasaidh Tam O'Shanter, by Acheo Bla Bheinn, were the result of the first litter bred by the Fowlers. Their second litter, this time by Ch Speywood Rowantree, produced Orasaidh An Gille Mhor, who in his turn sired Norwegian Ch Acheo Gavin Hastings (ex Ch Checkbar Jennifer Eccles).

Orasaidh Tibbie Dunbar produced a litter to Ch Mariquita Flashback in 1987, which gave Mrs Fowler her first homebred champion, Ch Orasaidh Cullen Skink, who has five Challenge Certificates and three Reserves. In 1991 he was bred with Orasaidh An Gille Mhor, who produced a litter of six pups, all of whom made their show debuts in 1992 with some success.

Ch Orasaidh Cullen Skink

Mr and Mrs T Richardson of Barnsley bought Ch Acheo Linsey Macdonald (Checkbar Joe Louis ex Acheo Inverie) in 1980, campaigning her to her title in 1983. Acheo MacKenzie (Acheo Bla Bheinn ex Acheo Inverie) also did some winning for the Richardsons.

Mrs Mary Watts of Ossett in Yorkshire is the secretary of the Skye Terrier Club and came into the breed in a very unusual way by adopting a Skye look-alike named Dougalina. Later she was delighted to find a breed which closely resembled her special dog and this led her to build up a successful kennel of Skyes. Kirkleyditch Gemma (Ch Kirkleyditch Dalesman ex Ch Kirkleyditch Petronella) won one Challenge Certificate and one Reserve CC before producing her first litter to Ch Speywood Rowantree from which came Caelum Sam Aon, the winner of one CC, and Ch Caelum Tom Truir, who became the kennel's first champion in 1991. The kennel is also home to Suncharm True Grit, a Junior Warrant winner with one Reserve CC, Caelum Feisty Fergus, who won his Junior Warrant at eleven months, and Caelum Happy Hogmanay, who has several Reserve CCs.

Mr and Mrs Vic Thomas of Peterborough have owned Skyes for many years. However, it was not until they became the owners of one of the most popular characters in the breed, Ch Drumfearn the Conjuror (Kirkleyditch the Wizard of Drumfearn ex Kirkleyditch Border Queen), and were advised to take up showing, that their hobby grew. Robbie, as he is known to his fans, is the winner of six Challenge Certificates, including one received just before his tenth birthday. He has also won well in veteran classes and has four times been the runner up in strongly contested veteran stakes classes at Championship Shows. As well as Robbie, the Thomas family own two bitches, Skyerise Silver Penny, and the homebred Skeitos the Comet who was awarded two CCs in 1992 and was the Crufts Reserve CC winner in 1991.

Mrs Jan Mason of Birmingham has owned Skyes since 1981, with Marjayn Melissa, Silhill Salome, Jeraro Heidi Hi, Caelum First Footer and Caelum Scotch Mist all earning places in the show ring for their owner. Ch Muffy of Marjayn (Ch Marjayn Mickey Mouse ex Silhill Salome) was bred by Mrs Mason, and was campaigned to her title by Miss Bailey. Solstice Scotch on the Rocks, from Mrs Mason's latest litter, made his debut in the show ring by winning Best Puppy in Breed in July 1992.

Mrs Ann Ankcorn, who also lives in Birmingham, bought her first Skye, Ch Kirkleyditch Maiden of Rona (Ch Spaceman of Skye Devil's Inn ex Kirkleyditch Annabelle), in 1981. After a litter in 1984 by Ch Kirkleyditch Marksman, which produced Pensford Lord of Arran, she returned to the show ring to win her qualifying Challenge Certificates in 1986 and 1987. During 1987 Orasaidh Cranachan of Pensford joined this small kennel and quickly won her Junior Warrant, and her first Challenge Certificate, in 1992. The latest addition to the Ankcorn household is Kirkleyditch Viking Star of Pensford who already has some excellent placings at Open Shows to her credit.

Mrs Joy French of Lincolnshire bought Hamish of Rasenglade (Acheo Foggy Bottom ex Rasenglade Bonnie Alithe) in 1981 followed by Fiataich French Marigold (Wee Jimmie frae Tarskavaig ex Vanghapara Gemma) in 1984, both doing well in the show ring. Wismar Lord of the Isles (Tarskavaig Pipes and Drums ex Tarskavaig Blanche Flower) joined the family in 1986 and is a class winner. After a lifetime involved with dogs Mrs French recently achieved her greatest wish: to own a champion. Ch Acheo Capercaillie of Joyscavey (Andy Irvine at Acheo ex Mariquita Flashader) was purchased in 1988 and gained her title in 1992.

Mr and Mrs D Struthers have shown Kerry Blues for many years. When their daughter, Hazel, expressed a wish to have a Skye of her own the Struthers went to the Balquhatston kennel returning home with Balquhatston Thunderbuster, (Ch Kirkleyditch Dalesman ex Ch Pendlebrook Lady Stair), in 1981. This young dog got off to a good start in the show ring, but sadly died young. Her second dog, Balquhatston Star Choice (Acheo Bla Bheinn ex Balquhatston Victoriana), born in 1982, won two Challenge Certificates and one Reserve CC, and later was shown by Mrs Struthers.

The partnership of Messrs Poulton and Blair enjoyed a great run of success during their brief association with the breed. Their first big winner, Ch Balqhatston Daredevil of Mallysmar, went on to take eight Challenge Certificates and three Reserve CCs, won Reserve in the Terrier Group at the Three Counties Championship Show in 1984 and was also Skye Terrier of the Year in 1984.

Their next show girl, Checkbar Justa Jiffy at Mallysmar, made a promising start but was retired early due to her reluctance to show. However, she proved an excellent brood bitch for the kennel. Further success came from Ch Rhosneigr Blond Returning to Mallysmar, and Ch Rhosneigr Blonde Reviver at Mallysmar who both gained their titles in 1985.

Home bred Ch Mallysmar the Dresser gained her crown in 1986, with Mallysmar Comedy Star going on to win one Challenge Certificate. Mariquita Charlie's Angel to Mallysmar was the winner of two CCs before she was exported to Japan. The kennel was disbanded in 1987, at which time several of the dogs joined the Norwest kennel where they have continued to do well.

Mr and Mrs Cyril Pay have built up their Betsett kennel into a success with stock from Rhosneigr, Kizzymarc and Mariquita bloodlines. Rhosneigr Cream Ravisher of Betsett and Kizzymarc Rag Dancer of Betsett were early winners for the kennel, and in 1988 Ch Mariquita Twilight at Betsett gained her title, taking six Challenge Certificates and four Reserve CCs. Knowlespring Flashdance at Betsett is the latest star of the Betsett kennel with several class wins to her credit.

Donnie Cameron of Inverness won one Challenge Certificate and two Reserve CCs with his dog, Orasaidh Tam O'Shanter (Acheo Bla Bheinn ex Acheo Can Seo at Orasaidh) and had several puppy class wins with Tarskavaig Candy Floss (Tarskavaig Pipes and Drums ex Tarskavaig Dear Blanche).

Mr and Mrs T Barrass started off with Balquhatston Ferry Boy (Acheo Bla Bheinn ex Balquhatston Victoriana) as a pet, but took him along to a few shows and got hooked! Their next Skye, Ch Balquhatston Ferry Girl of Gallondean, took her title in 1988, winning two of her Challenge Certificates at consecutive Crufts Shows in 1987 and 1988, one with Best of Breed. Ch Kirkleyditch the Crusader of Gallondean won his Junior Warrant and gained his title in 1991 with five Challenge Certificates and six Reserve CCs.

Gallondean have bred one litter to date, by Ch Crusader out of Ferry Girl, which produced the Reserve Challenge Certificate winning bitch Gallondean Golden Guinea, owned by Mrs Tingle. Mariquita Flashdancer of Gallondean (Ch Mariquita Flashlight ex Ch Skyecrest Lady of the Evening) and the latest addition, Galochsi Guiding Star of Gallondean (Ch Kirkleyditch the Crusader of Gallondean ex Acheo Poosie Nansie), complete the Gallondean kennel.

Carol Collins is the owner of the Skellgarth kennel, winning many prizes at Open and Championship shows with her Skellgarth Bonnie Wee Lass (Suncharm True Grit ex Skyecrest Prim and Proper) and Mariquita Flash Lady of Skellgarth (Mariquita Flashlight ex Skyecrest Lady of the Evening), who has a Reserve CC. Mariquita Ginny Ginero of Skellgarth and Mariquita Lady Caribella of Skellgarth, by Flashback ex Flash Lady, made their debuts in the show ring in 1992.

Mr and Mrs Don Miller own the famous Feorlig kennel of English Springer Spaniels and are currently enjoying a run of success with their Skyes. Their first, Marjayn Magic Moments (Ch Marjayn Marcus ex Marjayn Merry Xmas), won a Reserve CC before being bred. From her first litter by Caelum First Footer came Feorlig Quest For the Future and Feorlig Quite Charming, who battled it out for Puppy of the Year in 1990, Quite Charming coming out on top. In 1991 Feorlig Uigshader and Feorlig Undying Love (Ch Marjayn Moser ex Marjayn Magic Moments) made their debuts, both winning their classes at Crufts in 1992.

Mrs Pat Jones is best known for her Wellknowe kennel of Bearded Collies and, though she seldom exhibits them herself, her Skyes have done some notable winning. Ch Williamina of Wismar and Ch Wellknowe Wordsworth (Tarskavaig Ben Nevis ex Wismar Weeping Willow) who won his qualifying Challenge Certificate at Crufts in 1992 are both of hers, while Wellknowe Wizard, whom she kept, recently completed his championship. Wellknowe Cream Cracker at Dalgrain, yet another from this winning combination, has one Challenge Certificate.

Mr and Mrs T White own Private Eye of Kirkleyditch who has a Reserve CC, and Potinara Cherub and her litter sister Cymbidium Mimi, who is also a Reserve CC winner. Balquhatston Miss Marples has also enjoyed some good placings at Championship Shows. The latest Skye owned by Mr White is the exciting youngster, Skynoustie Magnum (Brassia Masculata ex Skynoustie Mini Ha Ha), who has won Best of Breed as a pup at Open Shows.

Mr and Mrs Westerholm of the famous Skyeline kennels in Finland came to live in Britain in the early 1980s, bringing with them the lovely Int Ch Rosagallica of Skyeline, Int Ch Drewsteignton Arlanda, and litter brother and sister Gallian Shadow of Skyeline and Skyeline Glimmer in Shadow from Whodeanie, who was campaigned to her British title, which included Best of Breed at Crufts in 1986, by Mr McCann of the Whodeanie Skyes.

Roshven Sligachan (Arym Call My Bluff ex Acheo Boc Beag).

Myra Robertson owns the small but successful Arym affix. Her first Skye, Ch Balquhatston Ghostbuster of Arym, gained his title winning five Challenge Certificates in all. His greatest moment of glory came in 1990 when he topped the entry at the Skye Terrier Championship Show on the Isle of Skye going Best in Show under Mrs Elspeth Clerc of Switzerland. Acheo Flower of Scots at Arym (Acheo Bla Bheinn ex Acheo Inverie) won one Challenge Certificate in 1986.

The first litter for the Arym kennel was born in 1989 with Arym Call My Bluff and Arym It's a Knockout both winning classes on the Championship Show circuit. Business commitments have curtailed Mrs Robertson's showing just lately and persuaded her to part with Arym It's A Knockout to Sweden, where he is currently chasing his title.

Mrs Julia Viles does not have a kennel and is the owner of just one Skye, Ch Kirkleyditch Arran (Ch Spaceman of Skye Devil's Inn ex Ch Balquhatston Silver Magic). However, Mrs Viles and Arran have had a long and successful show career with numerous Best Terrier and Best in Show awards at Open Shows. Arran collected the elusive third Challenge Certificate in 1992 and also has four Reserve CCs. He won his Junior Warrant at eleven months of age, was pup of the year 1985 and also Skye Terrier Dog of the Year 1985. Now a veteran, he still enjoys his shows and continues to win well.

Mr and Mrs B Evans, who own the Norwest Scottish Terriers, came into Skyes as the Mallysmar kennel was disbanded. The Evans own Ch Mallysmar the Dresser and Mallysmar Comedy Star, the winner of one Challenge Certificate. The Norwest kennel has produced some excellent Skyes, including Norwest Ayres and Graces and her litter brother, the cream drop ear Ch Norwest Wandering Star, who gained his title at the National Terrier show in April 1992.

Mr and Mrs Ormerod's first Skyes, Mallysmar Screaming Cream (Ch Rhosneigr Blonde Reviver at Mallysmar ex Checkbar Justa Jiffy at Mallysmar) and Mallysmar Top of the Bill (Ch Balquhatston Daredevil of Mallysmar ex Checkbar Justa Jiffy at Mallysmar) both produced winners for the Roban kennel. Roban Sparky won several breed puppy classes while Roban Denis the Menace has won a Reserve Challenge Certificate.

Mr and Mrs H Gay have had some good wins with Roban Alexis, and Roban Krystle who won several Best Puppy awards. Mariquita Isleback Basil has pressed hard for top honours and currently has two Challenge Certificates. Home bred Malsville Vienna was placed Best Puppy in Show at the Skye Terrier Club Championship Show in 1991, and won a Reserve Challenge Certificate in 1992. Kirkleyditch Viking Raider joined the kennel in 1990 and has had some encouraging placings. In addition to their Skyes Mr and Mrs Gay exhibit Glen of Imaal and Cesky Terriers successfully.

Mr and Mrs J Jessup already showed Poodles successfully before adding Skyes to their kennel. Rhosneigr Cream Megastar at Lissardo and Balquhatston Silver Ghost at Lissardo are the kennel's main winners.

Mrs A Spanner bred Delhorn Silver Knight in 1986. Since then she has gone into partnership with the Clewlows, and is co-owner of Ch Talyot Chloe at Delhorn who won Best in Show at the Skye Terrier Championship show in 1989. Kizzymarc Kamille at Delhorn in the latest winner for this partnership.

Mr and Mrs Peter Mitchell of Grangemouth got off to a winning start with Perlor Touch O' Class at Dalgrain who had many Firsts as a puppy. In 1988 he won his first Challenge Certificate at the Scottish Breeds Championship Show. Wellknowe Cream Cracker at Dalgrain (Tarskavaig Ben Nevis ex Wismar Weeping Willow) has also been successful for her owners, winning her first CC in 1991 with two Reserve CCs.

Mrs Isobel Tingle has owned a Skye for many years though work commitments prevented her from becoming an exhibitor. In 1986 she bought Acheo Poosie Nansie (Balquhatston Gangbuster ex Orasaidh Fernitickles) who won several puppy classes and Best of Breeds at Open Shows. The cream, Gallondean Golden Guinea (Ch Kirkleyditch the Crusader of Gallondean ex Ch Balquhatston Ferry Girl), joined the family in 1988 and has done much winning with five Reserve CCs to her credit. At the end of 1991 Acheo Poosie Nansie had a litter to Ch Kirkleyditch the Crusader of Gallondean, producing four pups. Gallochsi Hercules got off to a winning start under the noted Skye Terrier judge, Walter Goodman, at the Welsh Kennel Club Championship Show in 1992.

Photo: John Hartley

Acheo Ally Bain at Glorfindel.

Mr and Mrs Harry Newton, both relatively new Skye enthusiasts, had much fun showing Balquhatston Shona Beagh, who won many breed classes at Championship Shows and was awarded a Reserve Challenge Certificate. Mr Newton occasionally handled Tarskavaig Alfred the Great for his owner, Mr Allerton, who was unable to do so himself. The Newton's Tarskavaig Harbour Lights of Aitchjay (Ch Wismar Cream Delight ex Ch Tarskavaig Northern Lights) is at present the star of the kennel with one Challenge Certificate and three Reserve CCs, one of which was awarded at Crufts 1992. Tarskavaig Wish

Come True for Aitchjay has several puppy wins to her credit and is handled by Mrs Jeanne Newton. Mrs Janet Woodhead is another enthusiastic newcomer to the breed and won the Reserve Challenge Certificate at Crufts 1990 with home bred Knowlespring Double Cream. Knowlespring Black Magic won his Junior Warrant in 1990 and a Reserve CC at the Scottish Kennel Club Championship Show the same year. From her last litter Mrs Woodhead kept Knowlespring Sunflower (Ch Balquhatston Sunburst ex Rhosneigr Cream Regency) who is currently winning her classes at Championship Shows, as is litter brother, Sundance Kid of Silhill, who is owned by Mrs McCourt and is the winner of two Challenge Certificates.

Mr Peter Tear has owned a Skye since 1973 when his Silhill Sarona won one Challenge Certificate. Pressure of work prevented him from showing again until 1988 when Mrs McCourt began handling his Ch Balquhatston Sunburst, first to his Junior Warrant and then to his title in 1991.

Mr and Mrs Brian Johnson bought their first show dog, Ch Acheo Glittertind Morag of Skykim (Mariquita Flashman at Esgia ex Orasaidh Fernitickles), in 1987, and she amassed a great many Best of Breed awards at Open shows and won her title at Leeds Championship Show in 1992. Gallondean the Covenanter at Skykim joined them a year later and enjoyed a promising show career until liver disease struck when he was two years old. With loving care this game little dog has now come through the disease and is back in the ring again.

Recent newcomers to the breed include Gail Marshall of the Glorfindel Golden Retrievers whose Ch Silhill Bee Mine at Glorfindel (Ch Acheo Somerled ex Balquhatston Queen Bee) is one of the latest champions in the breed. In 1991 two more Skyes joined the kennel, Acheo Aly Bain at Glorfindel and Acheo Gallus Besum at Glorfindel. Both youngsters have made a good start to their show careers with Aly Bain winning several Best Puppy awards and also a Reserve CC.

Mr and Mrs Hadleigh of Wakefield are co-owners with Messrs Chappell and Stephenson of the imported dog Ch Elissa's Alexander (Ch Andrew Thane of Skyecrest ex Ch Olivia Europa). Determined to have a Skye of her own to show, Mrs Hadleigh began to campaign a daughter of Alexander, Acheo Alexina by Reigmakers (ex Acheo Houghmagandie), during 1992 with great success. So far she has achieved her Junior Warrant, and also her first Challenge Certificate while still a junior.

Geraldine O'Rourke has won well with her two bitches, Tarskavaig Suite Mairghead and Tarskavaig Candlelight, the latter having won two Reserve Challenge Certificates. In 1991 Tarskavaig Suite Mairghead was bred to Wellknowe Wordsworth. One of their progeny, Struanmore Silver Dawn at Clairwell, owned by Mrs Powell, is already a class winner.

Keith and Heather Alexander of Montrose have great plans for their two bitches, Kirkleyditch Viking Dawn and Orasaidh Tam Dhu, the latter already winning a Best Terrier Puppy award. Not to be outdone, Mrs Alexander (Keith's mother) has a Best Puppy in Breed award with her Kirkleyditch Pipe Major.

Photo: David Dalton.

Rhosneigr Duncans Dream, owned by Mrs Monica Barraclough.

The Skye Terrier is a very attractive breed and the show dogs have great personality as well as great beauty. These two qualities consistently attract newcomers to the breed and some of the recent recruits include Mrs Barraclough, who has already enjoyed excellent show results with Rhosneigr Duncan's Dream, winner of the huge Puppy Stakes class containing 89 pups at Bath Championship show in 1991.

Mr and Mrs Longbottom, whose Caelum Sam Aon has one Challenge Certificate, also own Mariquita Flashfire who has won well for them. Even more recent newcomers to the Skye Terrier breed are Mrs Lorna Duncan, whose Tarskavaig Dunkin Donut has made a promising start. Mrs Duncan recently added a new puppy to her home, so we obviously have another convert to the breed. In her spare time Mrs Duncan, who is an accomplished artist, likes to paint - Skyes, of course!

Mrs Powell, whose Staffordshire Bull Terriers are well known, changed her allegiance to Skyes with her Struanmore Silver Dawn at Clairwell already a class winner. Mrs Powell also owns the cream dog, Fairby Maximillian at

Clairwell. Mr Maclean of Edinburgh recently started showing, has already won a Reserve Challenge Certificate with Kirkleyditch Chieftain, and is the breeder of Silver Legacy of Silhill and litter sister Modern Abby, all of whom are making their presence felt around the show rings of Britain. In fact there is no doubt that the attractive, well presented Skye Terrier makes an impact not only in British show rings but also worldwide.

THE SKYE TERRIER IN THE UNITED STATES OF AMERICA

The first Skye Terrier to be registered with the American Kennel Club was named Romach. This bitch born in 1884, bred by Mr H Cornwall in England by Ch Kingston Roy ex Zulu, was imported by the Maizeland Kennels. The first champion in the breed, Sir Stafford, gained his title in 1890. He was sired by Sir Garnet ex Floss, and was also an import from England.

William P Sanderson of West Philadelphia owned several Skyes and exhibited Donald and Sanderson's Jim between 1882 and 1887. Another Philadelphian, Clifford A Shinn, imported Miss Pope, Elphinstone, Princess May and Wifie from Britain in 1884. Elphinstone (Falkirk ex Daisy) gained his championship title the same year. Mr McLell's Tom, Mr Sewell's Tatters and Mr Peabody's Boss were all exhibited successfully in the eastern states of America in the same era, while George William Donaldson, an early breeder/exhibitor, encouraged his sister, Mrs A C Kains, to show his strain in San Francisco around 1902.

By the end of the century as many as sixty Skyes were being shown and the future looked bright for the breed. However, numbers decreased in the first three decades of the new century until Michael Stillman of Arreton Farm in New Jersey took up the call. In 1927 Mr Stillman visited England and returned home with the bitch, Betsy of Peacehaven, for his wife, who was the daughter of the above mentioned George William Donaldson.

After a great deal of searching for a suitable male Betsy was bred with Thornton James (Quarrelton Lad ex Thistlebank Rose), a dog bred from Swedish stock owned by Mrs Elizabeth Sjostrom. The resulting litter was the first of many for the Arreton kennels which were to create an interest in the declining fortunes of the breed.

The Stillmans were devoted to the breed, a love that was shared by their daughter Frances, and at one time their kennel housed up to fifty dogs. Heather of Arreton, Ch War Aims of Arreton and the French import, Ch Du Bazizoo Celeste were all fine examples. Ch Scottish Chief of Arreton, by Ch Ballochmyle Togo ex Ch Du Bazizoo Celeste, was a great winner with a Best in Show award to his credit. Mrs Edward Spencer, another dedicated follower of the breed, exhibited many fine specimens which she had brought with her on returning from visits to England and Scotland in the thirties.

Mrs Earl's Iradell kennel holds a special place in the history of the breed in America. The first two Skyes bought by Mrs Earl were found on a trip to France. She called them Mickey and Minnie after the cartoon characters who were so popular at the time, but tragically they both developed distemper and died on board ship returning to the USA. Gregory of Arreton and Hector of Arreton, by Cato v d Ghersberg ex Dinah of Arreton, were bought in 1953 to replace Mickey and Minnie, and in the same year the Iradell affix was registered with the American Kennel Club.

A trip to Britain in 1937 resulted in an additional five Skyes making the trip across the Atlantic to join the Iradell kennel. In future years many Skyes from the Merrymount, Mynd and Bracadale kennels in England, and a few from Germany, were to join this successful kennel. Ch Gregory of Arreton gained his title in 1938 and an import, Ch Bracadale Tiggy of Iradell, holds the distinction of being the first Skye in the United States to win a Best in Show award, an honour she achieved in 1948. Later Ch Toby of Iradell won four such awards and Ch Ivory Jock of Iradell won eleven.

Although breeding and showing activities were curtailed during World War 2 Ch Bracadale Henry was placed second in the Terrier Group at the Westminster Show in 1943. When the war was over Mrs Earl recommenced importing stock from Britain, though the war years had taken their toll of the quality one normally expected. However, once British fanciers were able to resume their breeding programmes the standard soon improved and British stock was again eagerly sought on the other side of the Atlantic.

The lovely Ch Merrymount You'll Do (Wonder of Merrymount ex Merrymount Beetle) was imported and quickly gained his title, going on to win the Terrier Group at the Westminster Show in 1953, the first Skye to win the group at this prestigious show.

The list of champions owned and bred at Iradell is long, and a few may have been omitted. In addition to those already mentioned the roll call reads:

> Ch Jerry of Merrymount, Ch Bracadale Nanette, Ch Chum of Merrymount, Ch Rosebud of Merrymount, Ch Rattlin Willie of Iradell, Ch Jenny Lind of Iradell, Ch Didi v Rehsumpf, Ch Highland Harry of Iradell, Ch Cheddar of Iradell, Ch Bo'ness of Iradell, Ch Papa Stour of Iradell, Ch Fromage Monsieur of Iradell, Ch Bracadale Clementine of Iradell, Ch Merrymount Grey Dusk of Iradell, Ch Merrymount Charming Lady of Iradell, Ch Jerry of Iradell, Ch Bonnie Henry of Iradell, Ch Rip Tide of Iradell, Ch Jerry of Iradell, Ch Lady Jean of Iradell, Ch Kirkby King of Iradell, Ch Misty of Meerend and Iradell, Ch Queen Flora of Iradell, Ch Merrymount Desdemona of Iradell, Ch Kirkby American of Iradell, Ch Merrymount Old Andy of Iradell, Ch Ginger of Iradell, Ch Merrymount Setting Sun of Iradell, Ch Wee Jill of Iradell, Ch Merrymount Nizefella of Iradell, Ch Royal Henry of Iradell, Ch Roaring Storm of Iradell, Ch Rhosneigr River Toy of Iradell, Ch Merrymount Lyth Hill of Iradell, Ch John O'Groats of Iradell, Ch Merrymount Wise Lady of Iradell, Ch Sun Queen of Iradell, Ch Barry of Iradell, Ch Cute Meg of Iradell, Ch Rhosneigr Rising Star of Iradell, Ch Roxburgh of Iradell, Ch Ailsa of Iradell, Ch Kyle of Iradell, Ch Roberton of Iradell, Ch Merrymount Happy

Xmas of Iradell, Ch Merrymount the Best Silver of Iradell, Ch Lossiemouth of Iradell, Ch Major Ben of Iradell, Ch Pabbay of Iradell,Ch Burmar Drummer of Iradell, Ch Fawn Wonder of Iradell, Ch Portobello of Iradell, Ch Major Jock of Iradell, Ch Burmar Alexander of Iradell, Ch Fawn Lu of Iradell, Ch Burmar Sandman of Iradell, Ch Darvel of Iradell, Ch Alva of Iradell, Ch Gigha of Iradell, Ch Luce of Iradell, Ch Eilean Donan of Iradell, Ch Tarskavaig Great Scot of Iradell, Ch Portree of Iradell, Ch Wishau of Iradell, Ch Hollybush of Iradell, Ch Kirkmaiden of Iradell, Ch Bute of Iradell, Ch Mid Challenger of Iradell and Ch Ben Loyal of Iradell.

Mrs Earl's last import, Ch Tarskavaig Great Scot of Iradell (Ch Merrymount Gay Chummie ex Rhosneigr Rushing Dame), came from the Isle of Skye in 1964. A winner of two Challenge Certificates in Britain, he went on to sire some excellent stock before the Iradell kennel was disbanded at the end of the 1960s.

In the later 1930s Mrs Adele Goodman and her son, Walter, imported from France Laughing Clown de Luchar (Beauty Goldmine of Merrymount ex Corlie) and Ailsa of Merrymount from England. Both Skyes were shown but it was not until they purchased High Time Miss Gesty (Ch Chummie's Warman of Talisker ex Ch High Time Miss Gesture of Arreton) that Walter took up showing in earnest, creating a huge impact on the world of dogs with his style of showing and presentation. Miss Gesty was campaigned to her title and in 1950 became the first American bred Skye to win a Best in Show award.

In 1951 Ch You'll do de Luchar (Valère Du Clos de L'Ill ex Merrymount Moonbeam) was imported from France and began a successful show career. He was shown in Europe as well as in the States and won his French, Italian, American and International champion titles, was a Best in Show winner and won seven Terrier Groups.

Miss Gesty was bred to You'll Do and produced the Goodmans' first home bred winner, American, French, and International Champion Glamoor Going Up. This beautiful black dog won eighteen Terrier Groups and a Best in Show. His litter brother Ch Glamoor Yankee Doodle was also campaigned by Walter. A repeat mating produced Ch Glamoor Gaiety Girl, who was later bred to Int Ch Bistro de Saint Ludlin (R'école de Mandane ex Virginie du Clos de L'Ill) to produce the exquisite Ch Glamoor Wee Geordie who would have surely broken records had he not been tragically killed in a kennel fire at just two and a half years of age.

Ch Yule de Mandane (Ch Ursus de Mandane ex Wanda), a lovely cream import from France, although shown to his title was better known for his starring performance on Broadway in "Wonderful Town". Meanwhile yet another import had arrived from France, a stunning cream bitch named Evening Star de Luchar (Valère Du Clos De L'Ill ex Merrymount Moonbeam). Evie gained her title in 1957 and went on to win a staggering seventy-four Terrier Groups and an amazing twenty-one Best in Shows. As a brood Evie produced six champions, one to Ch Yule de Mandane, and five to Ch Glamoor Going Up.

The Goodmans' final import came yet again from France. This time the bitch was Ch Jacinthe de Ricelaine (Ch Earl de Luchar ex Ch Hortense de Ricelaine). Jackie went on to surpass the record breaking career of Evening Star by taking an outstanding ninety-seven Terrier Groups and thirty-five Best in Show awards: a truly magnificent achievement. Jackie was bred to Ch Glamoor Going Up and produced a litter of nine pups, all of whom went on to take their titles.

Ch Glamoor Good News (Ch Glamoor Going Up ex Ch Jacinthe de Ricelaine) not only won forty Terrier Groups and fourteen Best in Show awards but went on to win Best in Show at Westminster Show in 1969, the only Skye ever to have won this coveted award. Her litter brother, Ch Glamoor Go Go Go also enjoyed a successful show career winning a total of fifty-two Terrier Groups and was eight times Best in Show. He sired six champions, one of which, Ch Glamoor Gang Buster, won nineteen Terrier Groups and was three times Best in Show. Gang Buster and Good News were bred, producing Ch Glamoor Got To Be Good who took twenty-one Terrier Groups and was seven times Best in Show. Walter Goodman has now retired from showing and breeding Skyes but enjoys judging the breed at home and abroad.

The Glamoor kennels either owned or bred the following Skyes:

> Ch High Time Miss Gesty, Ch You'll Do de Luchar, Ch Glamoor Leading Lady, Ch Yule de Mandane, Ch Glamoor Yankee Doodle, Ch Glamoor Gaiety Girl, Ch Glamoor Happy Mood, Ch Glamoor Good Intention, Ch Jacinthe de Ricelaine, Ch Glamoor Yule Star, Ch Glamoor Shooting Star, Ch Glamoor Twinkle Star, Ch Glamoor Starry Knight, Ch Glamoor Winning Star, Ch Glamoor Gee Whiz, Ch Glamoor Go Lightly, Ch Glamoor Go Go Go, Ch Glamoor Good News, Ch Glamoor Going Good, Ch Glamoor Going Up Again, Ch Glamoor Goodness Gracious, Ch Glamoor Going West, Ch Glamoor, Glamorous Girl, Ch Glamoor Gang Buster, Ch Glamoor Good as Gold, Ch Glamoor Got To Be Good, Ch Glamoor Good Times, Ch Glamoor Too Good To Be True, Ch Glamoor Good as Always and Ch Glamoor Good Gracious.

In 1937, while on holiday in Monte Carlo, Mrs Robert Graff saw some Skye Terriers and promptly fell for the breed, returning home with several. Mrs Graff obtained additional stock from the Arreton kennels in her home country, and from the Talisker kennels in Canada. With these bloodlines the High Time kennels were established. Ch High Time Gesture of Arreton (Ch Bazizoo Beau Geste ex Ch Portia of Meerend) gained his title in 1942, with Ch High Time Laughing Mist (Laughing Clown de Luchar ex Talisker Marcella) following in 1946. Ch High Time Miss Gesty, owned by the Glamoor kennels, was the first

American bred Skye to win a Best in Show. In all six High Time Skyes gained their titles.

The Merrybrac kennels belonging to Mrs Eben W Pryne were established in 1938 with stock from the Merrymount and Bracadale kennels in England. Her affix was formed by combining the first syllable of the affix of each of the kennels she so much admired. One of her imports was the lovely Ch Bracadale Fidget (Ch Bracadale Henry ex Bracadale Betty) whom she mated to a German dog bought from the Iradell kennels, Ch Dido v Rehsumph, keeping from the litter a dog puppy, Safety Bet of Merrybrac. He was later bred to Ch Bo'ness of Iradell, producing Chs Merrybrac Moonshine, Maxine and Mustang. The Merrybrac kennels went on to produce Chs Merrybrac Manikin, Majesty, Mistery Maid, Mocha, Matador and Flora, as well as being home to Ch Hudson Queen and Ch Rhosneigr Right Winger of Merrybrac.

The Graecroft affix was registered in 1935 as a kennel for Scottish Terriers. In the mid-1940s Mrs Margaret Gray bought High Time Laughing Mist (Laughing Clown de Luchar ex Talisker Marcella) and later a cream male, Fromage Monsieur of Iradell. This combination produced Ch Graecroft Belle of Iradell and Graecroft Summer Storm, a bitch who was bred to Mrs Graff's Chummie's Warman of Talisker producing Ch Graecroft Weatherman. When Mrs Graff disbanded her High Time kennels Warman came to Graecroft and was campaigned to his title. He was bred to Ch Laughing Mist and produced the beautiful dog, Ch Graecroft Quicksilver. Mrs Gray also bred some fine drop ears, Graecroft Ivory Minx, who was campaigned, and Graecroft Skylark.

In 1945 Mrs W H Tompkins acquired her first Skye, Grey Angel of Letts Dhu (Ch Highland Thistle of What-Ho ex Letts Dhu Reckless Angel). She registered the Stonebrae affix and began to show the drop ear, Ch Little Dickens of Stonebrae (Ch Light Cloud of Letts Dhu ex Ch Babs of Letts Dhu). This remarkable dog gained his title in seven days, gaining three five-point majors. Incidentally, Ch Light Cloud of Letts Dhu (Ch Chummies Warcloud of Talisker ex Letts Dhu Reckless Angel) was a birthday gift to Mrs Tompkins from her husband. Ch little Dorrit of Letts Dhu joined the kennel and was successfully campaigned. Ch Little Cap of Stonebrae (Ch Little Dickens of Stonebrae ex Ch Gray Angel of Letts Dhu) enjoyed great success in the show ring, gaining fifty-one Terrier Groups, nine Best in Show awards, and a staggering 119 Best of Breed awards! His litter brother, the drop ear Ch Candide of Stonebrae, though not extensively campaigned, defeated his famous litter mate on one occasion. The Stonebrae kennel continued to take an active interest in the breed until the mid 1970s.

Mrs Leigh Bishop's Bonnyleigh kennel produced Ch Bonnyleigh's Martini (Ch Rhosneigr Sir Roger ex Bonnyleigh's Success) and Ch Bonnyleigh's the Gigalo (Ch Merrybrac's Mustang ex Ch Merrybrac's Flora) while Robert Hammond's Tweedsmuir kennel produced Ch Tweedsmuir Tikki of Quetzal in the fifties and early 1960s respectively.

The Abacus kennel belonging to Mrs William Frank produced some very good dogs. Her first Skye, a daughter of Ch Jerry of Merrymount (Ch Chummie of Merrymount ex Dairymaid of Merrymount) was bred to Ch Blacky Aus Dem Asgaard Clan (Bode v Schloss Oels ex Daisy v d Heiligin Brucke) and later to Ch Bracadale Henry (Holmesdale Bonnie Charlie ex Bracadale Berenice).

Mrs Frank imported two lovely dogs from France, Ch Ronny de la Chamardière and his grandson, Ch Allander de la Chamardière. The v Schlaraffenland kennel in Switzerland also sent stock to Mrs Frank. Ch Abacus Carl Campbell (Ch Ronny de la Chamardière ex Abacus Tinker Cameron) was a big winner. In all fourteen champions were owned and bred in this kennel.

Mrs Freelan enjoyed great success in the fifties with Ch Rip Tide of Iradell and Ch Kirkby King of Iradell, bred by Mrs Kirkby Peace in England. In 1958 Mrs Freelan bought Merrymount Albert of Iradell and showed him for a time before retiring from the scene.

The Skyemoor kennels belonging to Mrs Grace Moore were founded on Stonebrae stock in 1954. Ch Whirlwind of Skyemoor gained his title in 1966. Ch Prince Jasyn of Skyemoor (Midnight Star of Skyemoor ex Rhosneigr Blonde Mist), born in 1970, was one of the last champions from this kennel.

Gordon Jackson of The Rocks affix, an ardent admirer of the breed for many years, acquired his first Skye, Ben Neols of Dorvin, in 1958. Sadly this dog became a victim of distemper and was replaced by Victory Hill of Iradell,

Ch The Rock's Dicky, owned and bred by Gordon Jackson.

who was unshown. When the Merrybrac kennels imported the lovely Ch Rhosneigr Red Shoes from England Gordon knew he just had to have one of her pups when the time came for her to be bred, so in due course he bought Merrybracs Minnie Ha Ha. Unfortunately this lovely black bitch so hated to travel that she was rarely shown, but in due course she was bred to Ch Glamoor Going Up and produced two pups of which one, Ch The Rocks Dicky, gained his title and several group placements, and was Best Opposite Sex to Ch Glamoor Good News the year she went on to Best in Show at Westminster, 1969.

Gordon imported Rosmairi Acheo (Douce Granite ex Kirkby Harmony) from the Isle of Skye in 1962, and in 1965 Ch Acheo Eilean Dhu (Donas Acheo ex Kirkby Harmony) joined the kennel; she was successfully campaigned to her title, just beating Dicky to the post, and so became The Rock's first champion.

THE SIXTIES ONWARDS

The following kennels have all been active in the USA during the last thirty years. Some are relatively new to the show scene, and others have since retired or, sadly, are no longer with us.

ABERDEEN

This fairly new name in Skyes belongs to Diana Shaw. She has already made an impact with Ch Skyscot's Sweet N Low, who was bred to Ch Traeloch's Bobby McGee N Me, producing three champions to date: Ch Aberdeen's Mist on the Moor, Ch Aberdeen's Phineas J Woopee and Ch Aberdeen Midnight Nibbler.

AGONISTES

Some very nice dogs have appeared from this kennel. The beautiful black dog, Agonistes Black Magic (Druidmoor Mars De Midici ex Ch Quizas Black Jemima), was handled by Ken McDermott. Ch Agonistes the Diva Ryatti (Ch Beau Cheval Wichita Lineman ex Roylaines Riff Raff), Ch Agonistes Countess La Donna (Ch Beau Cheval Wichita Lineman ex Ch Druidmoor Baby Ruth) and Ch Agonistes Always Me (Ch Agonistes Ashley ex Skyecrest Lady Sheena) all gained their titles for the Agonistes affix.

AIRLIE

The Ogilvies chose the affix "Airlie" for their kennel as the seat of the Ogilvie family is found at Airlie in Scotland. Ch Rocheboise Alyson of Skyecrest (Ch Blanchskye's Wee Claymore ex Skyecrest Velvet Lady), Ch Skyecrest True Blue Luther, Abigail Duchess of Airlie (Ch Skyecrest True Blue Luther ex Ch Rocheboise Alyson of Skyecrest), Marsha of Airlie (Ch Talisker's Fairy Wonder ex Taliskers Little Snowflake) and Ch Cheltenham Charlie of Airlie (Ch Skyecrest True Blue Luther ex Ch Rocheboise Alyson of Skyecrest) were the Ogilives' pride and joy.

AMITY

Chris Crowell based her kennel on Talisker and Olivia bloodlines, which has proved to be a successful combination. Ch Amity Miss America (Ch Skye Ark Fearless ex Olivia Noblesse of Dunleigh) was her first home bred champion. Ch Amity Bark Beetle (Ch Skye Ark Fearless ex Olivia Noblesse of Dunleigh) and his brothers from her second litter, Ch Amity Bonanza and Ch Amity Break-a-Day, also gained their titles.

The third litter produced Int Ch Amity Columbus (Ch Olivia Perun ex Rolling Quizas O'Clair) who was exported to Germany where he had a splendid show career, winning the title of World Champion and siring many excellent show dogs. Ch Sweet Amity Display and Ch Sweet Amity Dreams of Skye Ark (Ch Olivia Nimrod ex Ch Skye Ark Pride and Joy) were the next stars to come from this successful kennel. In 1986 Ch Sweet Amity Display was bred to Ch Olivia American Dream producing Ch Amity Electra, Ch Amity Emperor and Ch Amity Esmeralda.

ANGELSKYE

Angela Budde of Colorado, whose stock is founded on Olivia lines, is the owner of the Angelskye affix. Her first two Skyes, Ch Olivia Dream of Snowfire (Ch Feather Duster of Morningsky ex Ch Olivia Miss Universe) and Ch Olivia Excalibur Wizardry (Ch Olivia American Dream ex Ch Chiquita of Morningsky), were both campaigned to their titles and were then bred from, producing in their first litters the Champions Angelskye Apollo's Dream, Angelskye Anderson Bobby, Angelskye Angus of Aberdeen and Angelskye Angelitos Negros. Ch Olivia's Dream of Snowfire's second litter to Ch Olivia's American Dream produced a most promising litter.

Ch Olivia Dream of Snowfire, owned by Angelskye.

Angela Budde of Angelskye with her first litter, three of which became champions.

ARGENT

Ch Gleanntan Argent Made O'Mist (Ch Gleanntan Go For It ex Ch Gleanntan Peaches and Cream) gained her title in the mid-1980s. In 1988 she was mated to Ch Gleanntan Going in Style (Heathermist Highlander ex Ch Gleanntan Goodness Knows) producing Ch Argent Stylish Cavalier who was successfully campaigned in 1990. A recent addition to this kennel is Ch Roblyns Ribbon of Steel (Ch Druidsmoor Sweeny Todd ex Ch Roblyn's Gonna Get Hot) who has done some excellent winning. The Argent Skyes are owned by Lynne Kuczynski of Pennsylvania.

Ch Roblyn's Ribbon of Steel, owned by the Argent kennel.

AVALAIRD'S

The Avalaird kennels produced a number of champions. Ch Avalaird's Daffodil (Ch Quizas Willard O'Bruce ex Winsdown Cookie Cutter), Ch Avalaird's Treebeard Wisteria (Ch Buffalo Tippermuir ex Avalaird's Rhiannon), Ch Avalaird's Allison and Ch Avalaird's Bairn of Maclean (Ch Buffalo Sidder Dhu ex Ch Avalaird's Daffodil) and Ch Avalaird's Flora MacIvor (Ch Gleanntan Monkey Business ex Avalaird's Miss Lucifer) are fine examples from the kennel.

BARRAGLEN

Four views of
Ch Barraglen's Brankie Birk.

Ann and Ross Bower's Ch Talakan Tapestry O'Barraglen (Ch Talakan Talisman ex Ch Kishniga's Miss Mischief) gained her title at eighteen months of age and went on to achieve her CD in Obedience. Mated to Ch Talakan Rover Run Easy Rider (Ch Gordon of Cherry Lane ex Petunia Fancy of Glenmere) she produced Ch Barraglen's Brankie Birk, Ch Barraglen's Bouquet and Ch Barraglen's Bobby Burns. A second litter by Ch Talakan Winterhawk (Ch Skyscot's Tweed of Rover Run ex Ch Talakan Tapestry O'Barraglen) produced Ch Barraglen's Aphrodite, Ch Barraglen's Astra and Ch Barraglen's Wee Bonnie Jean.

Ch/SF Ch Barraglen's Bobby Burns,
owned by Dr Donald Brown

BATTLEWOOD

Ch Royalist Fancy Free (Ch Gleanntan Coming at Ya ex Daisy Happy Days), Barbara Youree's first bitch, achieved some very good wins. She was then bred with Ch Glamoor Gang Buster producing the elegant Ch Battlewood Charlotte Russe, Ch Battlewood Buster's Fancy, Ch Battlewood Fancy's Buster, Ch Battlewood Silverspun G-Man and Ch Battlewood Buster's Fleur. Fancy Free's second litter, to Ch Gleanntan Monkey Business, produced Ch Battlewood Miss Muffet. Ch Miss Muffet is the dam of Ch Battlewood Babycham, Ch Battlewood Drambuie, Ch Battlewood Tanqueray, Ch Battlewood Black Velvet, Ch Battlewood Jack Daniel and Ch Battlewood Glenfidich, sired by Ch Brendan's Something Special.

In 1985 Kathryn Walling and her bitch, Ch Royalist Black Rose (Ch Bellwether's Boomerang ex Ch Battlewood Black Velvet), joined the kennel. Black Rose was bred with Ch Battlewood Jack Daniel, producing Ch Battlewood Black Jack, Ch Battlewood Bobby Naighlon, Ch Battlewood Black Bourbon and Ch Battlewood Royal Casey.

Ch Battlewood Fine and Dandy (Thistlwood Dauphin D'Argent ex Ch Battlewood Buster's Fancy) was campaigned by Kathryn to win fifty Best of Breed awards, one Group Two, one Group Three and four Group Fours. Ch Battlewood Better Believe It (Ch Dawn's Mr Adventure ex Jojacs Light and Lovely) gained his title in 1989.

BELLWETHER

Jane and William Bouton's Ch Twin Towns Winter Wizard (Ch Twin Towns Wise Guy ex Twin Towns Buttermilk Skye) and Ch Twin Towns Evil Eva (Ch Twin Towns Wise Guy ex Twin Towns Skye Lark) did a great amount of winning for their owners in the early 1970s. Eva went on to produce Ch Loyal Lane Ben Macdhui. In the mid 1970s the Boutons changed their affix to Bellwether, and have never looked back.

Ch Bellwether's Romach (Ch Glamoor Gang Buster ex Ch Twin Towns Evil Eva) was a Skye speciality Best in Show winner. Ch Bellwether's Boomerang (Ch Glamoor Gang Buster ex Ch Twin Towns Evil Eva), Ch Bellwether's Patent Pending (Ch Jojacs Happy Days ex Ch Bellwether's Grand Opera), Ch Bellwether's Blue Note (litter brother to Patent Pending), and litter mates Ch Bellwether's Grand Alliance and Ch Bellwether's Grand Opera (Ch Glamoor Got To Be Good ex Ch Bellwether's Romach) are all good examples of the outstanding Skyes this kennel produced in the 1980s.

BESDAM

Barbara and Ernest Koseff's first Skye, Gleanntan Morning Star, was a much loved pet. However, their second, Ch Gleanntan's Glory Hallelujah (Ch Gleanntan Monkey Business ex Ch Jojacs Rise and Shine), was campaigned to her title. Ch Battlewood Charlotte Russe and Ch Battlewood Bob-E's Tycoon (Ch Glamoor Gang Buster ex Ch Battlewood Bonnie Blue) joined the family in 1979. After a successful show career Charlotte Russe was mated to Ch Glamoor Got To Be Good, producing for the Besdam affix Ch Besdam No No Nanette, who gained her title at the tender age of one year. Nanette was bred to Bob-E's Tycoon, producing the exciting Ch Besdam Ralph Lauren, winner of sixty-nine Best of Breed awards and nine group placings, and Ch Besdam Nina Ricci, also a consistent winner.

BLANCHSKYES

The Blanchskyes produced three champions of note: Ch Blanchskyes Wee Exmoor, Ch Blanchskyes Wee Cuillin and Ch Blanchskyes Wee Claymore by Ch Skyecrest King Wonderful ex Skyecrest Princess Tamara.

BONNIEBROOK

Donald and Diane Watson produced five champions from their litter by Ch Roblyns That's A Plenty ex Ch Diaboliques Miss Conduct: Chs Bonniebrooks Happy Go Luckie, Peppermint Patti, Duncan, Prince Charlie, Golden Poppy and McTavish Utz of Bonniebrook in the late 1970s. In 1991 the Watsons imported a Tarskavaig puppy from Scotland, keeping their interest in the breed going.

BRANDYGATE

Beth and Barry Gates leased Ch Called Panther of Morningsky (Int Ch Olivia Wild West ex Ch Jennifer of Morningsky) from the Puddleby kennel and bred some litters in partnership. Ch Skyehaven's Ebony Gates (Ch Cinnabar The Cock of the North ex Skyehaven's Very Own Frostie) earned his title in good competition. Ch Gates Christmas Angel (Puddleby's Black Beard O'Gates ex Puddleby's Impetuous Ms Gates) and Ch Gates O'Heaven Amazing Grace (Ch Called Panther of Morningsky ex Puddleby's Be My Fortune) are two recent title holders for the Gates' affix. Two Skyes have been exported to Australia, namely Gates Impetuous Lady of Wuruf (Puddleby's Black Beard O'Gates ex Puddlebys Impetuous Ms Gates) and Gates Southern Lady of Wuruf (Ch Skyehaven's Ebony Gates ex Gates Ms Bonnie Love O'Skip).

BUFFALO

Avalairds Miss Lucifer was Betty Dickinson's first Skye. She was mated to Ch Gleanntan Monkey Business, producing Champions Buffalo Bodach Glas, Ian Nan Fonne, Sidder Dhu, Sossity and Ch Avalaird's Flora MacIvor. In 1980 Ch Buffalo Sossity was bred to Ch Gleantan Mon Rève (Int Ch Brendan's Something Special ex Ch Gleanntan Glory Seeker), producing five champions thus making her the top producing dam of 1984. Her offspring, Ch Buffalo Drumnacoub, Ch Buffalo Tippermuir, Ch Buffalo Otterburn Treebeard, Ch Buffalo Sauchieburn Maclean and Ch Buffalo Killiecrankie, all enjoyed successful show careers. Killiecrankie was bred to Ch Gleanntan Go For It in 1985, producing Ch Buffalo Rantin Rovin Robin and the lovely Ch Buffalo Blackberry Blossom, who was Best of Breed at the Skye Terrier Club of America's Specialty in 1989 under breed judge Donna Dale.

BUTE

The Bute affix is best known for producng Ch Bute's Coc-A-Bardy and Ch Bute's Wee Mischief (Ch Talakan Talisman ex Teakwood's Kissin Cousin) who gained their titles in 1989.

CALICOT

Judy Cottrell's first Skye, Ch Bonniebrook's Peppermint Patti, was handled to her title in the 1970s. Patti was bred to Ch Gleanntan Coming At Ya, producing a fine litter of six champions which included Ch Calicot's Pride and Joy, Ch Calicot's Mr McIvor of Utzmoor and Ch Calicot's Play It Again Sam.

CALUM'S

A least two champions have been bred at this kennel, namely Ch Calum's Ham and Haddie and Ch Calum's Bangers and Mash (Skyecrest Little Kilt ex Skyecrest Third Rose).

CELTICAIRES

Kathleen Scoggin's Ch Kakumee Rhinestone Cowboy (Canadian Ch Moonlitt's Promised Sunshine ex USA/Canadian Ch Myosho Peanut Butter) won his champion titles in America, Canada and the Bahamas, as well as winning several group one placements. Kennel mate, Ch Teakwood's Flyte O' Fancy (Ch Bellwether's Blue Note ex Ch Teakwood's Tickle My Fancy), not to be outdone, has her American and Bahaman titles too, and has also been placed in groups.

Chs Celticaires Storyteller and Celticaires Tiny Dancer (Ch Teakwood's Mountain Dew ex Ch Teakwood's Flyte O' Fancy) both gained their titles in 1991.

CHERRY LANE

The Cherry Lane kennel imported two Skyes from the Isle of Skye in 1968/69: Ch Tarskavaig Lord of the Isles (Ch Merrymount Gay Chummie ex Rhosneigr Rushing Dame) who won the dog Challenge Certificate at Crufts in 1968 and went on to gain his American title; and Ch Tarskavaig Glorious Twelfth (Merrymount the Rip ex Ch Tarskavaig Silver Birch), who won the bitch Challenge Certificate at Crufts '68 and gained her British title before being exported to the USA, where she added the American title to her name. The pair were subsequently bred producing Ch Gordon of Cherry Lane, who is behind many of the champions bred at Rover Run, and Ch Heath of Cherry Lane. Ch Rob Roy of Cherry Lane (Ch Tarskavaig Lord of the Isles ex Fern of Cherry Lane) was another example from this kennel.

CIMARRON

In the early 1970s the Cimarron kennel enjoyed considerable success with Ch Cimarron Sara Lone Wolf (Ch Taliskers Mr Wonderful ex Moonsongs Sheer Delight), Ch Cimarron Amy of Kenilworth and her brother Ch Cimarron Sarason Andrew (Ch Taliskers Bonnie Angus ex Ch Cimarron Sara Lone Wolf), the latter being a very big winner who collected many groups awards.

CINNABAR

Another kennel that enjoyed some success in the 1970s was the Cinnabar kennel with Ch Cinnabar Colonel Midnight (Taliskers Midnight ex Quizas Black Tjantik), Ch Rover Run Nonsuch of Cinnabar (Ch Gordon of Cherry Lane ex Ch Rover Run Droll Troll) and Cinnabar Brigadoon (Ch Cinnabar Colonel Midnight ex Karona Del Mar Solacia).

CLADICH

Ch Dunvegan Devil in the Kitchen (Ch Gleanntan Monkey Businesss ex Ch Gleanntan Lass Dhu O'Dunvegan) was Susan Parson's first Skye, quickly followed two weeks later by Ch Dunvegan Cladich Brigadoon (Ch Smiths's Wee Laddie ex Aust/USA Ch Danehill Gay Princess). Ch Cladich Candlewyck Kailyard (Ch Dunvegan Devil in the Kitchen ex Ch Skyehaven's Sara O'Candlewyck) was a later addition, followed a year after by her drop eared brother, Ch Candlewyck Printers Devil. Both these Skyes have earned their TT (Temporary Tested) titles in Obedience and are working towards their hunting certificates.

CLAN DONAN

Dr Donald and Ann Brown fell for Ann Bower's Barraglen Skyes and bought three! Ch Barraglen's A Wee Bonnie Jean and Ch Barraglen's Astra (Ch Talakan Winterhawk ex Ch Talakan Tapestry O' Barraglen) and Ch Barraglen's Bobby Burns (Ch Talakan Rover Run Easy Rider ex Ch Talakan Tapestry O'Barraglen) have all been campaigned to their American titles, with Bonnie Jean and Bobby Burns winning their Finnish titles in 1991. In 1990 Ch Tuukan Johnny Be Good (Int Ch Jopi ex Tuukan Highland Heaven) joined the Clan Donan kennel and added the American title to his Finnish one. In 1991, on a return trip to Finland, he won the group at Rovaniemi.

Ch Barraglen's Astra was bred to Ch Seumas O'Toole of Rover Run (Ch Rover Run Flying Scot ex Ch Rover Run Talakan Firebird), a drop ear, producing a litter of seven pups. Ch Baraglen's A Wee Bonnie Jean was taken to Finland to be bred with Ch Tuukan Albert, producing Ch Clan Donan Robert O' The Isle who gained his title in 1992. The Browns frequently visit Finland with their Skyes to compete.

CORCAIGH

In the mid 1980s the Corcaigh kennel imported Ch Y'Dreamer of Morningsky (Ch Amity Columbus ex Ch Fancy of Morningsky) from Germany. Y'Dreamer had a very successful career in the show ring with many group placements. Ch Sweet Amity Dreams of Skye Ark (Ch Olivia Nimrod ex Ch Skye Ark Pride and Joy) joined the kennel as did Ch Skye Ark Sailor Boy (Ch Skye Ark Sir Lancelot ex Ch Skye Ark Rona), who sired Ch Corcaigh's Pumpkin Pie and Ch Corcaigh's Puffin Stuffin (ex Dreams). Ch Corcaigh's Country Classic (Ch Y'Dreamer of Morningsky ex Ch Corcaigh's Pumpkin Pie) and Ch Corcaigh's Hearts Desire (Ch Corcaigh's Country Classic ex Ch Sweet Amity Dreams of Skye Ark) are the most recent stars of this kennel.

CRAGSMOOR

Eugene Zaphiris has bred some good winners with his Cragsmoor affix. Ch Cragsmoor Good N'Plenty and Ch Cragsmoor Plenty Good (Ch Gleanntan Coming at Ya ex Ch Glamoor Too Good To Be True) were placed in many groups. They were followed into the show ring by Ch Cragsmoor Take a Good Look and Ch Cragsmoor Gotcha Good (Ch Moormist Midsummer Knight ex Ch Cragsmoor Good N'Plenty) who also made a good account of themselves.

CROMLECH

Dick Kinnard was a great admirer of the drop ear and successfully campaigned several fine examples of this type. His most famous dog, Ch Milchrista's Dr Pem (Ch Abacus Carl Campbell ex Milchrista's Iris), was shown in the 1960s and won thirty- three Best of Breeds and twelve group placements. Dr Pem sired several drops, notable examples being Ch Milchrista's Moria (ex Milchrista's Ikare), Ch Cromlech's Jamie (ex Merrybracs Merryweather), Ch Paquebot (ex Elda de Fontguitard), Ch Malmgrem's Irma la Douce (ex Malmgrem's Valkyrie), Miss Muffin of Cromlech (ex Merrybracs Merryweather), Ch Carita's Gitano de Plata (ex Jojac's Merrydell Tippirinn) and Ch Milchrista's Dr Pem III (ex Ch Malmgrem's Valkyrie). Ch Paquebot is one of the few drop ears to have won a Best in Show, which he did in Canada in the 1970s.

CYMRIC

The Cymric Kennel bred Ch Cymric's Reveille (Quizas Moon Frost ex Ch Brian's Sweeper Girl) and continues to keep the Skye flag flying in the northwest corner of the States.

DAWNS

Glennda and Don Kountz own three Jojacs. Jojac Prime Time (Ch Glamoor Got To Be Good ex Bellwether's Grand Alliance), Ch Jojac's How Good It Is and Jojacs Light and Lovely (Ch Glamoor Got To Be Good ex Ch Bellwether's Grand Alliance), along with the home bred Dawn's Muppet of Mills (Ch Jojacs How Good It Is ex Wym-way Wraze the Flag), Dawn's Stormy Skye (Ch Dawn's Mr Adventure ex Jojacs Light and Lovely) and Dawn's Delightful Twink (Ch Battlewood's Fine and Dandy ex Ch Battlewood's Better Believe It.)

DRUIDMOOR

Charles W Brown imported Isoline de la Chamardière (Abacus Hector Maclean ex Abacus Wendy Cameron) from France and took her back there to be mated with Ch Bistro de Saint Ludlin (R'Ecole de Mandane ex Virginie du Clos de L'Ill), producing Ch Druidmoor Dubonnet and Ch Druidmoor Daiqiri. He went back to France to import the lovely black dog Ch Jimmy de Ricelaine (Earl de Luchar ex Hortense de Ricelaine) whose litter sister, Jacinthe, took the States by storm. Jimmy produced Ch Druidmoor Diabolique and Ch Druidmoor De Bussy (ex Ch Glamoor Going West).

Ch Druidmoor Mistral (Ch Ben Baines Mon Plaisir ex Druidmoor Doney Gal), Ch Druidmoor Sweeney Todd (Ch Glamoor Got To Be Good ex Ch Druidmoor Marilyn Monroe) and Ch Druidmoor Marilyn Monroe (Ch McTavish Utz of Bonniebrook ex Ch Moormist Mae West) are all fine examples from this kennel.

DUNVEGAN

Alice Smith has enjoyed success with both prick and drop ears. Ch Gleanntan Lass Dhu Dunvegan (Ch Glamoor Gang Buster ex Ch Jojacs Rise and Shine) was bred to Ch Gleanntan Monkey Business, producing Ch Dunvegan Devil in the Kitchen. Australian Ch Danehill Gay Princess (Ch Rhosneigr Blond Ever ex Ch Danehill Frigga), a cream drop ear bred in Australia, was imported from the Isle of Skye. She was bred to the drop ear Ch Smith's Wee Laddie (Bren-Wayn's Prince ex Ed's Little Virginia), producing the prick ear Ch Dunvegan Cladich Brigadoon. A later litter to Bonnimac's Dundee of Chattasey produced the drop, Dunvegan Remus.

ELISSA'S

The Elissa kennel got off to a good start with the bitch Ch Olivia Europa (Ch Olivia American Dream ex Ch Chiquita of Morningsky), who gained her title quickly. She was mated to Ch Andrew Thane of Skyecrest and produced an exciting black litter, Elissa's Alexander being exported to England. After serving the compulsory six months quarantine Alexander came out to win the puppy dog class on the Isle of Skye at the breed club Championship Show in 1990. In 1992 he won four Challenge Certificates, becoming a British champion. Littermates Ch Elissa's Alpha and Ch Elissa's Aindrea hold their American titles.

FANTASY

Debbie Gurling of Indiana is fairly new to the show scene but got off to a great start, finishing Ch Battlewood Black Bourbon (Ch Battlewood Jack Daniel ex Ch Royalist Black Rose). Her other Skyes include Calurian Fantasy Silver Lining (Ch Cinnabar Nonsuch as Tweed ex Gates Wee Bebe Beauty). Debbie bred her first litter in 1989 by Ch Battlewood Black Bourbon ex Calurian Fantasy Hot Topic.

FLAMBEAU

On a trip to England in 1974, James and Mary Kock paid a visit to Harrods Department Store in London and discovered a Skye Terrier puppy in the pet department. They bought Francis d'Orangis (Faygate Nijinsky ex Valerie de Mansart) and were hooked on the breed. When Andrew died in 1977 he was replaced by Ch Bonniebrook's Prince Charlie (Ch Roblyn's That's A'Plenty ex Ch Diaboliques Miss Conduct) who gained his title quickly with three majors. Ch Roblyn Bless Your Heart (Ch Windflower Mitten Drinen ex Ch Roblyn's Bhain Inghean) was purchased and shown to her title, and subsequently the pair were bred producing Ch Flambeau's Picayune, Ch Flambeau's Pain Perdu and Ch Flambeau Crepe Suzette. Suzette gained her title at the tender age of fourteen months and in due course held the title of top producing dam in 1986, with Ch Flambeau's Way Down Yonder, Ch Flambeau's Muskrat Ramble, Ch Flambeau's God of Mirth (by Ch Traeloch Bobby M'Gee N'Me) to her credit.

Ch Flambeau's Way Down Yonder was bred to Ch Olivia's American Dream producing Ch Flambeau's Cotton Picking Rag, Ch Flambeau's Lady Be Good, Ch Flambeau's Mac the Knife and Ch Flambeau's Oh What A Gal. At only six months of age Oh What A Gal won her first major defeating eleven bitches. At eleven months she completed her title with a five-point major under Walter Goodman. In 1990 she was No 1 Skye Terrier bitch and 1991 saw her continue her winning ways, going Best Opposite Sex to her brother, Mac, at the Westminster Show. At the Los Angeles Terrier Club Specialty in June 1991 she went Best of Breed in an entry of forty-five.

Not to be outdone, her sister, Lady Be Good, won a Best in Show in 1989, the first bitch to achieve such an award. In 1990 Mac the Knife was campaigned and finished the year with a Best in Show, many Group awards and No 1 Skye Terrier. In February 1991 he was Best of Breed at Westminster under the Honourable David Merriam. When not at shows the Flambeau Skyes are the much loved pets of their proud owners.

GAMIN

Chris Crabtree acquired her first Skye in 1971 and has been most successful with her kennel in Vancouver, Washington State. So far ten champions have been bred in this small, select kennel, including Ch Gamin's Gay Reflection and littermate Ch Gamin's Shadow (Ch Gamin-Koran Jack Falstaff ex Ch Gamin's Betsy Ross), Ch Gamin's Betsy Ross (Ch Talakan Rover Run Easy Rider ex Koran's Cobweb), Ch Gamin-Koran Jack Falstaff (Koran's Indomitable ex Ch Koran's Grey Gaylene), Ch Gamin Tuppence of Cymric (Ch Cymric's Reveille ex Ch Koran's Lady Macduff), and Ch Gamin Shooting Star (Ch Gamin-Koran Jack Falstaff ex Gamin's Betsy Ross). The kennel also includes Ch Koran's Grey Gaylene (Ch Sullivan's Gold Major ex Koran's Misty Eve), Ch Koran's Lady Macduff (Koran's Indomitable ex Ch Koran's Grey Gaylene) and Koran's Cobweb, from the same combination as Lady Macduff.

Chris Crabtree is an enthusiastic member of the Oregon Terrier Association and the Greater Clark County Kennel Club. With her mother and daughter she has succeeded in producing top quality Skyes renowned for their good temperament.

GLEANNTAN

Ben and Donna Dale were originally interested in Kerry Blues but changed their allegiance to Skyes with the arrival of Ch Jojac's Rise and Shine (Ch Glamoor Go Go Go ex Quetzal Querida) in the 1960s. She gained her title in 1970 and was bred to Ch Glamoor Gang Buster, producing Ch Brendan's Going Places, Ch Brendan's Starshine, Ch Brendan's Something Special, Ch Brendan's Travelin Man and Ch Brendan's Hello Sunshine. The Dales then changed their affix to Gleanntan, repeating the successful first mating with an even more successful litter comprising Ch Gleanntan Feather Duster, Ch Gleanntan Lass Dhu O'Dunvegan, Ch Gleanntan Ticker Tape, Ch Gleanntan Brendan and Ch Gleannan Coming At Ya, who has been an outstanding sire over the years, as well as gaining titles in Canada, America and Bermuda.

The Dales have continued to breed Skyes for three decades now and although there have been many individual outstanding stars from this kennel the following list of champions better describes the quality one expects from Gleanntan:

Chs Gleanntan Pongo's Mackintosh, Gotcha, Globetrotter, Monkey Business, Greta O' Enterprise, Gangleader, Abra, Peaches and Cream, Ghostbuster, Gizmo, Go For It, Gidgit, D'Skyes D' Limit, Glory, Glory, Glory Hallelujah, Glorybound, Gloryseeker, Mon Rève, Goblin, Argent Made O'Mist, Prudence Dictates, Glenaerie, Gamin, Great Jubilee, Black Watch, Gavotte, Touch of Class, Grizzabella, Galen, Monkeyshine, Glenlivet, Ruffles and Flourishes, Goodness Knows, Going in Style, Galewind, Gossamer, Gloria, Bennic Bandmaster, Grand Slam, Graduate, Got it All, Glenargent, T'Roc O'Gibraltar, Galavant, Gladrags, Going Strong, Goshawk, Glamour Girl, Grin And Bear It, Good Times, Gadabout, Gladtidings, Girlwatcher, Glenfiddich, Amazing Grace, Perriwinkle, Silverstreak, Glow of Heathermist and Gus of Gaylord.

GOLD COAST

This small kennel owned by James and Deedy Pierce has enjoyed considerable success with Ch Gold Coast Gideon (BC Richard of Skyecrest ex Ch Windflower's Gold Coast), Ch Gold Coast Flashdance, Ch Gold Coast Success Story and Ch Gold Coast Kandy Kiss (Ch Gold Coast Gideon ex Ch Skyscot's Strictly By Chance).

HEATHERMIST

This kennel is the home of Ch Gleanntan Glamour Girl (Ch Glamoor Gang Buster ex Ch Gleanntan Amazing Grace) and her daughter Ch Heathermist Happy Go Lucky by Ch Gleanntan Monkey Business. Latest addition and title holder is Ch Gleanntan Glow of Heathermist (Gleanntan Grand Design ex Gleanntan Gibson Girl).

HIGH SIERRA

Several champions have been produced under this affix, among them Ch High Sierra's Sassafras Sue (Ch Skyscot's Tweed of Rover Run ex Ch Moonshine Misty Lady), High Sierra's High Rider (Ch Talakan Rover Run Easy Rider ex Ch High Sierra's Sassafras Sue), Ch High Sierra's Ringo Kid and Ch High Sierra Shadow (Ch Utzmoor Rob Roy Du Biorn ex Utzmoor Carry'in On O'Weswyn.)

JAY-ROY

This kennel is a relative newcomer to the breed and specialises in creams. Ch Candlewyck Devil's Advocate (Ch Dunvegan Devil in the Kitchen ex Skyehaven Sara O'Candlewyck) has been a consistent winner with many good wins. Ch Rover Run Pot O' Gold (Ch Talakan Winter Hawk ex Rover Run Over The Rainbow) produced Ch Jay-Roy's Ready And Willing to Advocate and other progeny from this litter which are currently being shown.

JEFFERS

Janet Jeffers, always a very great admirer of the drop ear, has shown some lovely examples over the years. Ch Tormods Aindrea of Malmgren (Ch Lochy of Skyelark ex Ch Penny Too of Skyelark) was shown in the 1960s and produced Ch Malmgren's Valkyrie (ex Ch Malmgren's Lady Pem). Valkyrie was bred to the famous drop Ch Milchrista's Dr Pem producing Ch Malmgren's Irma La Douce and Ch Malmgren's Dr Pem III.

Janet Jeffers has recently changed her affix to her surname, and has continued to produce drops. Ch Jeffers Something Special (Ch Blanchskyes Wee Claymore ex Malmgren's Aquarius) is one of her latest successes.

JOJACS

In 1963 John and Jacqueline Macdonald bought Quetzal Querida (Ch Talisker's Prince Charming ex Talisker's Fairy Desire) as a show dog. However, she had other ideas as she hated shows, so Ch Highland Dancer of Kenilworth (Ch Talisker's Fairy Tale ex Ch Barry of Iradell) was bought and campaigned to his title. Querida was bred to Ch Glamoor Go Go Go, producing Ch Jojac's Pouring it On, Ch Jojacs Special Sparkle, Ch Jojacs Come A Long Way and Ch Jojacs Rise and Shine.

Ch Jojac's I'm the Real Thing (Ch Jojac's Pouring It On ex Druidmoor Dubois) gained his title in 1973. Others to gain their titles include Ch Jojac's Lady Be Cool, by Ch Druidmoor Debussy, and Ch Jojac's Happy Days (Ch Bellwether's Grand Encore ex Moormist Maelstrom).

KENILWORTH

William Clarkson has been involved with Skyes for many years and is a past president of the Skye Terrier Club of America. Past stars from this kennel include Ch Barry of Iradell (Ch Merrymount Nizefella of Iradell ex Ch Queen Flora of Iradell), Ch Lil Abner of Dontha Downs (Comus of the Mynd and Iradell ex Wills Dawn of Kenilworth), Ch Quetzal Quintessence (Ch Lil Abner of Dontha Downs ex Ch Quetzal Chianti), Ch Hyland Dancer of Kenilworth (Ch Barry of Iradell ex Ch Talisker's Fairy Tale), Ch Hi C's Little Bit of Kenilworth (Ch Talisker's Bonnie Angus ex Ch Talisker's Fairy Dream), Ch Hyland Piper of Kenilworth (Ch Lil Abner of Dontha Downs ex Ch Talisker's Fairy Dream), Ch Little Luv of Kenilworth (Ch Talisker's Bonnie Angus ex Ch Talisker's Fairy Dream), Ch Spitfire of Kenilworth (Ch Talisker's Mr Wonderful ex Quetzal Fancy Valentine), Ch Kenilworth's Puckeshetuck (Ch Talisker's Anders ex Ch Kenilworth Liza Doolitle), Ch Kenilworth Mr Bumble (Kenilworth's Rasputin ex Ch Kenilworth the Busy Body), Ch Kenilworth Lancelot (Ch Kenilworth Mr Bumble ex Ch Kenilworth Liza Doolittle) and Ch Kenilworth Perfect Prince (Ch Kenilworth Lancelot ex Kenilworth Star's Delight).

KUHL

Deborah and Michael Divis own the Kuhl Skyes. Their foundation bitch, Ch Ryatti's Really Me (Ch Talakan Rover Run Easy Rider ex Ryatti's Ravishing Rhea), is the dam of Ch Kuhl Breeze Lil' Hot Stuff and Ch Kuhl Breeze Silk Tuxedo (by Ch Talakan British Sterling). The Divis live in Wasilla, Alaska so their dogs should have no trouble growing coats!

KYLEAKIN

This kennel is owned by Julian and Carol Tinsley whose Ch Talakan Widgeon (Ch Skyscot's Tweed of Rover Run ex Rover Run Free Spirit) was bred to Ch Gleanntan Coming At Ya, producing Ch Kyleakin's Kohoutek and Ch Kyleakin's Extra Terrestial.

MACFERGUS

The lovely drop ear Ch Daskye Flapsdown MacFergus (Ch Skyecrest Laird Sylvester ex Ch Lady MacTuff Act Tafala) was the star exhibit for this small kennel. MacFergus did a great deal of winning and had many group placings before his death in 1992 at the ripe old age of fifteen years. MacFergus Brindle Stewart (Ch Talakan Talent ex Ch Talakan Pavielle of Kamal) is the latest breeding from this kennel to earn majors.

MACLEAN

Holly Thompson acquired her first Skye, Maclean's Maggie Mackenzie, in 1978. Maggie was solely a pet and was never bred. Holly Thompson then bought Ch Buffalo Sauchieburn Maclean (Ch Gleanntan Mon Rève ex Ch Buffalo Sossity) who achieved her title. She was bred to Ch Gleanntan Glenaerie (Ch Gleanntan Coming At Ya ex Ch Gleanntan Gotcha), producing Ch Maclean's Great Expectations, Ch Maclean's Chariot of Fire and Ch Maclean's Gone With The Wind.

MACLEOD

Champions holding the Macleod affix are Ch Paisley Macleod Price and Ch Macleod's Macdonald of Skye (Ch Macleod's Wee Kiltie of Skye ex Ch Christie Macleod of Skye). Ch Macleod's Wee Kiltie of Skye is by Ch De Medici's Pastafazoli ex Storey's Charade and Ch Christie Macleod is by Ch Lochy of Skyelark ex Ch Penny Too of Skye Ark.

MOORMIST

The Moormist kennel owned the lovely bitch Ch Druidmoor Mistral (Ch Ben Baines Mon Plaisir ex Druidmoor Doney Gal) who was bred with Ch Brendan's Something Special, producing in 1976 the talented litter which included Ch Moormist Maelstrom, Ch Moormist Mighty Quinn, Ch Moormist Mae West and Ch Moormist Mountain Laurel.

MYOSHO

This kennel is the home of Ch Kirkleyditch Myosho Tina (Ch Kirkleyditch Dalesman ex Rhosneigr Silver Ronde), who was imported from England. After gaining her title she was bred to Can/UK Ch Kirkleyditch King of the Road and produced the lovely cream, Ch Myosho Peanut Butter, who has done a great deal of winning in Canada.

NAESUCH

Joel and Louise Cohen bought Ch Nyteflyte Nefarious (Ch Y'Dreamer of Morningsky ex Nyteflyte Naughty Nancy) and showed her to her title. She was then bred to Ch Balquhatston Blockbuster, producing Ch Naesuch Silver Lining, who gained his crown in 1991.

NYTEFLYTE

The Nyteflyte affix is owned by Connie Clapp who bred Ch Nyteflyte Nicole (Rikaabah's Laird O'The Glen ex Acheo Katy Flora), Ch Nyteflyte Neon Lytes (Ch Corcaigh's Country Classic ex Nyteflyte Nu-Shootzie) and the trio of champions, Nyteflyte Nefarious, Nyteflyte Nighthawk and Nyteflye Nicolai by Ch Y' Dreamer of Morningsky ex Nyteflyte Naughty Nancy.

NORTHRIDGE

Over the years Dr Beverly Hayes has been involved with some rather special Skyes. Ch Sweetie Pie of Northridge (Ch De Medici's Pastafazoli ex Bonn Cassie of Lancaster) not only gained her title but also her UDT (Utiity and Tracking Degree) obedience title, always scoring very highly. Rocheboise Northridge Maggie (Ch Blancheskye's Wee Claymore ex Skyecrest Velvet Lady) gained her CD (Companion Dog) at nearly ten years of age. The latest star of the kennel is Northridge Annie (Ch Dawn's Mr Adventure ex Jojacs Light and Lovely) who has already earned her CD.

PIPERS

Bob and Sharon Trbovich were adopted by a Skye named Piper who would spend part of his day with them but preferred to return home for his dinner. Greatly impressed by this character they decided to have one themselves and bought Ch Gleanntan Glory Glory who was campaigned successfully to her title. Glory was bred to Ch Glamoor Good As Gold, producing Ch The Pipers Casablanca, Ch Pipers Desert Fox who was a multiple group winner and Ch Roblyn's Hotter Than That. Ch Pipers Blackgamma of Roblyn (Ch Roblyn's Gonna Get Hot ex Ch Gleanntan Going in Style) has recently won her Venezuelan title.

OLIVIA

The first part of the amazing success story of the Olivia kennel is recorded in the chapter on the former Czechoslovakia in Part 3.

In 1968 the Smids left their home in Czechoslovakia with four Skyes and waited in Germany for several months while the necessary paperwork for their refugee visas to America was completed. During those months Int Ch Olivia Jatagan died, and his younger sister, Ch Olivia Zinien, was diagnosed as having cancer and was left behind to end her days with Olga's sister.

Olga Smid with Olivia For Me Only, Olivia Furiant and Olivia Fortieth Anniversary at ten weeks old.

When the Smids finally flew to America they took with them Olivia Lacrima (Int Ch Jack v Bary ex Ch Olivia Zinien) and Olivia Jatagana, a daughter of the outstanding Ch Olivia Benfica.

Olga Smid with her dog and bitch CC winners on the Isle of Skye 1985.

On arrival in the USA problems beset the Smids immediately. The American Kennel Club refused to register the two Olivia Skyes because they had been bred in a communist country, and shortly after this devastating blow Olivia Lacrima died from a distemper virus, adding yet more misery to the Smids burden of sorrows.

Fortunately Mrs Adams of the Talisker Skyes in Canada came to the rescue. Already the owner of three Olivia Skyes who were registered in Canada, Mrs Adams gave Talisker's Vivat and Talisker's Olivia (Ch Olivia Hyperion ex Olivia Eroica) to Olga to enable her to establish her famous kennel in America. Later Ch Quizas Sorcha O'Bruce (Ch Quetzal Brucie O'Duff ex Ch Noelle de Larrimore), who also carried Olivia breeding, joined the Olivias from a breeder in Oklahoma. The rest, as they say, is history!

Ch Olivia American Dream, one of the all-time great stud dogs with many champion offspring.

Ch Rannoch Skye Swiss Account, bred in Switzerland, owed by Olga Smid.

In 1970 a litter by Talisker's Vivat out of Ch Quizas Sorcha O'Bruce produced the outstanding male, Ch Olivia Nimrod, with Ch Olivia Nomad also gaining his title and Olivia Noela winning several points towards hers. Nimrod was the first of many American champions for his owner and went on to sire eleven champions, five of them in America, and three international champions. From Nimrod's line have come Ch Olivia Vino Veritas, Ch Olivia Miss Universe, Int Ch Olivia Made In USA, Int Ch Olivia Wild West, Int Ch Olivia Xplosion, Ch Olivia Dukat, the outstanding sire Ch Olivia American Dream and his famous sister, Ch Olivia American Beauty Rose (Int Ch Olivia Xplosion ex Ch Olivia Thanks For The Memories). The bitch, Ch Skye Ark Princess Olga (Ch Talisker's Fearless ex Ch Talisker's Fanfralouche), has been a great asset to the kennel, producing many fine champions.

Ch Olivia Miss Universe with her newborn puppies.

Many world champions have been bred at Olivia, including Int Ch Olivia Wild West and Int Ch Olivia Silver Solo, both owned by the Morningsky kennels in Germany. The Olivia kennels have exported to kennels in many countries, including the Acheo kennels on the Isle of Skye, who have had three Olivias, two from Czechoslovakia and one, Olivia Radovan (Ch Talisker's Fearless ex Olivia Novela), who was imported from America in 1976.

In all the Olivia kennels have produced seventy-two home bred champions, and have owned some outstanding imports, including Ch Rannoch Skye Champagne and Ch Rannoch Skye Chummie from Switzerland and Ch Feather Duster of Morningsky from Germany.

Mrs Smid's judging talents are constantly in demand, taking her all over the world, and as she is now qualified to judge all breeds she is busier than ever. In 1985, despite losing her husband only a month previously, Olga Smid came to Skye, where a warm welcome, and over a hundred Skyes, awaited her at the Skye Terrier Club Championship Show. Not only was it a dream come true for Olga to judge the breed on its native Isle, but it was a great experience for exhibitors who value the opinions of this unique lady.

OUTLANDS

A relative newcomer to the breed, this kennel has produced three champions from a litter by Ch Talakan Rover Run Easy Rider ex Ch Talakan Agapanthas, namely Ch Outlands Long Walker, Ch Outlands Private Dancer and Ch Outlands Blues Brothers.

PUDDLEBY

Ruby Kathrin Patterson bought the bitch Ch Olivia Wonderful Dream (Ch Olivia Vino Veritas ex Ch Olivia Thanks For Memories) and imported Ch Called Panther of Morningsky (Int Ch Olivia's Wild West ex Ch Jenifer of Morningsky) from Germany. From this pairing came Ch Puddleby's Charming Chelsia. Ch Corcaigh's Black Olive was bred with Called Panther, producing Ch Puddleby's Memory to Joe Smid. Ch Puddleby's Laird Brodie, Ch Puddleby's Elegant Megeen and Ch Puddleby's Megan's Tweedledee (Ch Puddleby's MacGuffy O'Gates ex Ch Olivia Wonderful Dream) are just a few of the stars from this kennel.

QUIZAS

Jay Amann's first Skye, Ch Moonsong Tisket (Ch Allander de la Chamardière and Abacus ex Ch Abacus Phoebe Ferguson), was bought in 1960 and gained her title in 1963. Tisket was bred to Ch Chance de la Termitière, producing Ch Quetzal Caprice. In 1965 Ch Quetzal Brucie O'Duff (Quetzal Conquistador ex Talisker's Fairy Desire) gained his title and went on to win

Terrier Groups in the States and Mexico. Ch Quetzal Quintessence (Ch Lil Abner of Dontha Downs ex Ch Quetzal Chianti) also gained her title in 1965.

In 1966 the Quetzal affix was changed to Quizas, and since then many champions have been made up. Some of them are as follows:

> Ch Quizas Jolly Roger, Ch Quizas Tiger Lil, Ch Quetzal Chianti who gained her title after maternal duties, Ch Quizas Grey Mist, Ch Quizas Moon Blaze, Moon Minx and Moon Dust, Ch Quizas Sorcha O'Bruce , Ch Quizas Willard O'Bruce, Ch Quizas Cap'n Kid of Dunleigh and Ch Quizas Firefly of Dunleigh, Ch Quizas the Dragon Lady, Ch Quizas Casey O'Bruce who had a very successful show career winning his titles in America, Mexico, Venezuela and Columbia taking several groups and Best in Show awards, Ch Quiza's Snowball, a drop ear, Ch Quizas Marea of Taliqui, Ch Quizas Thistlissa, Ch Quizas Tweedledum and Ch Quizas Pippin Poppsiepetal.

ROBLYN

The Bouchers first Skye, Ch Little Luv of Kenilworth (Ch Talisker's Bonnie Angus ex Ch Talisker's Fairy Charm) gained her title in 1967 at four years of age. She was then bred back to her sire, Bonnie Angus, producing Ch Roblyn's Racy Rachel. Rachel was bred to Ch Glamoor Gang Buster and produced the lovely Ch Roblyn's Bhain Inghean, who won several Terrier Groups and went on to produce six champions, including Ch Roblyn's Ain't Cha Glad and That's A Plenty by Ch Glamoor Gang Buster.

Ch Roblyn's Ruby Tuesday (Ch Windflowers Mitten Drinen ex Ch Roblyn's Bhain Inghean) was the next star to emerge. The Roblyn kennel was home to Ch Glamoor Good as Gold (Ch Glamoor Gang Buster ex Ch Glamoor Good News), who sired Ch Roblyn's Hotter Than That (ex Ch Gleanntan Glory Glory), a Best in Show winner and the winner of several Groups. Ch Roblyn's Glascon Granite and Ch The Pipers Blackglamma of Roblyn took their titles in 1991.

The latest quartet to make a great name for themselves are Ch Roblyn's Rainbo Warrior, Ch Roblyn's Ribbon of Steel, Ch Roblyn's A Chorus Line and Ch Roblyns Glascon Gaviidae (Ch Druidmoor Sweeny Todd ex Ch Roblyn's Gonna Get Hot).

ROB ROY MACGREGOR

The Rob Roy Macgregor affix belonged to William and Margaret Counts in Texas who were admirers of the Merrymount type and loved both prick and drop ears. Their first Skye, Ch Moonsong's Nod (Abacus Abel Sinclair ex Ch Moonsong's Bouket), sometimes known as Flora Campbell, was soon joined by Merrymount Gay Pete (Ch Merrymount Midday Sun ex Ch Happyhill Gay

Gordon) who gained his title in 1956. Ch Abacus Phoebe Ferguson (Ch Abacus Carl Campbell ex Ch Abacus Mollie MacAlister) was then campaigned to her title. In 1968 Ch Rob Roy Macgregor's Gay Gavin (Ch Merrymount Gay Pete ex Ch Moonsong's Nod) took his title. Later Ch Burmar Drummer of Iradell (Burmar McGuffie ex Merrymount Happy Days), a cream imported from England by the Iradell kennels, joined the clan, as did Lady Iris Merrymount (Ch Merrymount His Grace ex Merrymount Gay Midwife) and Merrymount Mary Rose.

ROVER RUN

In 1965 Ch Wishau of Iradell (Ch Tarskavaig Great Scot ex Ch Portobello of Iradell) joined Walter and Carol Simonds' kennel of Corgis. This lovely dog gained his title in 1967 and that same year the Simonds acquired the bitch, Ram's Golden Sky (Hendean's Teddy Bear ex Hendean's Personality), who had been mated to Wishau, after her owner had decided to part with her before the pups were born and, fortunately, the Simonds stepped in. The litter produced the first of many Skye champions for which this kennel has become renowned, Ch Rover Run Droll Troll, Ch Rover Run Golden Cloud and Ch Rover Run Flying Nun from a repeat mating.

Ch Gordon of Cherry Lane (Ch Tarskavaig Lord of the Isles ex Ch Tarskavaig Glorious Twelfth) joined the kennel in 1972, later producing Ch Talakan Rover Run Easy Rider and Ch Rover Run Talakan Firebird (ex Petunia Fancy of Glenmere).

The Rover Run kennels have produced many more champions including Ch Rover Run Pot of Gold, Ch Rover Run Easter Parade, Ch Rover Run The Raider's Edge, Ch Rover Run Gold Digger, Ch Rover Run the Raiderette, the drop ear Ch Seumas O'Toole of Rover Run and the latest delightful cream, Ch Rover Run Gold Rush (Ch Talakan Winter Hawk ex Ch Rover Run Gold Digger).

ROYALIST

Karen Jenning's foundation bitch, Ch Jojacs Special Sparkle (Ch Glamoor Go Go Go ex Quetzal Querida), gained her title in 1968. She was followed in the show ring by the lovely black dog, Ch Druidmoor Debussy (Ch Jimmy de Ricelaine ex Ch Glamoor Going West), who gained her title in 1972 along with the bitch, Ch Cimarron Becky (Ch Jojacs Pouring it On ex Ch Cimarron Sara Lone Wolf). With these bloodlines the Royalist Skyes took off, producing Ch Royalist Free Spirit, Ch Royalist Fancy Free, Ch Royalist Too Tuff and Ch Royalist Black Rose.

Ch Royalist Flirtation, Ch Royalist Vixen of Calurian and Ch Royalist Revelation (Ch Royalist Too Tuff ex Calurian Sprite of Royalist) are the latest champions from this kennel. The Royalist kennel was also home to two outstanding dogs, Ch Bellwether's Boomerang (Ch Glamoor Gang Buster ex Ch Twin Town's Evil Eva) and the English import, Ch Littlecreek's Elgin (Skye Ark Sir Walter Scott ex Skye Ark Glamour Girl), who won many group placings.

Ch Sand Island Summer Soltice.

RYATTI

Ryatti's Ravishing Rhea has proved to be an excellent brood bitch, producing Ch Ryatti Resume and Ch Ryatti's Really Me to Ch Talakan Rover Run Easy Rider, Ch Ryatti's Rembrandt by Agonistes Black Magic, Ch Ryatti's Puttin' on the Ritz and Ch Rryatti's Racketeer by Ch Talakan Talisman.

SAND ISLAND

Carol Anderson's Ch Sand Island Solitaire (Ch Gleanntan Coming At Ya ex Ch Roblyn's Hotter Than That) gained her title in 1984 and also won several group placements. In 1985 she was bred to Ch Traeloch's Bobby McGee N'Me producing Ch Sand Island Burt Hill and Ch Sand Island Sam Fifield TD who took their titles in 1987. Sam has gone on to win at least forty Best of Breed awards and many group placements as well as his TD (Tracking Degree). In 1990 Carol imported four littermates from Finland, from a litter by Tuukan Highland Hero ex Ch Misting's Moonlight Mary. One of the litter, Ch Tuukan Sand Island Don, gained his title in 1991.

SHAWN-RAE

The Shawn-Rae affix is owned by Barbara Cline, a new admirer of the breed who has already made up one champion, Ch Shawn-Rae's Rocky Road (Ch Talakan Tambourine ex Talakan Krystal of Jo-Na-Da's). Hopefully Barbara will find the road smooth going in all her Skye activities.

SILVERSPUN

Fran and Bill Johnston have been involved with Skyes since 1972 when Ch Skycrest Laird Neil (Skyecrest King James ex Skyecrest Contessa) came into their lives. From their first litter in 1977, by Ch Dunvegan Tail Toddle ex Ch Gleanntan Silverspun, came Ch Silverspun Rosy Future. Ch Battlewood Silverspun G-man (Ch Glamoor Gang Buster ex Ch Royalist Fancy Free) did some winning for Fran in the early 1980s. Ch Silverspun Song of Spring (Ch Glamoor Gang Buster ex Ch Gleanntan Amazing Grace) was followed by her son, Ch Silverspun Four on the Floor, sired by Ch Gleanntan Monkey Business. Ch Olivia American Beauty Rose joined the Silverspun's and enjoyed a successful show career before producing Ch Silverspun Suncatcher, Ch Silverspun Starduster and Canadian Ch Silverspun Northern Star to Ch Gleanntan Globetrotter. A repeat mating produced the latest star in the family, Ch Silverspun Sundancer.

SKYE ARK

After seeing the film *Greyfriars Bobby*, Nicholas and Irma Juhasz decided they had to have a Skye. In 1965 they bought Taliskers Sunshade (Kirkby Sunshine of Talisker ex Talisker's Lovely Fairy), a drop ear. Ch Talisker's Fearless and Ch Talisker's Fanfralouche followed soon after and they were persuaded to show the latter two, which they did most successfully. Two further Skyes joined the Ark, Ch Glamoor Good Gracious and Ch Glamoor Good As Always (Ch Glamoor Gang Buster ex Ch Glamoor Good News), both successfully gaining their titles in 1973.

In 1974 the first Skye Ark litter was born, sired by Fearless ex Fanfralouche, producing four champions, Ch Skye Ark Fearless, Longfellow, Pride and Joy and Princess Olga. Ch Skye Ark Sir Lancelot (Ch Danters Different Drummer ex Ch Glamoor Good Gracious) was born in 1976, followed by the beautiful cream, Ch Skye Ark Rona, who in turn produced Ch Skye Ark Sea Breeze and Ch Skye Ark Sailor Boy by Ch Skye Ark Sir Lancelot.

SKYECREST

Dolly Stofer adopted a stray Skye while in England in 1945. However, it was not until the death of her husband in 1963 that Dolly renewed her acquaintance with the breed and built up her famous kennel.

Lady Tyke (Talisker's Brady Tyke ex Lady Susan MacKay) was bred to Ch Talisker's Bobby Burns, producing Ch Princess Pixie, Ch Duchess of Thai and Ch Wee Angus Duffy. Lady Tyke was then shown and gained her title in 1967. A repeat of this mating was made, and with the Skyecrest affix now registered, resulted in the first of many champions for the kennel, Ch Skyecrest Count Christopher.

Ch Skyecrest Lord MacKay (Ch Talisker's Mr Wonderful ex Ch Princess Pixie) gained his title in 1969. Included in the hall of fame are Ch Skyecrest Barefoot Contessa, Ch Skyecrest Prince Terrence, Ch Skyecrest Bonnie Heather, Ch Skyecrest Sassy Showstopper, Ch Skyecrest Princess Desire and Int Ch Rocheboise of Skyecrest (Ch Blanchskye's Wee Claymore ex Ch Skyecrest Velvet Lady) who was World Champion in 1980.

During the 1980s Dolly imported some excellent stock from Germany, Ch Fleur of Morningsky (Int Ch Olivia Silver Solo ex Int Ch Alpha of Morningsky) and Ch Eagle Black of Morningsky (Ch Olivia Wild West ex Ch Alpha of Mornngsky). Fleur gained her American title and produced some quality pups for Skyecrest before being exported to England where she went on to produce the top winning bitch in Britain, Ch Mariquita Flashfleur. Eagle Black has passed on his black genes to Ch Skyecrest Dark Knight an Ch Skyecrest Knight Rider.

The beautiful drop ears, Ch Skyecrest Rugby, Ch Skyecrest Lady Mona and Ch Skyecrest Lady of the Evening (the last of these joining her grandmother Fleur in England and adding the British title to her name) all easily gained their titles in their home country.

SKYSCOT

Leslie Becker's first Skye, Roylaine's Miss Elegant (Ch Talisker's Gray Laddie ex Roylaine's Sandy), won some points towards her title but it was a younger sister, Kimberley of Roylaine's, who set off on the glory road, gaining her title in 1966. The two bitches were bred to Ch Talisker's Dark Knight, with a dog, Skyscot's Jack Frost, being kept from one litter and a bitch, Skyscot's Miss Winnie the Pooh, retained from the other. This pair were later bred together to produce Ch Skyscot's Show Stopper.

Ch Gordon of Cherry Lane joined the Skyscot kennels in 1970 and was bred to Ch Kimberley of Roylaine's before later joining the Rover Run kennels. Ch Skyscot's Sir Thomas Moore (Ch Twin Town's Wise Guy ex Skyscot's Rebecca Lynne) enjoyed a great run of success in the late 1970s.

In 1983 Ch Skyscot's Patent Laddie (Ch Cimarron Quincy ex Ch Skyscot's Patience) quickly took his title and enjoyed many Group placings. Ch Balquhatston Blockbuster joined the kennel from Scotland and added his American title to that of his British one. Buster enjoyed a successful career on both sides of the Atlantic earning Group placings in both countries. Nowadays Leslie Becker devotes her time to her successful Norfolk terriers.

SNOWCASTLE

Snowcastle is the home of Ch High Sierra Snowcastle Buff (Ch Talakan Rover Run Easy Rider ex Ch High Sierra Sassafras Sue) and Ch High Sierra Sir Daggit (Ch Skyscot's Tweed of Rover Run ex Ch Moonshine's Misty Lady) and bred Ch Snowcastle Rover Run Willow (Ch Rover Run of the Raider's Edge ex Ch Misty Way's Calamity Jane).

TALAKAN

The Talakan Skyes are based on Skyscot and Rover Run bloodlines. In 1974 Rover Run Free Spirit joined Judy Davis' Afghan kennel. She quickly gained her title and was followed into the show ring by Ch Skyscot's Tweed of Rover Run, who was part owned with Rover Run kennels.

Ch Talakan's Rover Run Easy Rider, Ch Talakan Rover Run Sunbird and Ch Rover Run Talakan Firebird were a joint litter by Ch Gordon of Cherry Lane ex Petunia Fancy of Glenmere. Easy Rider has established himself as one of the top stud dogs of all time with over thirty champion offspring to date, including the lovely Ch Talakan Tempest, Ch Talakan Talent and Ch Talakan Tambourine.

Ch Talakan Rover Run Songbird was bred to Ch Skyscot's Utopia producing the top Skye of 1983, Ch Talakan Talisman, who enjoyed many Group placements during his career. Ch Talakan Twilight and Ch Talakan Tango have also been excellent representatives from this successful kennel.

TEAKWOOD

Larry and Laureen Ivey's foundation stock came from the Skyscot kennels and set them off to a successful start with the beautiful drop ear, Ch Teakwoods Dew Drop (Skyscot's Good Vibration ex Skyscot's Morag of Dunvegan), who was born in 1982 and had some really good placings at shows. Litter mate Ch Teakwood's Master Blend, a prick ear, was a group winner also. Ch Teakwood's Mountain Dew (Showboat's Onyx of Skyecrest ex Ch Teakwood's Dew Drop) was the next to gain his title. Further successful Skyes from this kennel include Ch Teakwood's Tickle My Fancy, Ch Teakwood's Flyte of Fancy and, most recently, Teakwood's Low and Behold who is fast chasing her championship.

TWIN TOWN

In the later 1960s and early 1970s the Twin Town Skyes, owned by Pat Maki, enjoyed much success with Ch Twin Town Skyrocket (Ch Graecroft Quicksand ex Twin Town Skye Lo), Ch Twin Town Earth Angel (Ch Twin Town Skyrocket ex Ch Twin Town Skye Lark), Ch Twin Town Margaret's Gaylord (Ch Twin Town Skyrocket ex Sunny Mop of Iradell), Ch Twin Town Wise Guy (Taliskers Wee Wise Guy ex Tam O'Shanter of Ethelwyn), Ch Twin Town Geordie Ross (Ch Twin Town Wise Guy ex Twin Town Buttermilk Skye) who had an outstandng show career, Ch Twin Town Evil Eva (Ch Twin Town Wise Guy ex Ch Twin Town Skye Lark) and the cream drop ear, Ch Twin Town Sweet William (Ch Twin Town Skyrocket ex Sunny Mop of Iradell), who was the first cream drop to earn his title in America.

WINDFLOWER

Ralph and Sandra Allen's first Skyes, Allen's Jane Eyre and Allen's Boris Gudunov, were much loved house dogs. In 1967 Ch Kirkby Hailstorm of Talisker (Kirkby Sunshine of Talisker ex Kirkby Heavensent), bred by Mrs Rhalou Kirkby Peace in England and imported by the Talisker kennels in Canada, joined the family and gained her title in the same year. Her only litter, to Ch Talisker's Fairy Heir, produced Ch Allen's Sissy Go Forth, Ch Allen's Zulekia Dobson, Ch Allen's H M Pulham Esquire and Ch Valentines Candy of Crispi. Ch Talisker's Apollo (Faygate Beetle of Talisker ex Talisker's Fairy Charm) next joined the kennel, gaining his title in 1971 and finishing as number three Skye Terrier in the annual ratings.

Barraglen's Baird.

The Allens' subsequently registered the affix "Windflower" and Ch Windflower's Judy Judy Judy (Ch Talisker's Chieftan ex Ch Allen's Sissy Go Forth), who gained her title in 1971, was mated to Ch Talisker's Apollo, producing Ch Windflower's Mother Goose. She was followed into the ring by Ch Windflower's Super Star (Ch Talisker's Apollo ex Ch Valentines Candy of Crispi) who did a great deal of winning and in turn produced Ch Windflower's Run Rocky Run to Ch Glamoor Gang Buster, and the big winner, Ch Windflower's Mitten Drinen. This dog sired the lovely dark bitch, Ch Windflower's Sylvia Sidney, ex Ch Windflower's Mother Goose, and the silver dog Ch Windflower's Gandy Goose ex Ch Windflower's Wonder Woman.

Olivia Iglesias.

Ch/SF Ch Barraglen's Bobby Burns.

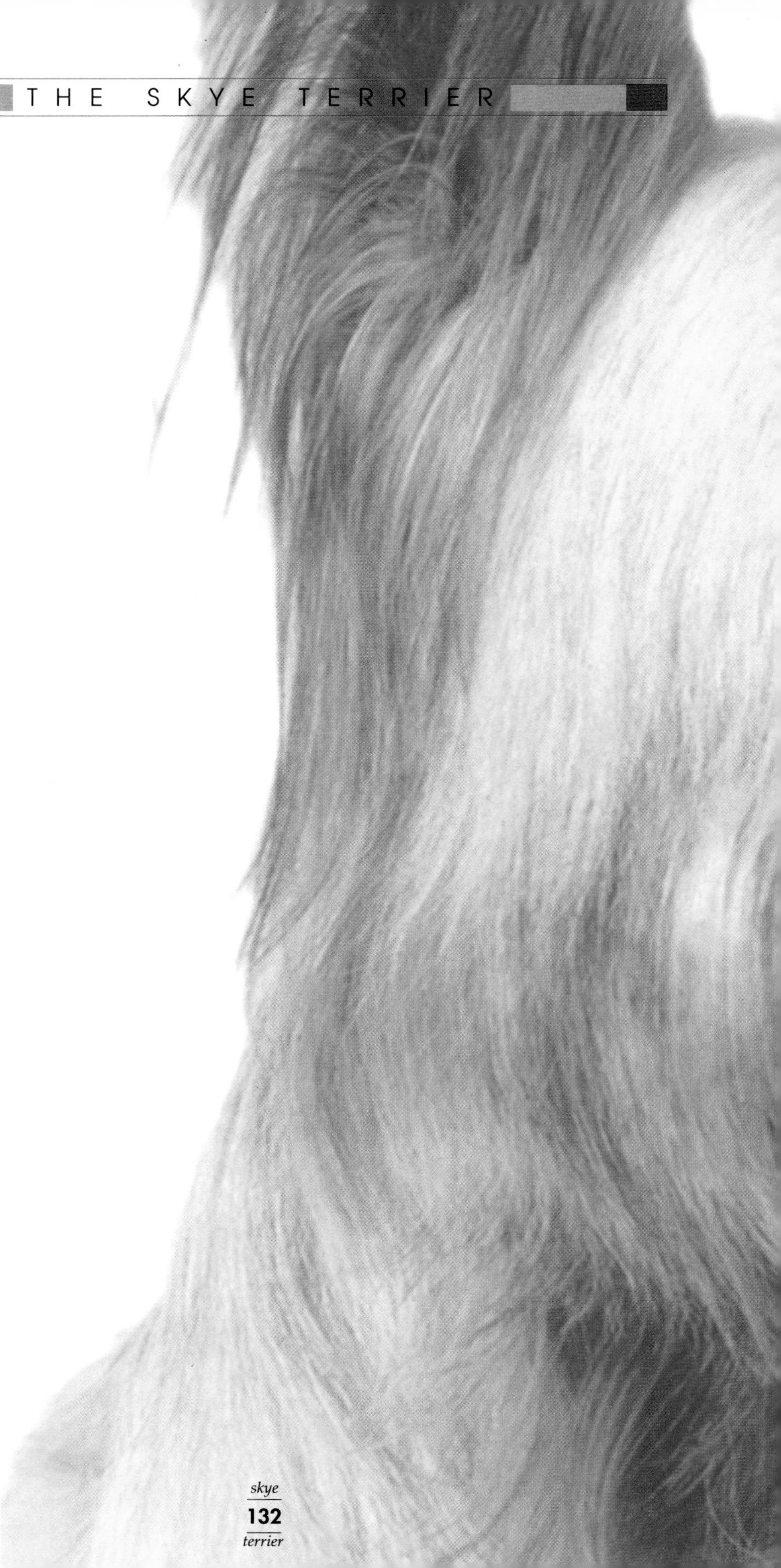

part **3**
WORLDWIDE
SKYE
TERRIER

AUSTRALIA

Skye Terriers were not established in Australia until the late 1960s but there is no doubt that early settlers introduced the breed to that country in the nineteenth century. Captain Allan Macdonald of Waternish joined his regiment, accompanying one of the immigrant ships to Tasmania in 1848; he took some of his terriers with him and is reported to have left several of them in Australia. A few years later, between 1850 and 1870, Captain Duthie of the famous Duthie Shipyard in Aberdeen took his Skye Terriers to sea but, on introducing them to Australia, found they did not take too happily to the heat.

The first registered imported Skye arrived in Australia in 1965. Acheo Seoras Beag (Marjayn Jock of Dornoch ex Merrymount Mid Ship) from the Isle of Skye was imported by Karen Brown. At that time the journey to Australia was a four week sea trip and, for the dogs, was followed by a spell in quarantine. Sadly this did not go well for the dog and he died at the early age of two years.

The following year brought an invasion of Skyes with Mr Barry Ross of South Australia importing a dog and two bitches from England. One of the bitches produced a litter of four pups en route. The dog, Rhosneigr Blond Ever (Ch Rhosneigr Rise Again ex Ch Rhosneigr Recamier), a prize winner in Britain before his exportation, and the two bitches, Rhosneigr Merrymount Only Wait (Ch Merrymount Mid River ex Merrymount Gay Princess) and Tarskavaig Scotskilt (Ch Tarskavaig Great Scot ex Sine Acheo), were to be the foundation stock for Mr Ross, who already bred Maltese.

Mrs Inge Skov Christensen had grown up with Skyes in her native Denmark, and already owned a successful kennel of Great Danes in Australia when she imported two bitches from the Isle of Skye in 1967. These two, Acheo Olga Olivova (Ch Acheo Olivia Whist ex Mo-cridhe Acheo) and Acheo Highland Wedding (Ch Acheo Olivia Whist ex Merrymount Mid Ship), were the foundation bitches for the Danehill Kennels in the southern hemisphere.

However, the first litter to be born in Australia was by Mr Ross' Rhosneigr Blond Ever ex Rhosneigr Merrymount Only Wait. One of the litter, Carolean Artful 'Arry, was shown for a time, but shortly after this litter was reared the dogs were put up for sale, Blond Ever and Only Wait going to Mrs Christensen and Scotskilt finding a good home with Mr Warby.

Mrs Christensen concentrated on showing Blond Ever and Olga Olivova to their Australian titles and then began breeding Skyes. Her newly-acquired stock produced Champions Danehill Frigga, Freya, Odin, Jock, Snaps, Kyleakin, Silver Sail, Gay Princess and Blond Bit, to name a few.

Ch Danehill Gay Princess, a cream drop ear, and Ch Danehill Silver Sail were sold to Sine Threlfall of the Acheo affix who lived in Western Australia from 1970. When Mr and Mrs Threlfall and their baby son returned to Britain in

1972 the dogs followed, having to undergo six months quarantine detention. Gay Princess was later sold to drop ear enthusiast Alice Smith in America, where she gained her title and produced at least one drop ear champion.

Towards the end of the 1960s Happyhill Mischief (Ch Happyhill Hokey Cokey ex Ch Happyhill Minnehaha) was imported from England by Mrs Vernon of Victoria. Mischief later produced Ch Vocalique Blue Haze. About the same time Mrs Cassidy of Queensland, a breeder of Australian Silky Terriers, imported Merrymount Skyrocket (Ch Merrymount Mid River ex Merrymount Rockette) and Merrymount Never Give Up (Ch Merrymount His Grace ex Merrymount Snowball) from England. Unfortunately Mrs Cassidy found the breed larger than she had anticipated, and had difficulty in accepting the temperament, though she bred some litters before admitting defeat and selling the dogs to Mrs Sonia Gardien, who has been successful with her Skyes.

During the 1970s several new kennels sprang from Danehill stock, Santlin, Gardony, Eljepa, Benhough, Giamba and Raldoris being the most notable. By 1975, when the last Danehill litter was produced, the breed was in desperate need of a blood transfusion!

In 1976 Jeanette Hattersley of the Raldoris kennel in New South Wales imported Kirkleyditch Lorna Doone (Ch Kirkleyditch King of the Road ex Hornblower Hoola-la) from England while Acheo MacPhail's Lament (Aust Ch Danehill Silver Sail ex Maid of the Loch of Acheo), bred on the Isle of Skye, was imported by the Benhough Kennels in Tasmania.

In 1979 Drewsteignton Avesta (Olivia Radovan ex Int Ch Larrikin's Iris of Drewsteignton) was the first import for the Santlin Kennels belonging to Maureen Cartledge, with Acheo's Robbie's Pride (Olivia Radovan ex Kirkleyditch Kittiwake) and Vanghapara Scot of Raldoris (Dracula's Luxy of Kirkleyditch ex Vanghapara Gay Duchess) joining the Benhough and Raldoris kennels

Rhosneigr Cream Pistol at 19 months, imported by Raldoris Kennels.

respectively. In 1981 Maureen Cartledge imported Tarskavaig Road to the Isles (Ch Tarskavaig Bonar Law ex Ch Tarskavaig Bonnie Scotland) to her Santlin kennel.

In the latter half of of the 1980s Mallysmar Stargazer (Mariquita Charlie's Angel to Mallysmar ex Checkbar Justa Jiffy at Mallysmar) joined the Skyepara kennel in South Australia, and Rhosneigr Cream Pistol (Ragged Robin of Rhosneigr ex Rhosneigr Blond Belle) arrived as the third import of Miss Hattersley's Raldoris kennel. With this addition of new blood entries increased at shows, more litters were registered and new kennels began to sprout. Skyes spread to all Australia's States except for the Northern Territory, and the breed was now being sought by fanciers in New Zealand.

In this decade the laws in Australia were changed to allow dogs from countries other than rabies free Britain to be imported. The Wanmirri kennel in Sydney belonging to Owen Clark imported Ch Rover Run Nova of Renaissance from America, but unfortunately this dog died only a year later, following surgery. However, a second dog from the Rover Run kennel, Am Ch Rover Run Go for Gold (Ch Rover Run the Raiders' Edge ex Ch Rover Run Pot of Gold), was imported by the Wanmirri/Santlin kennels with better results.

Gates Southernlad of Wuruf (Ch Skyehaven's Ebony Gates ex Gates Ms Bonnie Love O' Skip) and Gates Impetuous Lady of Wuruf (Puddleby's Black Beard O' Gates ex Puddleby's Impetuous Ms Gates) were imported from America by the Wuruf kennel in South Australia in 1989.

Listed above are the nineteen Skye Terriers imported into Australia. Another, a Happyhill dog, was imported to a pet home and three others were never used for breeding purposes. This means that breeders in Australia have to work hard to avoid too much inbreeding and the need to import quality stock is still very much a necessity. However, the breed is thriving and there are some outstanding dogs being produced which could trouble the best in any country. There are also some very fine drop ears in Australia though the prick ear is by far the most popular type.

Now is the time to get out your atlas and follow me on a tour of Skye breeders down under!

NEW SOUTH WALES

The Giamba kennel belonging to Mrs McGlynn was one of the most successful in the 1970s, starting with a dog from the Danehill kennels, Ch Danehill Snaps, who went on to take several Groups and was a Best in Show winner. This kennel bred some fine champions including Ch Giamba Skye Struanmore, Ch Giamba Skye Heather and Ch Giamba Skye Stornaway.

Two Raldoris Skyes.

Jeanette Hattersley, owner of the Raldoris affix, started with the Shih Tzu breed. In 1970 she purchased a Skye dog from the Danehill kennels as a pet, because showing was not a priority at that time. Fred, however, was quite a character and her interest in the breed deepened. When Fred died of cancer at the age of four years a bitch, Danehill Dizzy Blond, from the last litter bred by Mrs Christensen, was purchased with a view to showing. "Sarah", as she was known, had other ideas. She detested the show ring so much she would urinate all over the judge's hand, so her show career came to an early conclusion. Benhough Benjamin (Ch Danehill Jock ex Danehill Blond Bit) joined the kennel from Tasmania shortly after Sarah's retirement and later became the kennel's first Skye champion.

Ch Gildarre Lady Be Good.

In 1977 Kirkleyditch Lorna Doone was imported from England with Acheo MacPhail's Lament, who was bred to Danehill Dizzy Blond, making this a productive year for the Raldoris kennel. Lorna Doone enjoyed a successful show career gaining her title with little trouble. The following year Miss Hattersley imported the dog, Vanghapara Scot of Raldoris, from England. Breeding him to Lorna Doone resulted in some excellent Skyes, including the drop ear Ch Raldoris Boldantrue and Ch Raldoris Mlord Hamish.

Only six litters have been produced by the Raldoris kennels and showing has been limited due to lack of competition in the Sydney area. However, to keep the interest alive in New South Wales, Miss Hattersley imported Rhosneigr Cream Pistol (Ragged Robin of Rhosneigr ex Rhosneigr Blonde Belle) from England in 1987, thus injecting some fresh blood into the breed.

Skyeholm MacDougai.

Three new Skyes from Wanmirri joined the Raldoris kennel in 1991 when the former kennel went out of Skyes. Ch Gildarre Lady Be Good (Ch Eramosa Hairy Bear ex Ch Gardony Silver Lady), Wanmirri Wot No Nickers (Ch Santlin Spit Npolish ex Daycara Amy) and Ch Skyeholm Scarborough (Ch Skyeholm Wee Angus ex Skyepara Highland Girl) have all settled in, Scarborough taking Runner Up in the Group at her first show for her new owner. At the time of writing the Raldoris kennel owns thirteen Skyes ranging in age from two to twelve years, including a rescue dog whose ears were severely damaged by being flyblown, but who is now a happy member of the family.

The Skyeholm kennel belonging to Mr and Mrs Magnusson produced some very good Skyes in the 1980s, most notably Ch Skyholm Wee Angus who was a multi Group Winner, the lovely drop ear Ch Skyeholm Macdougal, Ch Skyeholm Rob Roy and Ch Skyeholm Highland Rose, to name but a few.

Betty and Owen Clark's Wanmirri kennel is noted for Smooth Fox Terriers, Cardigan Corgis and Skyes, having had some great wins during the 1980s and early 1990s. Their first American import, Ch Rover Run Nova of Renaissance, unfortunately died less than a year later afterwards following surgery, and the Wanmirri and Santlin kennel jointly imported Am Ch Rover Run Go for Gold (Ch Rover Run the Raider's Edge ex Ch Rover Pot of Gold) in 1990. Recently the Clarks came out of Skyes, which is a great pity for the breed; the kennel had built up a fine reputation, winning many Groups and Best in Show awards.

A Wanmirri Skye, owned by Owen Clark.

VICTORIA

Jean and Pat Baldwin have enjoyed great success with Ch Santlin Sigmund Freud who won many Group and Best in Show awards during his career and is himself the sire of nine champions for the Eljepa kennel. Among them are Ch Eljepa Skyway Express, a consistent winner, Ch Eljepa Skyenterprise, Ch Eljepa Road Tskye and Ch Eljepa Skyewayman.

Sonia Gardien has bred and shown some fine Skyes and among the stars her kennel has produced are the lovely drop ear Ch Gardony Silver Melody, Ch Gardony April Star, Ch Gardony Bolt Olitening and Aust/NZ Ch Gardony Pollyanna. Gardony Macduff, bred to Gardony Silver Bell, produced Ch Eramosa Hairy Bear, who was a big winner for his owners and sired several champion offspring.

David and Maureen Cartledge own the highly successful Santlin kennel. Beginning in the 1970s with Ch Vocalique Blue Haze, a daughter of Happyhill Mischief, the Santlin kennel is now the largest Skye Kennel in Australia. In 1979 Drewsteignton Avesta quickly gained her crown and took many Group awards. A second import, Tarskavaig Road to the Isles, followed in 1981, repeating Avesta's successes in the show ring and siring many top winners for the kennels including the multiple Best in Show winner Ch Santlin Sigmund Freud. Altogether the Santlin kennels have produced a positive galaxy of stars with many brilliant wins to their credit. These include: Ch Santlin the Skydiver; Ch

Santlin Ston-Col Sober; Ch Santlin Sealed With A Kiss; Ch Santlin S P Bookie, who was three times Top Skye in the Top Terrier Competition in Victoria; Ch Santlin Sowin Wild Oats; Ch Santlin Shotgun Wedding; Ch Santlin Singin Thblues; NZ Ch Santlin Star Tremember; Ch Santlin Stand 'N' Deliva (Ch Santlin The Shoplifta ex Ch Santlin Smarty Pants); Ch Santlin the Streaker and Ch Santlin the Senterfold (Ch Santlin Sugar Daddy ex Gardony Lady Angela); Ch Santlin Speako the Devil; Ch Santlin Sign of the Times; Ch Santlin Spunky Trunks; and the drop ear Ch Santlin Spit N' Polish.

Mrs Jackie MacKay emigrated to Australia from Scotland in 1985 and when they decided to have a dog they remembered an aunt's Skye and decided to purchase one. Ch Gardony Reb was their choice and, although he was initially bought as a pet, they took him to a show, where he went Best Puppy in Group. From that day in October 1987 Jackie was hooked, and Bobby now has amassed many awards. The Silver bitch, Santlin Starsesn Whispers, born in 1990, joined the MacKays's home and amassed an impressive number of Puppy Group wins on her way to her title.

SOUTH AUSTRALIA

The Asyut kennel belonging to Mrs Maureen Fox and Mrs Diana Lose are best known for their Schnauzers and Chihuahuas, though Mrs Lose had long expressed an interest in Skyes, purchasing her first, Gardony Tiger Lily, in 1981. She was soon followed by Gardony Little Warrior, whose show career had an untimely end when a fight left him minus an ear before he had completed his title. The first Skye litter born in the Asyut kennel produced two champions, Ch Asyut Streak O' Lightening, a cream, and Ch Asyut Moon Shadow, a silver.

Mrs Pat Girdler had been involved with German Shepherds and Pembroke Welsh Corgis for ten years before adding Skyes most successfully to her Gildarre kennel. In 1980 she bought Gardony Silver Lady who went Best Puppy in Group at her very first show, and later went on to become the first Skye in South Australia to win Best in Show all breeds, gaining her title easily. Silver Lady produced three litters for the Gildarre kennel, Ch Gildarre Mylady Jane and drop ear Ch Gildarre Mr Wonderful from the first litter gaining their titles. The second litter produced Ch Gildarre Belladonna, and the third produced Gildarre Lady Be Good, who was sired by Eramosa Hairy Bear. Mrs Girdler also bred Ch Gildarre My Lady O' Skye and Ch Gildarre Lady Primrose among other winners.

The Skyepara kennel owned by Kim and Helen Flaherty imported Mallysmar Stargazer from England. They also own the well known Ch Gildarre Belladonna and the black drop ear Ch Gildarre Mr Wonderful, who sired two champions for the kennel, Ch Skyepara Cool Edition and Ch Skyepara Sheer Lace. Belladonna is the dam of Skyepara Bonnie Bell.

Lyndon and Teresa Smith bought their first Skye, Gardony Blue Bryony, after Lyndon fell for Gardony Tiger Lily, who belonged to Mrs Lose, Teresa's mother. Gardony Bolt O' Lightening joined the family, gaining his title in 1984.

The first litter for the Wuruf kennel, by Ch Santlin the Sandman out of Blue Bryony, produced the extrovert Ch Wuruf Wolf Man Jack, their first home bred title holder. A second litter, born on Christmas Eve 1985, produced Wuruf Stormy Weather, who was sold to Lorraine Golding to start the Woodrush kennel. When Stormy Weather was bred to Wolf Man Jack one of the litter, Woodrush Jack Daniels, was bought by the Smiths, who campaigned him to his title in 1990.

Ch Wuruf Wolf Man Jack, owned by Asyut Kennels.

In 1989 the Smiths imported two bitches from America, Gates Impetuous Lady O' Wuruf and Gates Southern Lady of Wuruf. Southern Lady gained her title within a year and Impetuous Lady produced an interesting litter to Ch Asyut Streak O' Lightening in December 1989. From this litter Wuruf King Creole was retained and has been shown sparingly.

Skymanor Benson owned by Woodrush Kennel

The Woodrush kennel is owned by Lorraine Goulding, who became interested in the breed through seeing Mrs Smith's Skyes at shows and subsequently acquired Wuruf Stormy Weather (mentioned above) and Asyut Moon Shadow. A visit to the Gardony kennels in 1989 resulted in the purchase of Gardony Silver Melody, a silver drop ear who gained her title in 1991 after a battle to have her ear type recognised. She is the first drop ear champion in the State.

Wuruf Las Vegas joined the kennel in 1990 making a successful start in the show ring until struck by an illness which caused coat loss and kept him out of the ring until it grew again. In 1991 he was bred to Wuruf Stormy Weather, producing a fine litter from which three offspring are currently being shown in South Australia, while Woodrush Hit the Jackpot is attracting a lot of attention in Victoria and Woodrush Casino Capers has been exported to New Zealand where she has already started on a successful show career. The most recent addition to the kennel is the beautiful two year old cream drop ear, Skymanor Benson.

WESTERN AUSTRALIA

Skyes were introduced to Western Australia in 1971 by Sine Threlfall from the Isle of Skye who spent two years in the state and bought the silver prick ear Ch Daneshill Silver Sail and the cream drop Ch Danehill Gay Princess. During her stay the dogs won several Group awards, Gay Princess going Best in Show at a Parade.

Eight years later Mrs Boekelman bought Gardony MacGregor, followed by Gardony Skye Lab, who both gained their titles. Some time later Ch Acheo Robbie's Pride and Ch Benhough Faberge, a cream drop ear, were bought after the Benhough kennel was disbanded. Unfortunately Mrs Boekelman's marriage broke up, which resulted in another move for the dogs, Skye Lab, Robbie's Pride and Macgregor going to Gina Moller. MacGregor was subsequently stolen from the Moller's home leaving her without a stud, so Eljepa Skyewayman was purchased from the Baldwins in Victoria, quickly gaining his title.

Wuruf Edge O' Reality.

Mrs Boekelman's daughter, Louise, campaigned Llanyddy Lucky Lady, a birthday gift from her mother in 1987, to her title. In 1989 Gina Moller offered Louise all seven of her Skyes, including old favourites Skye Lab and Robbie's Pride. Louise was happy to accept this offer.

A litter of six pups born in 1991 from a cream dog, Jentol Skye Illusion, was retained. Having eight dogs, all closely related, Louise went to the Smiths in South Australia for Wuruf Edge O' Reality, who is out of imported bloodlines. Both Illusion and Edge O' Reality are well on their way to their championships.

Other Skyes currently being shown in Western Australia are Eljepa Skye In The West and Santlin Slightly Sozzled. Kate Bronomyer's Skye is currently doing her CD title.

Aust/NZ Ch Skyeclan Shake Dis City, Aust/NZ Ch Santlin Stand N Deliva and Ch Skyeclan Blu Suede Shus.

QUEENSLAND

Apart from a brief spell in the late 1960s when Mrs Cassidy imported two Merrymounts from England, Merrymount Sky Rocket gaining his title, little was heard of the breed gaining headway in

Queensland until Mrs Helen MacGregor and her Skyeclan kennel took up the call. Ch Santlin the Senterfold (Ch Santlin Sugar Daddy ex Gardony Lady Angela) produced some outstanding offspring, including three drop ears, one of which, NZ/Aus Ch Skyeclan Shake Dis City by Ch Santlin Stand 'N' Deliva, won Best in Show awards in both countries.

NZ/Aus Ch Santlin Stand 'N' Deliva (Ch Santlin the Shoplifta ex Ch Santlin Smarty Pants), their first big winner, took twenty-four Best in Shows,

Aust/NZ Ch Skyeclan
Lapo The Gods.

nineteen Reserve Best in Shows and one-hundred-and-five Best in Group awards in an outstanding career. His tally of Best in Show awards is yet to be equalled in Australia. He also won his New Zealand title and rounded off his career with the top award at the Sporting Terrier Club of Queensland, his last show.

The Skyeclan Kennel have bred twenty-six Champions to date, including Ch Skyeclan Nite Raider (Ch Benhough Benjamin ex Ch Santlin the Senterfold) from their first litter; Ch Santlin Stand 'N' Over (NZ/Aus Ch Santlin Stand 'N' Deliva ex Ch Santlin Solo 'N' So Fair), Ch Santlin Blu Suede Shus (Vanghapara Scot of Raldoris ex Ch Santlin the Senterfold), NZ/Aus Ch Skyeclan Lapo The Gods (NZ/Aus Ch Skyeclan Great Pretender ex Skyepara Seventh Heaven) and in New Zealand several have gained their titles including Ch Skyeclan Bold Baron (Ch Skyeclan Reo Speedwagon ex Ch Santlin the Senterfold), Ch Skyeclan

Thunda Down Unda (Ch Skyeclan Blu Suede Shus ex Skyeclan Night Moves) and Ch Skyeclan Toucho Paradise (Ch Skyeclan Blu Suede Shus ex Ch Skyeclan Standn Proud). Of the twenty litters the MacGregors have produced, seventeen Skyes have gained their Australian titles with twelve taking their titles in New Zealand and three having dual titles.

Skyeclan Dragon Slaya.

The Skyeclan kennel have produced a number of drop ears who have gone on to win their championships, among them NZ Ch Skyeclan Bohemian Rhapsody (NZ/Aus Ch Skyeclan Great Pretender ex Skyepara Seventh Heaven) and the trio NZ Ch Skyeclan Fantasia, Ch Skyeclan Neva Endn Story and Ch Skyeclan Racing Snail by Skyeclan Nite Stalker ex Skyepara Seventh Heaven, both drop ears.

Salli MacGregor is just as enthusiastic as her parents as far as dogs are concerned. At Crufts dog show in 1993 she competed in the Junior Handling finals, representing Australia. Salli recently obtained the Bel-Ria affix after the death in New Zealand of Lyn Staig, who established her kennel with Skyeclan stock and on whose death the Skyes returned to the MacGregors. Bel-Ria Freddie Mercury and Bel-Ria Isle-O-Mist, bred by Lyn Staig, will be campaigned by Salli.

TASMANIA

Mrs Bev Houghton's first Skye, Danehill Blond Bit, was bought in the mid-1970s. Her first litter to Ch Danehill Jock produced Ch Benhough Benjamin. In 1977 Acheo MacPhail's Lament was imported and gained his title; he was followed by Acheo Robbie's Pride in 1979 who also went on to gain her crown. Mrs Houghton had to give up her Skyes in the early 1980s after the sudden death of her husband in an accident at work.

AUSTRIA

Archduchess Maria Terezia of Austria, Queen of Hungary and Bohemia (1717-80), mother of the ill fated Marie Antoinette of France, is reputed to have owned the first Skye Terrier in Austria. Just before the first World War the first registered imports came from Germany, and were of Swedish and British bloodlines. Frau Kraus was the first acknowledged Austrian breeder with her Schluesselburg kennel, and Count Colloredo was known to have kept a kennel of drop ears.

Frau Janisch with Ch Crown Prince Charles of Meerand, Jacob of Meerend, Moritz of Apenborg, Little Peter of Apenborg and Lucy of Meerend with judge Miss Rosabel Watson at the World Show in Frankfurt 1935.

Roddie of Meerend and Queenie of Meerend were imported during the 1930s. Frau Janisch was a great supporter of the breed, housing many good Skyes, including the English import, Crown Prince Charles of Meerend, who was the winner of the World Champion title at the World Show in Frankfurt 1935, under Miss Rosabel Watson of the Luckie affix. Frau Janisch's affix, v d Hagenau Lainz, graced many winners. Also in 1935 Fraulein Passeger, who enjoyed considerable success with her Skyes in Austria, sold some of her v d Schrottenburg puppies to buyers in America.

Frau Tschebul's famous v Schlaraffenland kennel was established in 1933 with the English import, Peacehaven Jorrocks, and the German import, Pracha v Sonnwendhofe. Pracha was bred with Crown Prince Charles of Meerend, producing the well known winner, Int Ch Amor v Schlaraffenland. The v Schlaraffenland Skyes were considered to be of high quality and were well respected throughout Europe.

Herr Steinbacher's affix, Austria, dates from 1947 with the Canadian import Talisker's Wee Ambassador, a big winner in his day and World Champion at the Dortmund World Show of 1956. Another import from the Canadian kennel was Chummie's Sunlight of Talisker. Other famous names from this kennel are Ch Austria's Claudia, Ch Austria's Fairy Queen, who was exported to Mrs Adams' Talisker kennel and was a particular favourite of Mrs Adams, and Austria's Hokus Pokus who was a well known winner.

Another established name in Austria was the St Barbara kennel belonging to Frau Uibeleisen, who bred Ch St Barbara Noblesse, St Barbara Alligin and St Barbara Wirbelwind in the late 1940s and early 1950s. Baronin v Gagern produced the noted Ch Gin v Gross Poellach in his kennels, also during the 1950s.

Dr Gogi, of the v Muspelheim affix, bred some litters in the 1970s, among them litter mates Birrius v Muspelheim and Bumblebee v Muspelheim who won the Junior World Dog and Bitch titles at the World show held in Innsbruck in 1976. The latest enthusiast in the breed is Otto Krcal of Vienna who owns Rannoch Skye Gwyneth, already the winner of Junior CCs at fifteen months of age.

Belgium

The first Skye registered in Belgium was named Samy, bred by Mark Gretton of Hull, England. Born in 1878, Samy was owned by M Art Gantois of Brussels, and won a second prize at a show in Ostende in 1883. Little other early information on the breed in Belgium is available but it is recorded that Baronin Wykerlooth's Bauet kennel imported Skyes from the Sunny Sky kennel in Luxembourg, and the O' Craighmor kennel in Scotland, before the second World War.

International Ch Arline owned by Mr and Mrs Van de Roer.

In the 1960s the famous Shaggy Wonder Skyes belonging to Mrs Mewis de Ryck became known, Ch Shaggy Wonder Off You Go becoming a big winner for Mrs Dereymaeker who founded her Glenlivet kennel with this bitch. One of the best known Skyes bred by Mrs Dereymaeker is Ch Glenlivet Quarry who, along with Ch Glenlivet Tempest and Ch Glelivet Tartan, did much winning.

Ch Arline's Magic Mr Muzzle.

Baronne M M de la Fosse et L'Espierres bred Skyes under the de Mansart affix in the 1970s, with Valerie de Mansart coming to Britain with her owners. Jean Luc Bour built up a very successful kennel known as the de Grimsby Skyes. His import from England, Ch Littlecreek Reay, had a very successful show career before joining the Isle of Skye kennel in the Netherlands where she took up maternal duties. Ch Reggae of Foggy Plain was also a big winner for her owner and went on to produce Ch Jocrates and Ch J'Anais de Grimsby.

Resident in Belgium is Herma Van de Roer with her Arline Skyes; they are also registered in the Netherlands, and are covered in the chapter on Skyes in that country. This energetic lady is responsible for the huge entries at the Belgian Terrier Show due to her unstinting efforts to attract exhibitors from all over Europe to this event.

Ch Arline's Fizgig Flash.

Pyon Floating High was imported from England by Hilde Taeymans, and has been shown with some success. In 1990 she produced her first litter to Ch Arline's Goliath The Giant, and several of the litter are currently being shown.

Int Ch Arline's Fizgig Flash with Int Ch Arline's Goliath the Giant bred by Herma Van de Roer.

CANADA

Skye Terriers have been recorded in the Canadian provinces of Ontario and Nova Scotia (where some of the earliest Scots settlers landed) since the latter half of the 1800s, but the name which is always associated with Canada is that of Mrs Marjorie Adams and her Talisker kennel, although she died more than twenty years ago.

As a young lady in 1904 Marjorie Townsend imported Oban Jock from Scotland, followed by Talisker Belle and Talisker Prince, exported by James Monroe of Glasgow. These three were the foundation stock of the famous Talisker kennel, and in 1909 Talisker Belle won a Blue Ribbon at the Westminster Show.

Talisker's Dark Prince and Talisker's Charming Heiress with Mrs Adams 1965.

After a break of several years from breeding and showing, during which time she married and raised a family, Mrs Adams, as she now was, took up the breed again in the 1930s, importing Ch George of Merrymount, Ch Marielou of Merrymount and Ch Skyhigh Lady Fay of Talisker (Ch Togo of Merrymount ex the Merrymount Ghost), the latter proving to be a great brood bitch for the Talisker kennel.

During the 1950s Mrs Adams imported British Ch Alison of the Mynd, who quickly gained her Canadian title. "Sonny" was later joined by another cream from Austria, Austria's Fairy Queen, who also gained her title and was a particular favourite of Mrs Adams. These two creams produced some outstanding Skyes, including Ch Talisker's Black Prince (Talisker's Dream Baby ex Ch Alison of the Mynd), the winner of seven Terrier Groups, and Ch Talisker's Fairy Wonder (Ch Talisker's Black Prince ex Ch Austria's Fairy Queen). This combination also produced Ch Talisker's Fairy Heir, Ch Talisker's Fairy Tale, Ch Talisker's Lovely Fairy, Ch Talisker's Fairy Dream and Ch Talisker's Adorable Fairy.

Situated in beautiful surroundings, the Talisker kennel was home to over seventy Skyes, several of them imports from around the world. Among them were Faygate Guy Fawkes and Faygate Beetle from Miss Alexander in England, Adelia Sweetheart from Adela Straubert in Yugoslavia, Ch Rhosneigr Redoubtable from Mrs Crook in England, Kirkby Hailstorm of Talisker from Mrs Kirkby Peace in England and Ch Olivia Hyperion from Olga Smidova's kennel in Czechoslovakia.

The Talisker kennel bred many outstanding champions including Ch Talisker's Mr Wonderful, Ch Talisker's Mr Wonder, the two sisters Ch Talisker's Fanfralouche and British Ch Talisker's Ciboulette, the latter and Ch Talisker's Peter Piper accompanying kennel manager Megan Rees on her return to Wales after the death of Mrs Adams in 1972.

Dr Meen's Kishniga kennel has enjoyed great success with his line having been established on Gleanntan stock. Home bred champions include Ch Kishniga's Going Strong, Ch Kishniga's KKKatie, Ch Kishniga's Shortbread and Ch Kishniga's Skywalker from the excellent brood Ch Gleanntan Glory Be (Ch Gleanntan Monkey Business ex Ch Jo Jacs Rise 'N' Shine). In 1992 Dr Meen imported Brilliant Whispers Gentle Gesture from the Netherlands and Finnsky Ringleader from Finland.

During the 1970s Donald Drury enjoyed much success with Ch Valhalla Keltic Robbie, a Best in Show winner and winner of four Groups. Talisker's Hermia, bought by the Drurys in 1972, later produced Ch Ceilidh's Ceol Na Mara.

Carol Prokopowich of Ontario is the owner of the Kakumee affix which has bred some big winners. Carol owns Ch Myosho Peanut Butter (GB/Can Ch Kirkleyditch King of the Road ex Kirkleyditch Myosho Tina) and bred Ch Kakumee Rhinestone Cowboy. The beautiful drop ear, Ch Kakumee Nonchalant, by Ch Olivia Vino Veritas was the result of Peanut's first mating.

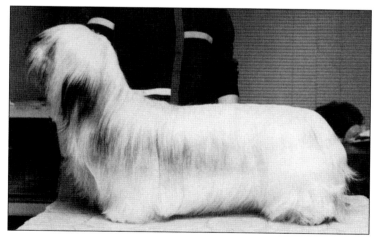

Ch Kakumee Nonchalant.

Her second, to Ch Olivia American Dream, produced Ch Kakumee Misleading Lady and Ch Kakumee Pineapple Pete. The bitch Olivia Heart to Heart (Ch Olivia Dukat ex Ch Chiquita of Morningsky) joined the kennel in the late 1980s.

Don and Sandra Smiley's Rusalka kennel is situated in British Columbia and was started with Amity Bonanza (Ch Skye Ark Fearless ex Olivia Noblesse of Dunleigh) and Olivia Radost (Ch Talisker's Fearless ex Olivia Novela) in 1977 who both gained their Canadian and American championships. Rusalka's Berneray, from this pair's first litter, was exported to Switzerland.

The Smiley's next Skye, Ch Olivia U'Neke from Rusalka, easily gained her title and was then bred to Ch Feather Duster of Morningsky, producing for them their first home bred champions, Rusalka's Extra Terrific, Rusalka's Sir Echo and Rusalka's Ebony. Ch Skyecrest Onyx of Rusalka (Ch Eagle Black of Morningsky ex Ch Olivia Zuleika) joined the kennel, and went on to win her crown before

Ch Rikaabah's Annie Laurie, bred by Jack and Elaine White.

being bred to Extra Terrific to produce Am Ch Rusalka's Glorious Gizelle, Ch Rusalka's Great Expectation, Ch Rusalka's Gaylord Ravenal and Chs Rusalka's Gigolo and Gladiator, both drop ears.

Karen Mathieson of Delaware enjoyed much success with the glamorous silver, Ch Olivia Primaballerina (Ch Talisker's Fearless ex Olivia Novela), who was Number One Skye bitch in Canada in 1977. In 1979 she was bred to Ch Olivia Nimrod producing the silver drop ear, Ch Rikaabah's Annie Laurie.

The Goldenwire kennel owned by the Geisenhafers of Michigan has been one of the most successful in recent times with the English import, Ch Littlecreek's Lisa, who went on to win eight titles in all: USA, Canadian, Bermudan, Champion of the Americas, Puerto Rico, Dominican Republic, Bahamas and International Champion. On top of all these titles she won the Terrier Group in each country in which she competed: a remarkable record! Lisa in not the only star in this kennel. Fellow title holders are Am/Can Ch Rob Roy of Cherry Lane (drop ear), Am/Can/Bermuda Ch Littlecreek's Maree, Int Ch Maclean Going My Way, Am Ch Myosho Milli the Mouse, Am/Can Ch Goldenwire's Buddy and Am/Can Ch Goldenwire's Babe.

Carol Gregoire is a newcomer to the breed with the highly successful Ch Silverspun Northern Star (Ch Gleanntan Globetroter ex Ch Olivia American Beauty Rose) who is a Best in Show winner. Carol is also the owner of Northern Star's litter sister who is a drop ear.

Mary Secord, owner of the Marelsa kennels, has bred some very good dogs including Ch Marelsa Fergus (Ch Kirkleyditch King of the Road ex Kishniga Marelsa Tisket), Ch Marelsa's Polly Moppet (Ch Myosho My Marelsa Bruce ex Kishniga Marelsa Tisket) and Ch Marelsa's Antiqued Silver (Ch Marelsa'a Rudyard Kipling ex Ch Marelsa's Polly Moppet).

CZECHOSLOVAKIA

During the 1960s the name of Olga Olivova Smidova and her Olivia Skyes began to filter through to the British dog scene from the unlikely setting of what was then Czechoslovakia. Madame Smidova had become involved with the breed in the 1940s when her husband, Joe, had acquired for her the dog Tell Splendid (Bill z Hebrid ex Thekla v Schwarzenbach). In a short time his new owners were completely hooked with his character which led to Olga making up her mind to introduce the breed to Czechoslovakia.

Her second Skye, Iduna v Schlaraffenland (Int Ch Amor v Schlaraffenland ex Ch Silver Maid of Merrymount) was imported from Austria, with Netti Dimgod (Uli v Schloss ex Cilla Dimgod) coming from Switzerland. These three formed the foundation on which the world famous Olivia kennel was built.

One of Olga's first big winners, Ch Beauty of Scalpay (Tell Splendid ex Cilla Dimgod), was a great stud dog, siring the famous Ch Olivia Blues (ex Iduna v Schlaraffenland) who won top honours in her country from 1949 to 1955. This lovely bitch, a grandaughter of Ch Silver Maid of Merrymount, is behind all the great winners from the Olivia kennel.

During the 1950s Madame Smidova imported Vivat v Schlaraffenland from Austria (Austria's Correct ex Koenigskind v Schlaraffenland). He and Ch Olivia Blues produced a litter from which the bitch, Olivia Harmonie, became the first Skye to be exported from Czechoslovakia. Harmonie went to Madame Allard's kennel in France and won her French championship.

Because of the political situation in her country Mme Smidova could not sell directly to France, so exchanges were made, Chin Up de Luchar and Elfe de Mandane coming from France and the English dog, Merrymount Gold Digger, coming from Holland in 1956. Later in 1957 Gaiety Girl de Luchar joined the now flourishing Olivia kennel, all four helping to establish some outstanding Skyes.

Int Ch Olivia Jatagan (Olivia E-Moll ex Chin Up de Luchar) was undoubtedly the outstanding star of the kennels in the late 1950s. A dog of great substance and looks, he won just about every award on offer. He sired twelve litters in all, with fifty-five champion offspring, twenty-one of which were exported, including one to the Isle of Skye who later became a British champion. Jatagan sired thirteen champions in Czechoslovakia, Poland, East and West Germany, Luxembourg and Britain, and is therefore behind many of the European winners of today.

Olivia's next big winner, Int and World Ch Olivia Night Star (Elfe de Mandane ex Olivia Intermezzo), gained titles in many countries and caught the eye of well known British judge, Stanley Dangerfield, who wrote in 1965, "....here was a Skye who could compete with the best in Britain".

The beautiful Champion Olivia Benfica (Ch Acheo Olivia Whist ex Int Ch Olivia Night Star) was a big winner in 1965/66. Ch Olivia Hyperion, a younger brother to Benfica, was exported to the Talisker kennels in Canada, to join Olivia Desdemona and Olivia Eroica who were already there. Had it not been for Mrs Adams the Olivia kennel may not so easily have become established in America.

In 1966 recognition of Mme Smidova's judging talents was rewarded by an invitation to judge at the National Terrier Show in England, followed two years later by an invitation to judge Skyes at the City of Birmingham Championship show. One month before she was due to arrive in England the invasion of Czechoslovakia took place, and with communications cut no-one knew whether the appointment would be fulfilled. However, those who knew Olga know that nothing stands in the way of dogs; she arrived in England with two pups, Olivia Laska and Olivia Lyric, who were both placed in quarantine until arrangements could be made to forward Lyric to her new owner in Switzerland, with Laska going to the Acheo kennels on the Isle of Skye.

Olga Smid judging at the World Show at Brno, with World Chs Rannoch Skye Superstar and Proud Black Rose of Morninsky.

Shortly after returning home from Olga's judging engagement in England the Smids made the big decision to leave Czechoslovakia and move to America. With them they took four Skyes, leaving the rest with their family, and, each taking only the basic necessities so that they would not alert the authorities, they made their escape separately and successfully. Many beautiful trophies and personal belongings had to be left behind, but they considered their freedom to be of greater value.

For twenty-one years the Olivia Skyes had dominated the terrier scene in Czechoslovakia, producing many champions at home and in other countries. The Olivia stock is behind many kennels in the area that was Czechoslovakia, including Silesian Castle, Gladiator, Silver, Reimer, Marimen and Garuda, but could the Olivia kennel be as successful in America? For the answer refer back to the chapter on Skyes in the USA.

Marie Mencakova bought Olivia Avanti in 1963, showing her in her home country and in East Germany, where she became a champion. After Avanti's death in 1975 Madame Mencakova bought Korosparti Very Nice from Dr Répássy in Hungary. Very Nice was mated to Dr Répássy's American import, Int Ch Olivia Red River (Ch Talisker's Fearless ex Olivia Novela), to start up the Marimen kennel. From her first litter in 1980 came Ch Areta Marimen and Ch Ariel Marimen.

The Tamesis kennel belongs to Dr Pavcik who guided Ch Areta Marimen to her title and who is the foundation bitch of his kennel. Areta was bred to the German import Ch Farid of Morningsky (Int Ch Olivia Silver Solo ex Int Ch Alpha of Morningsky), producing a litter containing five champions: Ch Adonis Tamesis, Ch Arete Tamesis, Ch Apolena Tamesis, Ch Ambra Tamesis and Ch Axamit Tamesis.

Ch Apolena Tamesis was bred in Germany to Fetish v Silberblauen See in 1968. Tamesis Boston from that litter went to Russia where he is one of the top winning Skyes. Tamesis Britania was exported to Hungary. In 1991 Dr Pavcik imported the American Skye Olivia Independent Spirit (Ch Silverspun Sundancer ex Ch Rannoch Skye Olivia).

The most recently established kennel in Czechoslovakia is that of Josef Korber who owns the Armadale affix. His Ch Ambra Tamesis gained her title and is the foundation bitch for the kennel. Her daughter, Armadale Bianca, had a litter of four pups by Ch Tamesis Axamit in 1992.

Argus Armadale, bred by Josef Korber.

Denmark

The earliest imports in Denmark came from Scotland and were owned by Harald Christensen of Fredrickshavn. Tibbie, born in 1883, was bred by Mr Miller of Edinburgh and was the earliest recorded prize winner of the Silver Medal at the Copenhagen Show of 1886, along with her son Lion.

Towards the end of the nineteenth century, Skye, bred by Mr Murray, Tibbie II bred by Mr Sanderson, and Lady Flora bred by Mr Smail, all from Edinburgh, were registered by Johan Knudsen and Mr Christensen. The next recorded registration was that of Freddy vom Hardtwald who was imported from Germany.

During the 1920s a number of Swedish Skyes were imported and were shown in Denmark. The Swedish breeder, Dagmar Lagerroth, exhibited many of her Skyes at Danish shows, including her Scottish import, Ch The Cuttie. Directør Hedi Dam, owner of Isabella Lambda and Mimi Lambda, exhibited in her native Denmark in the late 1920s.

Paul Andersen established his Darwins kennel in the early 1930s with Swedish imports Arabella av Tornø (Ch Mac of Merrymount ex Silver Jill av Tornø) and Iron Tassie av Tornø (Ch Bob of Peacehaven ex Brenda av Tornø). Some of the noteworthy dogs which came from his Darwins kennel include Darwins Iron Queen (Ch Mac of Merrymount ex Iron Tassie av Tornø), Darwins Adonis (Henry of Peacehaven ex Iron Tassie of Tornø) and, from a later litter to Adonis, Darwins Luckie Henry.

Nanny Dønvig's Skylarking kennel was founded with the bitch Lola av Barva (Ch Bob of Peacehaven ex Lady Nathalia av Tornø) bred by Commander Gustav Celcing of Barva. This kennel produced many good Skyes including Skylarking Reif, Sylarking's Sardy, Sylarking Billy and Skylarking Mug.

Schmidt and Stallknecht owned the successful Rookes kennel whose import from Sweden, Mascot av Tornø, and the home bred pair, Rookes Smut and Rookes Toddy, were noted prize-winners in the 1930s.

Arthur Eriksen's Belles affix registered just one litter in 1936 by Lilbjergs Mucki ex Rookes Stormy Weather. Preben Engberg bred several Skyes including Engbergs Pero and Engbergs Pjusker, two excellent dogs.

Eric Werner imported Boss of Merrymount (Ch Chummie of Merrymount ex Flora of Quarrydale) in 1936 from Lady Marcia Miles in England. Mr Werner's kennel bred some fine dogs including Skarabergs Chummie (Boss of Merrymount ex Daisy av Tornø) and Skarabergs Theodora (Ch Bob of Peacehaven ex Miramar Isadora). Alfred Brunso's Helmarhjos affix, Leif Jorgensen's Asta affix and Fru Jensen's Bisgaards kennel all produced excellent types of Skye.

Between 1940 and 1945 Ingeborg Kjær Nielsen bred several litters with her Jyllingehøjs affix, including the winners Jyllingehøjs Hanne and Hera, (Skyarking Mug ex Skylarking Lena) as did Fru Ego Koefoed's Ego kennel. Ch Ego's Queen Bess was exported to Norway, and won her champions' title. Other prize-winners included Ego's Sweet Sussi and littermate Ego's Golden Darling.

Gunnar Neilsen got his first Skye, Bisgaaed's Molly, from the Bisgaaed's kennel in 1939. Molly was by Helmarhojs Bamse out of Helmarhojs Mille. His next Skye, imported in 1966, was the English import, Rhosneigr Blond Cloud (Ch Rhosneigr Rise Again ex Seamab Petrol). In 1989 Mr Neilsen became the owner of Ch Acheo Alice Springs (Acheo Bla Bheinn ex Acheo Inverie) and in 1991 Int Ch Florian of Morningsky (Int Ch Olivia Silver Solo ex Int Ch Alpha of Morningsky) joined his kennel.

Søren Neilsen imported several Rhosneigr Skyes from England in the early 1960s, including Rhosneigr Pjevs (Ch Rhosneigr Rise Again ex Rhosneir Rollright) and Rhosneigr Brormand (Merrymount Wot No Cream ex Rhosneigr Rare Poppy), to establish her Thorsvang kennel. Notable Skyes from this kennel are Thorsvang's Bimse and Thorsvang's Sweet.

Lars Staunskjaer imported Ch Olivia Intrika (Ch Olivia Belcanto ex Ch Olivia Zinien) from Olga Olivova Smid of Czechoslovakia in 1966. In 1970, having gained her title, she was bred to the Swedish dog, Heater av Tornø, producing Kattegat's Gaston, a well known winner.

Rhosneigr Pjevs and Torsvang's Bimse.

The Jyllingehøjs Skyes belonging to Mrs Greta Sørensen's aunt, Inger Kjær Neilsen, made such an impression on her young niece that she vowed that she, too, would have Skyes of her own one day. Today Mrs Sørensen has the biggest kennel of Skyes in Denmark.

In 1976 Mrs Sørensen imported the sweet grey dog, Skyelab Gillmore (Int Ch Silhill Sea Breeze ex White Rose of Skyeline) from Sweden, and he went on to gain his title. From Finland came Jacaranda of Skyeline (Int Ch Silhill Sea Breeze ex Int Ch Katinkullan Any) in whelp to Int Ch Rhosneigr Silver Flash, and in 1976 she produced the first of many successful litters for the Augustea kennel. Of the seven pups born five went on to gain their titles, including Ch Augustea's Alexia. Jacaranda was campaigned to her Danish title after this litter. Her second litter, to Ch Skyelab's Gillmore in 1977, produced Ch Augustea's Aymus.

Jacaranda was accompanied to Denmark by Tulipa of Skyeline (Int Ch Xeres of Skyeline ex White Lady of Skyeline), a lovely cream who went on to become an International Champion and was placed in many Groups.

In 1983 Mrs Sørensen imported Int and Nord Ch Wallflower of Skyeline (Int Ch Rhosneigr Silver Flash ex In Ch Tarskavaig Mary Morrison) in whelp to Gallion Shadow of Skyeline, and she subsequently produced a litter of five puppies from which Mrs Sørensen kept the lovely cream dog Ch Augustea's Adonis. Happening of Skyeline (Int Ch Drewsteignton Arlanda ex Int Ch Wallflower of Skyeline), who also gained his Danish Title, completed the imports from Finland in 1983. Ch Augustea's Anais (Ch Happening of Skyeline ex Ch Augustea's Aymis) was the next to win top honours for the kennel.

The German import, Ch Flirtation of Morningsky, a beautiful black bitch by Ch Easy Rider of Morningsky ex Ch Umbrella du Petit Tanagra, joined the kennel in 1986, followed by the Dutch import Ch Zenith Zed of the Isle of Skye (Int Ch Olivia Wild West ex Int Ch Cimmaron Czigana v d Litsberg). These two quickly gained their championships. Other title holders at present in Mrs Sørensen's very successful kennel include Ch Augustea's Amazing Amanda, Ch Augustea's Amity, Ch Augustea's Aniara and Ch Augustea's Antoinette.

In 1973 Lis Møller imported a dog and a bitch from the Isle of Skye, Acheo Donald Angus (NZ Ch Acheo Scottish Nationalist ex Tarskavaig Jeannie McColl) and Acheo Flower of Scotland (Ch Vanghapara Wild Highlander ex Coruisk Kilmandy). Both won certificates, and the bitch produced a litter in 1975, from which one pup, Muggi, was shown. Sadly Flower of Scotland died young, and Donald Angus was sold to Grethe Hojsgard and Lille Skensved, who also imported Silhill Satara from England. The pair produced a litter in 1976 and Acheo Donald Angus was later campaigned to his title.

Ch Flirtation of Morningsky.

Jytte Bjorn imported Fantomen (Int Ch Florian of Morningsky ex Int Ch Acheo Alice Springs), a drop ear, from Sweden in 1986. Fantomen went on to win his title.

Connie Damm and Steen Laursen Godstrup of the Nicandra Cairn Terrier kennels also have an interest in Skyes, as they own Esmeralda (Ch Zenith Zed of the Isle of Skye ex Bornholm's Sidse Hajsky) and the English import, Ch Kirkleyditch Rebaldus (Kirkleyditch Randison ex Kirkleyditch Sunflower), who joined them in 1989. Their next imports came from America in 1990, the litter mates Kuhl Breeze's Keelar and Kuhl Breeze's Maggee (Ch Talakan British Sterling ex Ch Ryattis Really Me), and Corcaigh's Korielle (Corcaigh's Heart's Desire ex Nyteflyte Nirvana).

Two litters were born in 1991, Ch Kirkleyditch Rebaldus to Esmeralda, and Kuhl Breeze's Keelar to Corcaighs Korielle, with Nicandra's Big Boomer from the Keelar/Korielle litter winning Best Junior in Show at the Belgian Terrier Club Show in 1992.

The Bornholm kennel belonging to Bente Lehmann Nielsen imported the beautiful cream, Ch Tuukan Glamour Girl (Ch Kirkleyditch Border King ex Juuliska), from Finland in 1983. She did a great deal of winning before producing a litter to Ch Augustea's Adonis in 1985. From this came the winners, Bornholm Lucy in the Sky, Bornholm Happy New Year Whiskey and Bornholm Zia in the Starry Sky. Mr Erwin Gisselfeldt is the owner of Mariquita Noble Splash (Ch Mariquita Flashback ex Mariquita Divine Madness) the winner of two Challenge Certificates. A great supporter of the Skye, Mr Gisselfeldt is frequently seen at the Skye ring side at British shows.

Tina Toft Andersen, a new Skye enthusiast, has already tasted success with her two dogs. Ch Augustea's Anjoy (Ch Happening of Skyeline ex Ch Flirtatiom of Morningsky), a cream bitch, has won five Best of Breed awards, has twice been Best in Show at an event where no CCs were on offer, and has won Best in Show four times at a Danish Terrier Club Show. Ch Augustea's Amigo in Action (Ch Zenith Zed of the Isle of Skye ex Ch Augustea's Amazing Amanda), a lovely black dog, has already enjoyed a successful career, gaining his first certificate at nine months of age, and a further four before he moved into the Open class. He became a Danish champion at nineteen months, and has so far won two Best in Show awards in the brace class with his sister and two Best in Show awards in

Ch Augustea's Anjoy.

the junior class at a Danish Terrier Club show. Miss Andersen's first litter from the pair will be registered under her Skyewalker affix.

At the time of writing the most recently registered Danish affix is Bournanville, owned by Anita Lonskov Sørensen of Copenhagen. Her Finnish import, Finnsky Orchidee, (Int Ch Rannoch Skye Superstar ex Ch Finnsky Glacier), was bred back to her sire, Superstar, producing a litter in 1991.

E IRE

Skyes have been exhibited in Eire since the 1870s with British exhibitors crossing the Irish Sea to exhibit at the Dublin Show, and similarly Irish exhibitors regularly crossing to compete at British shows. Some of the first Irish exhibits included in the early Stud Books include Mr John Gealy's Wasp (Douglas ex Fan), Mr A Crowther's Badger (Reeky ex Ross), Mr R Dwyers's Lilly, Mr Whitestone's Prinny and Mr R Boyles's Skye and Smut bred by the Marquis of Breadalbane.

In the old days owners did not always accompany their dogs to shows but sent them by train and boat. On arrival at the show a handler would exhibit the dog and later send it back to its owner. Things did not always go smoothly, as can be seen by the case of Venus' trip to the Dublin Show. Venus was an outstanding young bitch who had won all her classes at her early outings. Her owner had entered her at Dublin so she was duly dispatched by rail, arriving safely, winning her classes and the cup. Expecting her home in four days, her owner met every train, only to be told, "No dog". A telegram was sent to the Show Secretary, who replied that he had taken her, with several other British exhibits, to the railway station several days previously. After two weeks of constant worry her owner sought legal advice and was told to claim compensation from the Railway Company. A writ for £50 was brought against the Company, who suddenly found the missing bitch, whereupon she was duly returned to her owner, none the worse for her experience. Under present regulations unaccompanied dogs are no longer accepted at shows.

Lochinvar the Laird.

In Eire one of the most successful kennels belonged to the Misses Briscoe, who travelled and competed against the best in Britain. Their drop ears, Ch Pied Piper of Valclusa and Ch Sweet Brenda (Ch Adel Monk ex Zentha), won Challenge Certificates in Britain, as did the prick ears Ch Neddie and Ch Miss Chummie in the early 1920s.

The Skye's popularity in Eire then fell for many years until a number were brought over from England in the 1970s. The first of note was Kirkleyditch Tiggy Winkle (Ch Tarskavaig Clansman ex Happyhill Jemma), Skye Terrier bitch of the year in 1970, a Challenge Certificate winner and one of the earliest to re-establish the breed in Eire.

Mrs Peggy Cronin, of the Chipper affix, was the earliest to breed Skye Terriers in any number again and Chipper Kirsty (Kirkleyditch Kings Ransome ex Chipper Niddrie) won well for her owner, Lesley Bullock. At about the same time Mrs Alison Stevens of County Wicklow was adopted by Dougal, a three year old Rhosneigr dog whose elderly owner was no longer able to keep him. In 1977 Skye Terrier puppies were advertised for sale in the Irish Times and Mrs Stevens was tempted into buying another. This time the Stevens chose a bitch, Brora Belle (Tarskavaig Gille Caluim ex Chipper Gille), who won nine Green Stars.

In 1980 Mrs Stevens bought Kirkleyditch Misty Moon (Dracula's Luxy of Kirkleyditch ex Rhosneigr Silver Ronde) from Jill Bower in England. Misty Moon sired seven litters in Eire, two of them to Brora Belle, and Mrs Stevens kept one dog, Dougal II.

In 1984 Tasha Tam O'Shanter (Littlecreek McIvor ex Krystal Arbroath Smokey) joined the Stevens' home, subsequently winning eight Green Stars. In 1987 Tasha was bred to Littlecreek Harris, and Lochinvar the Laird and Lassie of Lochinvar were retained in the home kennel. From a repeat mating in 1989 the Stevens kept two more Skyes, Wee MacGregor and Ishbel of Lochinvar. At the present time Mrs Stevens does very little exhibiting, preferring to let her dogs lead an active life chasing squirrels, rabbits, deer and pheasants.

Mr Dominic Harris bought Littlecreek's Cady (Ch Kirkleyditch Dalesman ex Silhill Golden Way of Littlecreek), and Littlecreek MacIvor (Littlecreek's Cady ex Littlecreek Thomasina) in the late 1970s from England. He later bred Krystal Arbroath Smokey with Littlecreek MacIvor, producing the green Star winner Tasha Tam O'Shanter mentioned above.

Alan and Ann Cowie of Dublin bred three litters from Chipper Gille. Her first, to Tarskavaig Gille Caluim produced Brora Belle; the progeny from her second, to Vanghapara Aristocrat, and her third, to a Vanghapara dog, were all sold as pets due to a disappointing lack of interest in the breed at that time.

During the 1970s, when quite a number of Skyes appeared on the Irish scene, the Skye Terrier Club of Ireland was formed. The club is still in existence, but at the time of writing is dormant. In the past the Irish club produced interesting newsletters containing articles written by well known breeders in England and Scotland, and hopefully the club will prosper once again and continue its good work.

The 1980s saw Littlecreek's Randy of Kirkleyditch (Ch Kirkleyditch Dalesman ex Silhill Golden Way of Littlecreek), owned by Jill Bower, at many of the Irish shows, where he quickly gained his Irish title. Among his awards were two Group wins and Reserve Best in Show at the St Patrick's Day Show in 1982.

With her Krystal kennel, Lesley Bullock has been one of the most successful breeder/exhibitors in Ireland. In 1980 she took Chipper Kirsty to be mated with Ch Kirkleyditch Dalesman, which resulted in Chs Krystal Ambrosia, Krystal Angus McTavish and Krystal Aphrodite, who all won their Irish titles. A second litter produced Krystal Black Velvet who won two Challenge Certificates for Jill Bower in England.

The most consistent Skye Terrier winner on the Irish show circuit in recent times came across the sea from Scotland. Mr Charlie McLean's Balquhatston Equaliser (Ch Balquhatston Skyjack ex Balquhatston Lianora) has won several Green Stars, including one at the Dublin 1992 show, and took the Terrier Group at the Clonmel Show during the summer of the same year.

FINLAND

According to the Stud Book the first Skyes reached Finland in the 1890s when two imports from Britain, Gyp and Vega, were bought by the Skye Terrier Company in Porvoo. Unfortunately no more information on this company is available and it does not appear that any breeding was undertaken as the only other dog mentioned at this time was Kingie, belonging to a Mr Fraser, also of Porvoo. The next mention of the breed was in 1922 when an import from Sweden was the sole Skye entry at a show.

In the mid-1930s Mrs Jeanne Oldenburg imported Bracadale Pompey (Highland Laddie ex Highland Lassie) and Bracadale Henrietta (Holmesdale Bonnie ex Bracadale Berenice) from England. She bred a litter from them in 1939 registering the puppies under the affix Of Olden. Although the breed aroused some interest at this time war prevented any hope of progress.

A Hungarian import named Buksi was next registered in 1946, followed by the Swedish imports Tsedy in 1947 and Rag av Tornö (Teddy Bear av Tornö ex Mimosa) in 1948. The German bred Assi vom Föhrenhang (Askan v Gerogirenof ex Betty v Mittelweg) arrived in 1954, and the English bred Merrymount Queen Anne (Ch Rhosneigr Redoubtable ex Merrymount Sunsets Ann) in 1958.

With these imports the Skye Terrier population slowly began to grow with the affixes of Lill-Knuts, Iivantiiran, of Pellonpää, Sirkankallion, Kotitalou, of Auanbajo and von Alahovi appearing on the scene.

OF SKYELINE

Photo: Henri Oksauen.

Photo: Harri Lehkonen.

Int Ch Kirkleyditch Border King, imported by the Skyeline Kennels.

Mrs Hjördis Westerholm with four of her lovely champions.

Mrs Hjördis Westerholm bought her first Skye, a bitch named Stella Jacqueline (Kil of Auanbajo ex Oona-Bettina-Soraya), in 1963, and with her Skyeline affix went on to build up the most successful kennel in Scandinavia in her day. Ch Kavillan Tytti (Ch King of Auanbajo ex Ch Villa of Pellonpää), her foundation bitch, produced five International Champions.

During the 1960s and 1970s Mrs Westerholm imported many Skyes from Britain, carefully choosing dogs who would blend with her already high quality

Skyes. The imports, Int Ch Tarskavaig Royal Scot, Int Ch Tarskavaig Mary Morrison, Ch Merrymount Sun Myth, Int Ch Rhosneigr Silver Flash, Int Ch Rhosneigr Recovery, Int Ch Silhill Sea Breeze (co-owned with M-L Varis), Ch Silhill Sparky of Zapangu (co-owned with Mrs Rose Envall of Sweden), Int Ch Silhill Silver Shadow, Int Ch Kirkleyditch Border King and Int Ch Drewsteignton Arlanda, all appear in the pedigrees of many of today's top winners in Finland.

Int Ch Captain Scot, Int Ch Heavenly of Skyeline and Carol of Skyeline.

Of the dozens of champions bred at the Skyeline kennel Int and Nordic Ch Rosa Gallica of Skyeline, Int Ch Opulus of Skyeline, Int and Nordic Ch Dancer of Skyeline, Int and Nordic Ch X-ett of Skyeline and Int Ch Wallflower of Skyeline are just a few examples of the quality which graced the show ring. Int Ch Rhosneigr Silver Flash, Int Ch Rosa Gallica of Skyeline and Int Ch Wallflower of Skyeline all went on to win Best in Show awards at All Breed Shows.

In the early 1980s the Westerholms retired to England, bringing with them Rosa Gallica, Arlanda, Gallion Shadow and his lovely sister, Glimmer in the Shadow who was handled to her British title by Dave McCann of the Whodeanie kennels, and included Best of Breed at Crufts in 1986 in her list of top honours. Though the Skyeline affix has been absent for the ring for some time it is possible that Kirsi Sainio, who is co-owner of the affix, will breed a litter in the future.

HALLEBERGETS

Int and Nordic Ch Hällebergets Hep-Othon.

The Hällebergets affix owned by Sven and Solveig Söderholm started with stock from the Skyeline kennel. Their Ch Baby of Skyeline (Ch Kil of Auanbajo ex Ch Kavillan Tytti) was bred with Ch Rhosneigr Silver Flash, producing Int and Nordic Ch Hällebergets Hep-Othon, Int and Nordic Ch Hällebergets Flipper-Japp, Int and Nordic Ch Hällebergets Glaciär-Lili, Ch Hällebergets Cliff, Ch Hällebergets Clair and Ch Hällebergets An-Emy. Other champions from this kennel include Int and Nordic Ch Hällebergets Dolly, Ch Hällebergets Fortuna and Ch Hällebergets Eddy. Although the Söderholms have not played an active part in the breeding of Skyes for some time they are co-owners of the recent Swiss imports Int and World Ch Rannoch Skye Superstar and his sister Ch Rannoch Skye Surprise (Ch Olivia American Dream ex Int Ch Olivia Vamp), both impressive winners in the ring.

FINNSKY

Keeping Skyes in the family are Mrs Söderholm's brother, Rolf Dahlbom, his wife Thea and their family of enthusiasts. Mr and Mrs Dahlbom's first show Skye, Hällebergets Hep-Othon, became an International and Nordic champion.

Int and Nordic Ch Finnsky Casanova.

Their next big winner, Int and Nordic Ch Hällebergets Dolly, enjoyed a great show career into her teens and produced some worthy offspring including Ch Finnsky Anaisa and Ch Finnsky Amorine (by Int Ch Hällebergets Hep-Othon) and from her second litter Int and Nordic Ch Finnsky Baccus and Ch Finnsky Barracuda (by Nordic Ch Hällebergets Eddy). The next litter for the Finnsky kennel, the "C" litter, produced Ch Finnsky Casanova, Ch Finnsky Conzales and Ch Finnsky Cleopatra.

Over the years the Finnsky kennel has built up a reputation for producing some outstanding champions. Among the most noteworthy are Int Ch Finnsky Fabian, Int Ch Finnsky Galaxy, Int Ch Finnsky Glacier, Ch Finnsky Heartlove, Int Ch Finnsky Madonna and Int Ch Finnsky Manfred Man. Chs Finnsky Oliver, Olivia and Odette were from a repeat mating of Madonna and Manfred Man.

Outstanding show results for the kennel have been achieved by imported Skyes, including Ch Hovagårdens Gule Garm from Sweden, who has been a big winner with a Best in Show award in 1992. From Switzerland the Dahlboms imported Ch Rannoch Skye Surprise and her brother Int Ch Rannoch Skye

Int and Nordic Ch Finnsky Galaxy.

Int and Nordic Ch Finnsky Fabian.

Finnsky Tazee.

Superstar, the latter going on to amass an outstanding record of wins including Groups and Best in Show awards, winner of the Contest of Champions and winner of the title World Champion at the World Show in Brno, Czechoslovakia in 1990 under the noted breed specialist Olga Smid. He proved his worth at stud by siring several champions for the kennel, and for other well known kennels also.

The Dahlboms next import came from the Netherlands with Ch Glenbrittle Heights Luxury Liner gaining his title in 1991. The most recent import, Ch Olivia Inspiration (Ch Silverspun Sundancer ex Ch Rannoch Skye Olivia) from America, recently gained her title and continues to display the type of Skye for which the kennel is noted.

Ch Finnsky Odette (Int Ch Rannoch Skye Superstar ex Int Ch Finnsky Glacier) was bred by artificial insemination to the English owned Ch Elissa's Alexander (Ch Andrew Thane of Skyecrest ex Ch Olivia Europa), an import from America, and this interesting combination of bloodlines should bring further honours to this adventurous kennel. Finnsky Ringleader was exported to the Kishniga kennel in Canada in 1992 and Finnsky exports to the Netherlands, Norway, Sweden, Denmark and Japan have all been successful in their new countries.

Int Ch Jopi and Ch Tuukan Glittery Star.

TUUKAN

The Tuukan kennel was founded by Miss Taimi Ylitalo who imported several Marjayn Skyes from England in the late 1960s, including Int Ch Marjayn Coruisk Fancy (Ch Acheo Sea Sprite ex Kirkby Harmony) and Ch Marjayn Dougal (Ch Merrymount the Rock ex Ch Marjayn Meta). After the death of Miss Ylitalo her cousin, Mrs Toni Rajaniemi, took over the affix and has built up a very successful kennel indeed. One of the first big winners was Int Ch Jopi (Elliot of Pellonpää ex Tuukan Mayflower) who was Skye of the year in 1984, Terrier Veteran of the Year 1984 and Top Veteran all breeds in 1985. Jopi was shown for much of his career by Toni's daughter, Nina, who with Int Ch Tuukan Queen Anne became the top Junior Handler of the year, competing in the Grand Final in England showing one of Miss Bailey's Marjayn Skyes.

Prominent among the Tuukan Skyes are Int and Nordic Ch Tuukan Charlie, a multiple Group winner (Int Ch Kirkleyditch Border King ex Juuliska), and, from a repeat mating, Int and Nordic Ch Tuukan Glittery Star, Int and Nordic Ch Tuukan Gala Queen and Int Ch Tuukan Glamour Girl, who was exported to Denmark and now lives in the Netherlands. Int Ch Tuukan Son of Saturday (Int Ch Jopi ex Int and Nordic Ch Tuukan Queen Anne) went Best in Show at the Skye Terrier Specialty in 1987 under Jill Bower of the Kirkleyditch kennels.

Int Ch Jopi.

Int Ch Tuukan Albert has been another big winner for the kennel with many Group wins and a Best in Show at an All Breeds show. Int Ch Misting's Moonlight Mary (Int Ch Jopi ex Ch Misting's Manzanilla) has an excellent show record and has produced some exciting winners to the American dog Ch Barraglen's Bobby Burns, including Tuukan Gral of Clan Donan who was World Junior Champion at the World Show held in Valencia, Spain, in 1992. Gral is owned by Mr and Mrs Hummel of Germany.

In addition to her successful export to Germany Mrs Rajaniemi's Tuukan Skyes have fared well in Denmark where Int Ch Tuukan Glamour Girl gained her title, and in America where Ch Tuukan Sand Island Don (Ch Tuukan Highland Hero ex Int Ch Misting's Moonlight Mary) gained his title with Ch Tuukan Johnny Be Good (Int Ch Jopi ex Tuukan Highland Heaven) who, at the time of writing, is among the top winning Skyes in America being in third place in the Breed Points system.

SKYROYAL

The Skyroyal kennel was established in 1970 when Mrs Terri Blomqvist bought the bitch Hällebergets Glacier-Lili (Int and Nordic Ch Rhosneigr Silver Flash ex Ch Baby of Skyeline) followed by Int Ch Xeres of Skyeline (Int Ch and Nordic Ch Rhosneigr Silver Flash ex Int and Nordic Ch Heavenly of Skyeline) who both gained their International and Nordic titles.

The Swedish imports O'Luxy Royal (Int Ch Opulus of Skyeline ex Int and Nordic Ch Biskyea Kismet) and Bonette Sable (Int and Nordic Ch Brabant ex Xanta of Skyeline) from the kennel of Åsa Svensson have played an important part in the breeding programme for the Skyroyal kennel over the past twenty

Nordic Ch Misting's Handsome Hugo with Int and Nordic Ch Misting's Chic Cecilia.

Int and Nordic Ch Misting's Chic Cecilia.

Int and Nordic Misting's Hazel bred and owne by Mrs Tuula Taipale.

years. The kennel produced Int and Nordic Ch Skyroyal Sunscot, Int and Nordic Chs Skyroyal Real Queen and Real Duke, Int and Nordic Ch Skyroyal Luxy Lady and Ch Skyroyal New Glacier. In 1991 Mrs Blomqvist imported Tarskavaig Dream Come True from Scotland to join her well known kennel.

MISTING'S

The Misting's kennel belonging to Mrs Tuula Taipale is famous for its Scottish Terriers, with the Skyes pressing hard for the number one position. Mrs Taipale bred her first Skye champion, Ch Misting's Manzanilla (Int Ch Silhill Sea Breeze ex Hällebergets Fortuna) in 1979. She gained her title easily before being bred to Int and Nordic Ch Jopi, to whom she produced three litters in all. From the first litter in 1984 came Int and Nordic Ch Misting's Handsome Hugo and the great bitch, Int and Nordic Ch Misting's Hazel, who is now a force to be reckoned with in veteran competition. Manzanilla's later litters produced Ch Misting's Music Molly, Int Ch Moonlight Mary and Ch Misting's Midnight Mandy.

Ch Susky's Butterscotch owned and bred by Mrs Annamari Salokannel.

Chs Misting's Chic Cecilia, Guttersnipe and Gamester are just three recent champions from the kennel. The Misting's kennel is also home to two imports, Mariquita Flashnite (Mariquita Flashlightning of Kirkleyditch ex Skyerise Solitaire) came from England in 1988, followed by SF Ch Acheo Roy Laidlaw (Andy Irvine at Acheo ex Mariquita Flashader) in 1991, the latter gaining his title during 1992.

SUSKY AND MASTERTEAM

Susky's Royal Tartan.

Annamari Salokannel owns the Susky affix of Skye and Cairn terriers while her daughter, Susanna, owns the Masterteam affix. Mrs Salokannel's first Skye, Ch Tuukan Charlotta (Int Ch Kirkleyditch Border King ex Juuliska) gained her title and was bred to Int and Nordic Ch Jopi in 1985. The resulting litter produced the drop ear, Susky's Butterscotch, a CC winner, and Ch Susky's Marshmallow. In 1986 Mrs Salokannel imported Acheo Local Hero (Balquhatston Gangbuster ex Orasaidh Fernitickles) from the Isle of Skye, campaigning him to his Finnish title. Her next import, Mariquita Flashader (Ch Mariquita Flashlight ex Am Ch Fleur of Morningsky), was imported in whelp in 1989 and one of the litter, Susky's Royal Scotchman, is a CC winner. Her most recent import is from Germany, Elaisa of Bumble Bee Castle, who joined the kennel in 1991.

Susanna has enjoyed great success as a junior handler, and has worked abroad at the famous von der Bismarckquelle kennel in Germany, and with the well known professional handler, Wood Wornall, in Califoria. Now back in Helsinki, Susanna has established a successful trimming shop and makes trips to Estonia to teach dog enthusiasts there how to trim their dogs. Miss Salokannel has judged in Moscow and Scotland.

SKYEMOOR

The Skyemoor kennel is owned by Mrs Armi Vitasaari whose foundation bitch, Int and Nordic Ch Skyroyal Luxy-Lady (Skyroyal Highnoon ex O'Luxy Royal), has had a very successful show career and has proved her worth as a brood by producing Ch Skyemoor Lucky Scot and the drop ear Ch Skyemoor

Lucky Love (by Int and Nordic Ch Skyroyal Sunscot) in 1983. Further success came with Ch Skyemoor Jolly Jonathan and Ch Skyemoor Jolly Jumper who gained their titles in 1986.

A litter by Ch Finnsky Heartbreaker out of Int and Nordic Ch Skyroyal Luxy Lady contained eleven pups, several of them attaining their championships, including Ch Skyemoor Funny Girl, Ch Skyemoor Fairytale, Ch Skyemoor Fanfyr and Ch Skyemoor Fontana. The Skyemoor kennel has also bred a number of drop ears, including Skyemoor Hot Capuccino, Skyemoor Good News and Skyemoor High Hope.

LONGWEILER

Mrs Erja Partanen owns Rottweilers and Skyes. Her first Skye, Ch Tuukan Patricia (Tuukan Nevil ex Ch Marjayn Mandy), gained her title and was followed by the drop ear Tuukan Zinaida (Int and Nordic Ch Jopi ex Tuukan Diana). Zinaida was bred to Ch Skyemoor Lucky Scot, producing Ch Longweiler A'Hoy and Ch Longweiler Aristos in 1989. Susky's Royal Scotchman (Andy Irvine at Acheo ex Mariquita Flashader) joined the kennel and is a CC winner. He and Zinaida produced a litter in 1991, and Longweiler Binnie and Benetta are currently being shown.

NAPOS

The Napos kennel belonging to Mrs Eila Kropsu is situated in Maksniemi in Northern Finland, not far from the Arctic circle. Despite the distance she has to travel to compete with other Skyes Mrs Kropsu has enjoyed considerable success with Ch Napos Adonis (Ch Finnsky Ikaros ex Finnsky Heartrose) from her first litter.

Ch Finnsky Odette (Int Ch Rannoch Skye Superstar ex Int and Nordic Ch Finnsky Glacier) is co-owned with the Dahlboms and is a big winner currently holding the title of World Champion from the World Show held in Valencia, Spain in 1992. Odette was then bred to Ch Elissa's Alexander in September of the same year.

SKYELIGHT

The Skyelight affix was registered by Penti and Pirjo Aaltovirta who own the successful trio, Ch Finnsky Madonna who is a Group winner, Ch Finnsky Nightbaron and Ch Finnsky Promise. Mr and Mrs Aaltovirta bred their first litter in 1991 by Ch Glenbrittle Heights Luxury Liner out of Ch Finnsky Madonna, producing Skyelight Aramis, Skyelight Aamor, Skyelight Athene and Skyelight Afrodite, all of which are winning well in the ring. Madonna, now back in the ring again, won her Swiss title during 1992.

MARQUEE

Marika Gustafsson, owner of Ch Misting's Wait For No-One (Int and Nordic Ch Tuukan Charlie ex Int and Nordic Ch Misting's Hazel), imported Acheo Grand Slam (Andy Irvine at Acheo ex Orasaidh Fernitickles) from the Isle of Skye in 1990. The Marquee Skyes share their home with a Polish Lowland Sheepdog.

M-PEE's

Markku Penttinen's first big winner was Int and Nordic Ch Adonis of Skyeline (Ch Rosa Hugonis of Skyeline ex Ch Hällebergets Carmen-Chic). After some years' absence from the ring he returned most successfully with Misting's Baleful Bolero (Ch Finnsky Heartbreaker ex Ch Misting's Hazel) who quickly gained her title. A litter to Ch Hovagårdens Gule Charm in 1991 resulted in just two pups, but a second litter by Ch Misting's Guttersnipe in January 1992 produced seven lovely puppies.

FRANCE

Little information is available on early breeders of the Skye in France though we learn from Baroness Burton, who judged the Terrier Show in Paris in 1923, that Tweedside Moonlight, owned by Mesdames Perrier and Manbre, was one of the best of his breed that she had ever judged. Favourable remarks were also passed on Jerry du Tholonet owned by Monsieur Goultenoir de Tourq.

M and Mme Chamart-Herault's kennel de la Chamardière was established in the 1930s. Already well known for their West Highland White Terriers they quickly made an impact with Skyes imported from the Meerend kennels in England and the Von Borke kennels in Germany. They bred their first litter in 1933 which produced Lessy de la Chamardière, a CC winner and winner of the International Beauty Certificate. In 1936 the lovely Ch Holmesdale Fergus (Holmesdale Sinbad ex Holmesdale Pamela) and two bitches were imported from Mrs Sandwich's kennel in England and Fergus quickly added French and International Champion titles to his name.

Lessy de la Chamardière was bred with the Scottish import Colin O'Craigmohr and one of the litter, Lady Lydia de la Chamardière, was exported to America in 1938. For her second litter Lessy was bred to another British import, Ch Peter Pan of Meerend, producing the kennel's first home bred champion, Ch Intran de la Chamardière. Marie and Bonnie Jean O'Craigmohr were the next imports from Scotland and Bonnie Jean attained her title. Phoebe O'Craigmohr also joined the kennel and became a French and International Champion.

During the Second World War the Chamarts had to find homes for fifteen of their puppies, but somehow managed to keep eight adults in spite of food rationing. In 1943 a litter by Limo II de Mandane out of Miss Meg de la Chamardière was bred to keep the kennel going. This produced the beautiful Ch Ronny de la Chamardière who was later exported to Mrs Frank's Abacus kennel in America.

In the 1950s Allander de la Chamardière (Nono de la Chamardière ex Violet du Pirujo) joined Mrs Frank's kennel in America where he quickly gained his American title. He then returned to France to win his French and International Championships before leaving once again for America. Ch Bonnie de la Chamardière also made her name with Mrs Frank.

In the 1930s the du Bazizoo kennel belonging to Monsieur Basilewsky was reputed to be the largest Skye Terrier kennel in the world. Importing quality stock from Scotland, England, Sweden and Germany was a recipe for success with many outstanding Skyes being produced. Several of M Basilewsky's dogs were given individual diets adjusted to suit their specific needs, and notes were kept on the health and general condition of each dog.

When war came M Basilewsky was notified that he must destroy all but six of his dogs. Keeping even six proved difficult with food in short supply, but the kennel survived, with Ch du Bazizoo Celeste and Ch du Bazizoo Beau Geste going on to top honours in America in 1941/42. Ch Yucco du Bazizoo also gained his title in America in 1942.

Mme Williamson established her world famous Luchar kennel in the 1930s with imports from the Merrymount kennels in England. Ch Goldmine of Merrymount, Ch Silver Lass of Merrymount and Ch Murdie of Merrymount were early noted winners for the kennel. During the war the Williamsons moved with their dogs to the South of France which was less stressful, and there managed to breed an occasional litter to keep the strain going. Ch You'll Do de Luchar (Ch Valère du Clos de L'Ill ex Merrymount Moonbeam) and his famous young sister, Ch Evening Star de Luchar, both took America by storm with Evening Star winning a record number of Best in Show awards.

The Mandane Skyes belonging to Madame Allard were also a force to be reckoned with during the 1940s, 1950s and 1960s, breeding some outstanding Skyes. Chs Yasmile and Yule de Mandane and Ch Vulcain de Mandane are just three examples. Ch Yule de Mandane was owned by the Glamoor kennel in America, and apart from being a top show dog he appeared on Broadway in the musical, *Wonderful Town*..

There is no doubt about it, our friends from America had a knack of discovering outstanding Skyes in France. The Goodmans imported Ch Jacinthe de Ricelaine (Earl de Luchar ex Hortense de Ricelaine), bred by Madame Elie who previously was unknown to the rest of the world. Jackie was to change all that by exceeding Evening Star's remarkable record of Best in Show awards and becoming the top winning Skye Terrier of all time. Mme Elie also bred Ch Jimmy de Ricelaine in the same litter, and he later joined Mr Chuck Brown's kennel in America.

In the 1960s Madame Nicole Trelut established her de Neuville Mousseaux kennel with stock from the v Bary kennel in Germany. The cream dog Int Ch Puck v Bary (Ch Olivia Largo ex Heidi v Bary) and Int Ch Olga v Bary (Ch Olivia Largo ex Ch Ferry v d Golden Hohe) were big winners, and also produced some lovely litters. From their first, Ovide, Ossian and Odile de Neuville Mousseaux all became International Champions. A repeat mating produced more champions, including Ch Quillan de Neuville Mousseaux. In 1976 at the World Show in Innsbruck, Austria, Ch Upton de Neuville Mousseaux took the title.

Tiburce du Petit Tanagra.

Madame Ganet's kennel du Petit Tanagra produced some lovely Skyes in the 1980s. Mme Ganet bought Ch Bumblebee of Morningsky (Int Ch Amity Columbus ex Ch Larrikins Rusty) in whelp to Int Ch Olivia Silver Solo, which

Ch Twenty-Two Violets du Petit Tanagra and Olivia Windsong.

gave her her first champion, Int Ch Tiburce du Petit Tanagra. Chs Umbrella and Uvee du Petit Tanagra came from her second litter, and in 1982 she bought Olivia Windsong from America and Nscho Tshi of Morningsky, followed by Olivia Xplosion in 1984 and Olivia Big Surprise.

Nicole Birembaut's Des Petits Grys kennel is based on the Grimsby lines belonging to Jean Luc Bour who lives in Belgium. Madame Birembaut's Int Ch J'Anais de Grimsby is a well known winner as is Foch des Petit Grys.

Madame Helène Garoni owns the Of Miss Liberty kennel and is the breeder of Ch Demetan of Miss Liberty and Evann of Miss Liberty, both well known winners. In 1990 she imported Ch Acheo Somerled (Acheo Bla Bheinn ex Acheo Inverie) from England, showing him to his International title, and in 1992 imported a Mariquita puppy by Ch Elissa's Alexander out of Skyerise Solitaire.

The affix of Foggy Plain belonging to Madame F Rosseel is very well known, having bred the lovely Ch Reggae of Foggy Plain. Madame F Anthoine of the du Val de Saynans affix is the breeder of Int Ch Chalimar du Val de Saynans. Two other notable kennels are the Decortes de Molina and Moquet's au Dolmen, both of which are active in the show ring.

Int Ch Umbrella du Petit Tanagra.

Germany

Germany has been the adopted home of the Skye Terrier since the turn of the century. One of the earliest breeders, Frau Schroeder, imported Andra O'Craigmohr and Braw Lassie O'Craigmohr from Miss Murdoch's kennel in Scotland in 1929 to establish the Trillup kennel. This fine pair produced Int Ch Mac Trillup, a big winner who was later bred with the English import, Grey Mist of Merrymount, producing Int Ch Trillup Aida.

Several kennels were established in Germany during the 1920s and 1930s, including Princess Pless' v Schloss Fuertenstein kennel, Crown Princess Cecilia's v Schloss Oels kennel, Countess Kalnein's v Schloss Bork kennel and Frau Leutke's v d Heiligen Bruecke kennel which imported Belinda of Merrymount and the drop ear Ch Piper of Merrymount from England. Other kennels of this era are Frau Schwendler's Orkney kennel, Frau Stiller's v d Sonnwendhoffe kennel and Frau Braunschweig's Apenborg kennel which imported several top winning Skyes from England.

Ch Susan of Meerend (Julian of Meerend ex Ruby of Meerend), owned by Frau Braunschweig, was the first Skye bitch to win the World Champion title, at Frankfurt in 1935. Jacob of Meerend and Susan of Peacehaven were another two imports who won well for the Apenborg kennel.

Many kennels were based on Apenborg stock including v Finowfurt, v d Reiterralp, v d Spreeweise, v Rehsumpf, v Dornek, Islay, v d Schnick and the v Muencher Kindl Kennel belonging to Frau Dillis who established her

Kiss-Girl v Engelmohr

kennel with Gibsy v Apenborg (Jacob of Meerend ex Susan of Meerend) and Hurlwind v Apenborg (Evan of Peacehaven ex Pilrock Iona of Meerend).

Frau Dillis built up an impressive kennel, initially with imports from the Merrymount and O'Craigmohr kennels, and in 1965 she imported Tarskavaig Flying Scotsman from the Isle of Skye and then in 1968 two from Czechoslovakia, Olivia Komedian (Ch Olivia Belcanto ex Queeny v Schlaraffenland) and Olivia Hesione (Ch Acheo Olivia Whist ex Int Ch Olivia Night Star).

In 1976 Gloriette v Muencher Kindl took the title of World Champion at the World Show in Innsbruck under judge Olga Smid. Gloriette had previously taken the title in 1973: a remarkable achievement.

Frau Drauz' kennel vom Pilgrimsbrunnen was established in 1937 with stock from the v Schlaraffenland and v Muencher Kindl kennels. Herr Drauz made his living as a building engineer so the Skyes lived in their own luxurious house complete with thatched roof. The star of the kennel was the well known Eskimo v Pilgrimsbrunnen (Rumpelstilzchen v Muencher Kindl ex Zwergenfee v Muencher Kindl).

Int Ch Pretty Paws of Morningsky

In 1941 Fraulein Steppat registered her zum Faulen Pelz affix after purchasing St Barbara Alligin (Int Ch Amor v Schlaraffenland ex Ch St Barbara Noblesse) who went on to gain his title and several Best in Show awards. Ch Rupert of Meerend (Ch Challenger of Meerend ex Joan of Meerend), imported from England, gained his championship in 1947, the first post war import to do so.

Yet more kennels appeared in the 1950s, including v d Elmsburg, v Bollensdorf, v Hochberg, v d Golden-Hohe (owned by Frau Benedix-Gutheil and remembered for Ch Akbar v d Golden-Hohe and Ch Ferry v d Golden-Hohe, both big winners), v Eisbach am Englischen Garten, v Palast des Silbergrauen Skye and Elfengrund (remembered for the lovely Ch Prinzess v Elfengrund and Int Ch Strick v Elfengrund). The v Bary affix belonging to Frau Krueger produced many champions including Peggy v Bary, Int Jack v Bary, Int Ch Puck v Bary, and Int Ch Olga v Bary.

Moving forward to the 1980s and 1990s it can be seen that the Skye is still very popular in Germany with many kennels producing top class exhibits. Georg Schott's v Engelmohr Skyes are noted for their temperament; Georg is renowned for arriving at shows with six or seven Skyes on leads, all getting along with each other most amicably! Noted dogs from this kennel include the famous Int Ch Aki v Engelmohr, from the kennels' first litter in 1973, and Ch Dusty Girl v Engelmohr. Two Kirkleyditch Skyes, Kirkleyditch Musicman and Kirkleyditch Hideaway, joined the kennel from England in 1991. Herr Hollmann's v Torweisenhof kennel is noted for Ch Babuschka v Torwiesenhof (Int Ch Aki v Engelmohr ex Wostod of Kenstaff), Ch Adular v Torwiesenhof (from an earlier litter to Babuscha) and Ch Cecil v Torwiesenhof, who is also the holder of an Obedience Certificate.

Herr Ufer, owner of the v d Hardthohe affix, is the breeder of Ch Dave v d Hardthohe (Ch Winter Whisper of the Isle of Skye ex Current Magic of Morningsky) and Gibsy v d Hardthohe, who is currently chasing top honours. In 1987 the Ufers imported the bitch Balquhatston Amazing Grace from Scotland.

The Hummels are an up-and-coming name on the German Skye scene with their Bumble Bee Castle kennel. They are the owners of Int Ch Pretty Paws of Morningsky (Int Ch Olivia Wild West ex Umbrella du Petit Tanagra), whose offspring by Int Ch Olivia Big Surprise, Chs Baron and Babsy of Bumble Bee

Castle, have been recent winners. Another of their winners is Ch Nickky (Ch Flair Fellow of the Isle of Skye ex Arline's Gentle Georgy).

A litter in 1990 from Ch Babsy by Olivia Heartbeat produced Elvis and Elliot Earl, and their sister Elaisa who was exported to Finland. All members of this litter were well placed at their first shows. Tuukan Gral of Clan Donan was imported from Finland in 1991 and was the World Junior Winner at Valencia, Spain in 1992.

Mention should also be made of the v Picht, v Völkersloch, Solitaire, Unter dem Nordlich, Canis Familiaris, v Musikwinkel, v d Fahrlaender Meuhie, v Kleinen Zampano and v d Sangerstadt kennels, who are all currently active on the dog scene in Germany. However the most famous kennel in the last decade has undoubtedly been the Morningsky kennel owned by Elke Spinnrock.

Two Skyes from the Bumble Bee Castle kennel

The foundation bitch of the Morningsky kennel, Larrikin's Rusty (Sir Henry Doodle of Cimarron ex Int Ch Larrikin's Iris) from the Netherlands, was joined by the American import, Int Ch Amity Columbus (Ch Olivia Perun ex Rolling Quizas O'Clair), who quickly gained his International and World Champion titles. The first Morningsky litter, bred in 1977, produced their homebred star, the outstanding Int and World Ch Alpha of Morningsky, who won the World Champion title twice, in 1978 and 1981, and who is behind most of the top winners on several continents today. A repeat mating produced Ch Belinda and Int Ch Bumblebee of Morningsky.

Ch Belinda and Ch Bumblebee of Morningsky

Over the years Morningsky has imported several quality dogs: Columbus was followed by Int Ch Olivia Silver Solo and Int Ch Olivia Wild West from America, Ch Umbrella du Petit Tanagra from France, and the most recent import from America, Olivia Heartbeat. From a mating between Int Ch Silver Solo and Int Ch Alpha of Morningsky came a litter full of champions: Am/Can Ch Feather Duster, Am Ch Fleur, who was subsequently exported to England, Int Ch Florian in Sweden, Ch Farid in East Germany and Int Ch Fancy.

Morningsky is remarkable for the outstanding blacks it produces, though some excellent creams have also been bred here. The kennel is also noted for its impressive number of champions in Europe and America, among the most recent of whom are Int Ch and World Ch 1991 J'Kind as Paint of Morningsky (Int Ch Brilliant Brisk of the Isle of Skye ex Int Ch Proud Black Rose of Morningsky) and Ch What A Feeling of Morningsky (Int Ch Olivia Wild West ex Ch Free and Easy of Morningsky).

Bautz v Musikwinkel and Elvis of Bumble e Castle, owned by Mr and Mrs inke of Dresden

In 1990 Mrs Gisele Dalrymple of the Balquhatston Skyes in Scotland returned to live in Germany, taking with her Ch Balquhatston Skyjack, Balquhatston Lianora, and Balquhatston Victoriana. Ch Balquhatston Skyjack was shown at the World Show in 1991.

Hong Kong

The Skye Terrier is known to have reached Hongkong as early as 1927 when Lady Marcia Miles' husband reported back to his wife that he had seen one on the streets there.

However, the show Skye was unknown there until just recently when Mrs Brenda Banbury, who was on a judging trip to the colony, discovered a Skye and made it the winner of the Terrier Group. As terriers are somewhat rare in Hongkong the win seems all the more remarkable. The Skye, Ch Skye of Tsang Man Shing, is owned by Mr Tsang Man Shing of New Territories, and is out of Australian stock.

Hungary

During the period 1933-1943 Skye Terriers were very popular in Hungary with several imports being shown. Mr Peter Hatvany owned the Sarvar kennel which housed Busy of Meerend, Bess of Meerend (Silver King ex Susanne of Meerend) and Derick of Merrymount (Ch Chummie of Merrymount ex Jellulah of Peacehaven). Mrs J Tüköry's Nagylapos kennel owned the British import Fanling Tana (Ch Chummie of Merrymount ex Bright Lassie). During this period 150 Skyes were registered in Hungary, András Herzog's Double Hill kennel, Mrs J Dávidházy's Alba Regia kennel, Mrs S Dóra's Dorpic kennel and Mrs G Rupp's Lucky Home kennel all being well respected names. Many Skyes travelled to shows in Hungary, particularly from Austria. The well known Ch Crown Prince Charles of Meerend, Ch Peacehaven Yorrocks, Ch Phoenix of Meerend, Ch Silver Maid of Merrymount and Princess Ida of Meerend all made the long journey to the Hungarian shows successfully.

After the second World War the Skye was rarely seen until 1958, when Dr and Mrs Répássy became interested in the breed. For over twenty years the Répássy's Körösparti kennel kept the Skye Terrier to the fore in Hungary. Importing stock from the Olivia kennel in Czechoslovakia they built up a fine kennel of sound and attractive Skyes.

Their first pair were Olivia Knight Teddy (Elfe de Mandane ex Olivia Hallo) and Olivia Manon (Merrymount Gold Digger ex Olivia Hallo) who both became champions. Among their progeny are Ch Körösparti Abszint and Ch Körösparti Bambino. Other famous names from the kennel are Ch Körösparti Very Nice and Ch Körösparti Sex Appeal.

Paloma z Cieplic was imported from Poland in the early 1970s, followed by Olivia Red River (Am Ch Talisker's Fearless ex Olivia Novela) from America in 1976, who was their last big winner. Korospari Skyes are behind all the winning Hungarian kennels right up to the present day.

Tiborne Thaly's Hobby kennel did some breeding in the late 1960s, Hobby Cindarella (Olivia Unicum ex Körösparti Ines) being exported to America. The Harangvirag kennel, owned by Gyulane Clair, produced some good Skyes, including Harangvirag Alfi Gripp and Tuzer Sztiri, who was a big winner in the 1960s.

Laszlo and Mary Safar enjoyed great success with their two Skyes in the late 1970s. Ch Körösparti Talisman (Palomai Ariel ex Körösparti Nicolette) and the Scottish import Ch Pendlebrook Prince Fergus (Dracula's Luxy of Kirkleyditch ex Acheo Kalgoorlie Kate) were both big winners.

Dr and Mrs Répássy, with six-week old puppies ex Olivia Red River, 1979.

Among the other kennels which sprang up in the 1970s were Julianna Kapri's Szayer kennel, Bela Csiszer's Bálványkerti kennel and Tibor Treiner's Mártonközi kennel, from which Mártonközi Black was exported to Austria. Antaine Szany's Szelesháti kennel produced Szelesháti Adonisz, a well known winner. Vilmos Salamon's Tengerparti kennel exported Tengerparti Apollo to Rumania and Tengerparti Aladdin to Yugoslavia in 1976 from a litter by Körösparti Parade out of Bálványkerti Amaryll. Sandorne Aba's Palomai kennel produced some excellent winners including Palomai Ara Dzseki (Olivia Unicum ex Paloma z Cieplic) and Palomai Beatrix (Ulli up z Cieplic ex Paloma z Cieplic).

Istvanne Pavlicsek's Boldoghegyi kennel has been active since 1970 with Boldoghegyi Alexandra (Olivia Unicum ex Hobby Beauty), a big winner. Mrs Pavlicsek's kennel currently houses Gaylord of Bumble Bee Castle (Olivia Heartbeat ex Nickky), an import from Germany, Tamesis Britannia (Fetisch v Silberblauen-See ex Tamesis Apolena) from Czechoslovakia, and Darling (Palomai Euripides ex Boldoghegyi). The Day Dream and Tóköz-menti kennels bring us up to date with the Skye Terrier fanciers of Hungary.

I TALY

The Castel Martini kennels, owned by Giulio Poggi Banchieri, were the first to make an impression on the show scene in Italy. In the 1940s Buli di Valrisano and Diddi della Vigna were the foundation pair for the kennel and produced some excellent stock, including the champions Brontoia, Brontola and Betti di Castel Martini, all from the same litter. Two Merrymounts, one of them Ch Merrymount Sunrise, were imported from England in 1951, adding some new blood to the kennel's already successful line.

Ch Fairy
Wonder di Villa
Bellaria, with
Dr Montanari
Miccoli.

Signora Federici built up a successful kennel with Tarskavaig St Nicholas (Merrymount Wot Airs ex Tarskavaig Fionnghal), who was imported from the Isle of Skye in the late 1960s and went on to win his title. Her next import, Reminder of Skyeline (Int Ch Rhosneigr Silver Flash ex Filipendula of Skyeline), was imported from Finland. This pair later produced a litter, the drop ear Ch Bettina di Monte Aguzzo gaining her title, the only one of this variety of ear set to do so in Italy. The di Monte Aguzzo kennels are also famous for their two World Champions, Int Ch Fiore di Monte Aguzzo (Int Ch Black Prince di Villa Bellaria ex Ch Cate di Monte Aguzzo) and Int Ch Jula di Monte Aguzzo (Ch Black Prince di Villa Bellaria ex Chiara di Monte Ingino).

Guiliana Mondani, who started breeding Skyes in the early 1960s, is generally acknowledged as the one whose lovely Skyes brought the breed to the attention of showgoers throughout Europe. Guiliana imported Ch Rhosneigr Blond Lad (Ch Rhosneigr Rise Again ex Ch Rhosneigr Blond Bit) from England, and Ch Talisker's Little Treasure (Ch Talisker's Fairy Wonder ex Ch Talisker's Wanda) from Canada, and both gained their titles. Treasure was bred to Ch Poker de la Chamardière, producing five puppies of which two, Ch Black Prince and Ch Silver Bell di Villa Bellaria, appear in nearly all Italian pedigrees today.

In 1980 Signora Mondani imported two Skyes from Germany, Elliott of Morningsky and Ch Fawn Lou of Morningsky, who gained their titles and later produced a litter of ten! The famous black male Ch Fairy Wonder di Villa Bellaria owned by Montanari Miccoli, and Ch Fleck di Villa Bellaria from this litter were to be the last of a long line of champions bred by Signora Mondani, but in the 1970s several new kennels based on the di Villa Bellaria strain grew and prospered.

Laura and Andrea Pizzi's dell' Antica Caledonia Skyes, established in 1980, have built up a strong reputation and currently lead the way in Italy. Their foundation stock contained Talisker, Villa Bellaria, Morningsky and Kirkleyditch blood. Bright Sun (Eggpunch di Villa Bellaria ex Festival di Villa Bellaria) and Ch

Maila (Porthos ex Anni), who was bred by M T Quilghini, gave them their first litter in 1984 which included Int Chs Blond Dream, Blue Boy and Bryght Moon.

Ch Maila was later bred to Int Ch Bubi Boris, litter brother to Bright Sun, producing three champions including Int Ch Cassandra, who was World Junior Champion in 1986 under noted breed specialist Olga Smid. Int Ch Crystal also came from this litter. In 1985 the Pizzis imported Polly Perkins of Morningsky

from Germany and she went on to win Italian, International, European and World Champion titles as well as three Best in Show awards. Unfortunately she never produced any puppies.

Int Chs Guendalina dell' Antica Caledonia, Gallant dell' Antica Caledonia and German Gift

Int Ch Olivia Heartbreaker.

dell' Antica Caledonia were produced by Ch Olivia Wild West out of Int Ch Cassandra. Two years later Cassandra was bred to Int Ch Brilliant Brisk of the Isle of Skye producing four pups who have many CACs between them.

Int Ch Olivia Heartbreaker, imported from America by Laura Pizzi.

Olivia Heartbreaker (Ch Olivia Dukat ex Ch Chiquita of Morningsky) joined the kennel from America in 1989. This latest addition has done a great deal of winning, gaining his champion's title and winning several Terrier Groups too. Heartbreaker was bred to Holland dell' Antica Caledonia, giving three Italian champions, including India dell' Antica Caledonia. The latest youngster to show promise is Joshua dell' Antica Caledonia who has had many excellent placings in junior classes.

Signor Luciano Vezzani's Atreyu kennel is home to the beautiful grey Int Ch Bubi Boris, and to Ch Fleck di Villa Bellaria, as well as to her sire and dam, Chs Elliott and Fawn Lou of Morningsky.

Signora Maria Teresa Quilghini's La Perla del Tirrena kennel was established with stock from the Kirkleyditch kennels in England. Several champions and international champions were bred in this kennel, all cream, including Ch Maila and the famous Ch Murdok.

JAPAN

While on a formal visit to Japan in 1963 Dame Flora MacLeod of Dunvegan Castle met, among others, Mr Yoshida, the former Prime Minister of Japan. Discovering she was from the Isle of Skye Mr Yoshida quickly made firm friends with the Clan Chief, discussing his favourite breed of dog, the Skye Terrier, though it is not known if Mr Yoshida ever owned any Skyes.

In the late 1960s a sudden demand for pedigree dogs of all breeds arose from Japan and dealers offered above average prices for puppies. This tempted some people in Britain who, rightly or wrongly, decided to take advantage of this opening to establish their strain in Japan. Thirty-four Skyes, mostly puppies but including one stud dog, were exported from Britain to Japan during this period.

Ch Kirkleyditch Silver Dollar, imported from Britain by Mr and Mrs Yoshimoto.

Later distress stories of abandoned dogs, and even worse accounts of cruelty, resulted in anguish for the breeders who had sent stock to the Far East. With the dealers disappearing from the scene almost as fast as they had arrived the export trade to Japan was suspended.

No country is free from cruelty as the newspapers tell us every day, but with anti-cruelty laws somewhat lacking in Far Eastern countries many clubs, including the Skye Terrier Club of Great Britain, find it unacceptable for any of their members to export to Japan.

However, the breed is thriving in Japan, and in the hands of enthusiastic and caring people. We must not forget that many excellent dogs have come out of Japan and should not make judgments too harshly. It is to be hoped that those who have Skyes can be accepted as fellow enthusiasts, and helped in every way to foster the understanding of our breed and place the dogs in good homes in Japan, just as we would try to do here.

The Kirkleyditch kennels sold two Skyes, a dog and a bitch, to great enthusiast Sazugo Ugai in the early 1980s. These were Ch Kirkleyditch Silver Rune (Ch Kirkleyditch Dalesman ex Ch Kirkleyditch Petronella) and Kirkleyditch Silver Dollar (Ch Spaceman of Skye Devils Inn of Kirkleyditch ex Kirkleyditch Annabelle), who both quickly gained their titles. In 1984 Olivia Yamour was bought by Mr and Mrs Toshio Mizuna of Tokyo, who were then living in Germany but subsequently returned to Japan with their Skye.

Ch Kirkleyditch Silver Rune, imported from Britain by Mr and Mrs Yoshimoto.

In 1991 Sazugo Ugai imported Finnsky Quickstep (Ch Hovagardens Gule Garm ex Ch Misting's Baleful Bolero) from Finland. The Tuukan kennel, also in Finland, exported two of their Skyes to Japan in 1985. The new owners were so keen to learn as much as possible about the upkeep of their dogs that they invited their breeder, Nina Rajaniemi, to come to Japan, all expenses paid, to demonstrate her grooming and handling technique for all interested Skye owners. Records show that in 1990 thirteen Skyes were registered with the Japanese Kennel Club.

LUXEMBOURG

The only available information on the Skye Terrier in Luxembourg dates from 1920 when Miss Mayrisch's Sunny Sky kennel was established with stock from the O'Craigmohr kennel in Scotland. For many years Miss Mayrisch bred good, sound terriers, but on her retirement the breed faded into disappearance in Luxembourg.

Netherlands

The first record of Skyes in Holland came in September 1874 when eight were entered at a Netherlands show. It was not until 1890, when dogs were first registered, that we discover Mac, sired by Foxie ex Lassie Lyncs, and bred by Mr H Dundas who later became Viscount Melville. Mac was owned by Mr E Smit, and was five and a half years old at the time of registration.

Skyes were quite rare in Holland until Mr van Hout began his Woodfeet kennel in the 1940s, though initially he did not register his litters. The first Dutch bred litter to be registered was bred by Mr L H J van der Graaff who owned the Van Geestenborch kennels. His litter of four pups was sired by Hanno von der Alten Bergstadt ex Burgere von der Alten Bergstadt, both imports from Germany.

During the war, at the time of the liberation of Rotterdam, when the German army were taken prisoner, one officer was seen clutching a dog in his arms. Fearing for the safety of the dog he approached a young lady in the crowd and asked her to look after his dog whose name was Prosty, and told her that she would find Prosty's papers at German headquarters. The person who was handed the dog had no idea what breed it was until she saw a picture in a magazine and realised she was the owner of a Skye Terrier. The lady, Mrs J C Iordache Brazilay, was completely won over by the breed.

When Prosty died Mrs Brazilay bought Rex Hannover van Het Skyenhof, a dog who went on to win his title and was Best Terrier at Breda in 1951. Girly was the next addition; she won many championships, including a Best in Show award. From Germany Mrs Brazilay next bought Baeat Boheme who enjoyed a great show career. Girly's first litter in 1953, by Baeat Boheme, produced four pups one of which, Ch Dracula's Ursele, went on to take Best in Show at Utrecht in 1957.

Many fine Skyes were bred at the Dracula kennels including Ch Dracula's Orion, Ch Dracula's Floria Tosca, Ch Dracula's Luxos, and Dracula's Luxy of Kirkleyditch, who was exported to England where he won two Challenge Certificates and had such a great influence on the breed in Britain.

Mrs E Vieryra Liesveld owned the Hilgersmount kennel which was home to many outstanding imports from the Merrymount kennel in England. In 1955 she bought Ch Merrymount Coquette (Ch Merrymount You'll Do ex Rebecca of Merrymount), Merrymount Wise Lady, Merrymount Gold Digger and the beautiful dog, Merrymount What's Wanted (Ch Merrymount Old Andy ex Merrymount Desire), who quickly gained his title in Holland.

The following year Mrs Liesvald bought Merrymount Summers's Day (Ch Merrymount Happy Jack ex Ch Merrymount Sunset), winner of the

Challenge Certificate and Best of Breed at the West of England Ladies Kennel Show (WELKS) in 1964, and the outstanding cream drop ear Ch Merrymount Sungleam (Ch Challenger of Meerend ex Ch Merrymount Sunset) who had a very successful show career in Holland and quickly became a Dutch Champion. Only three litters were bred by Mrs Liesvald, the first in 1956 by What's Wanted ex Merrymount Coquette. Later she exported Merrymount Gold Digger to Olga Smidova in Czechoslovakia and imported Olivia Kay from Mrs Smidova.

Mrs W E M Westerman Dalhuijsen's first Skye, Girly Van Het Ludenbosch (Gnom v d Jacht ex Dracula's Carmen), was the foundation bitch for her Iron Cape kennel. Girly was bred to Ch Merrymount What's Wanted in 1957 producing some excellent Skyes. Proud of the Iron Cape was considered an outstanding bitch and Int Ch Never Too Late of the Iron Cape was the outstanding dog of his day.

Int Ch Top Secret of Devils Inn.   Photo: Tim Hogendouru.

Mr J Wijkstra's Larrikin kennel was founded with the bitch Adelaide of the Quint and the Czech import Olivia Larrikin. They produced Ch Larrikin's Boukje and Ch Larrikin's Chiquita. Chiquita was bred back to Olivia Larrikin and produced the beautiful Int Ch Larrikin's Iris who gained her title and was later exported to England where she quickly gained her British title.

In the 1970s a kennel which was to create a lot of new interest in the breed in the Netherlands appeared on the scene, the Skye Devils Inn kennel of Hans Boot. His first Skye of note, Ch Dracula's Natalia, was a big winner with fifteen Challenge Certificates. His next move was to import Kirkleyditch Diamond (Dracula's Luxy of Kirkleyditch ex Happyhill Jemma) in whelp to the Crufts Group winner, Ch Silhill Silver Secret, from England. From this litter came the beautiful Int Ch Top Secret of Skye Devils Inn and Int Ch Secret Charm of Skye Devils Inn.

Diamond was campaigned, gained her title and was then joined by Kirkleyditch Satan Bug who also went on to take her Dutch title. Int Ch Top Secret of Skye Devils Inn was bred to Dracula's Funny Girl, producing Champions Secret Power, Glamour Girl, Topping Fun and Spaceman of Skye Devils Inn. The last of these was exported to the Kirkleyditch kennels in England where he was campaigned to his British title. The Skye Devils Inn dogs were noted for their glamorous coats and expert presentation.

Mr J Van Leeuwan's first litter in 1978 was by Int Ch Amity Columbus ex Larrikin's Ofelia, starting the Van De Litsberg strain. Only three litters were bred by Mr Van Leeuwan, but this kennel is remembered for producing Ch Amarous Ofelia's Son van de Litsberg and Int Ch Cimarron Czigana van de Litsberg (Ch Amarous Ofelia's Son van de Litsberg ex I'm a Lady of Skye Devils Inn) who has been a very influential breeding bitch in the Netherlands.

Present day kennels in the Netherlands are:

ARLINES

Herma van de Roer's Arline Skye Terriers are Dutch registered although they live just across the border in Belgium. Herma's first Skye was bought as a surprise for her husband in 1976. As Frits had always been mildly allergic to dogs Herma decided to conceal the puppy for a couple of days to test for any adverse reaction! Fortunately all was well and Ripper was welcomed into the house although he would have nothing to do with Frits whenever Herma was present. However he always weakened when left alone with him: a typical Skye reaction! Ripper was of Dracula lines, and although not a show dog was a great character. When he died after an accident at just three years of age the van de Roers decided that as no other dog could replace him they would have a bitch. With the help of the President of the Dutch Terrier Club a litter was traced in the south of Holland. The puppies were sired by Baramis von de Litsberg out of Larrikin's Ofelia, and from the breeder, Mrs Fick, they acquired Arline whose litter brother, Angus, helped establish the Glenbrittle Heights kennel.

Arline and Herma began their show career at club meetings where they met another new enthusiast, Lia Obee, who was also just starting in Skyes. The two ladies teamed up, travelling together to many shows to campaign their Skyes. Arline went on to gain her Junior winner, Dutch, Yugoslavian and International titles along with the German Bundessieger. She was bred to Int Ch Amity Columbus with a bitch, Cherokee Rose, being kept to campaign. Rose gained her title and in turn was bred to Arline's Chicka Saw Chief from which came the dark grey bitch, Arline's Fizgig Flash, who has been campaigned to her International title. Another from this litter, Ch Arline's Cheerful Dame, though not shown until two years of age, went on to take her title and Best in Show in Brno, Czechoslovakia.

Ch Arline's Magic Mr Muzzle and Ch Arline's Miss Marple gained their titles in 1990. In 1991 Int Ch Arline's Fizgig Flash was bred to Int Ch Brilliant Brisk of the Isle of Skye with a bitch, Arline's Baby Boom Beverley, being kept to continue this winning line. The Arline kennel has exported two pups to Russia. The first unfortunately succumbed to a distemper virus, but a second, Arline's Yessica, is faring well.

Although providing a home for four Skyes Herma and Frits make a great effort to socialise their dogs, taking them everywhere they go as members of the family. Therefore the dogs are always on their best behaviour and thus attract a great many admirers to the breed. Herma van de Roer has done much to encourage the breed's popularity in Belgium and is an enthusiastic member of the Belgian Terrier Club. Through her efforts the Belgian Top Terrier Show in 1990 had an entry of 53 Skyes, the second highest entry at the show, so it was most fitting that the Skye, Int Ch Brilliant Brisk of the Isle of Skye, went Best in Show. In 1992 the breed entry rose to 65 with the Skye again winning Best in Show. The successful dog, Brilliant Whispers Skye Adventure, is a son of the 1990 Best in Show winner.

Mrs van de Roer is at present producing beautiful hand painted T-shirts to raise funds to feed and cover the health care of the Russian Skyes, who are sadly lacking in the basic things we all take for granted. Skye Terrier enthusiasts in Europe are very eager to support her efforts.

BRILLIANT WHISPERS

In the early 1980s John and Monique Janssen owned Briards and Bobtails. Then they heard of a five month old Skye Terrier who was in desperate need of new owners and changed the puppy's fortune by giving him the chance of a loving home. The puppy was Wesley of Movin Channel (Ch Amarous Ofelia's Son v d Litsberg ex Chiba v d Litsberg) and despite the unhappy life to which this pup had been subjected previously he soon adjusted to his new surroundings and became a very loving character. Sadly his was a very short life, and when the Janssens' old Briard and Bobtail also died there was only one breed to consider as a replacement.

Whisp and Basil: Int Ch Winter Whisper of the isle of Skye and a drop eared son.

Bjorn (Angus ex Charmaine v d Litsberg), a grey, was bought first, and as Monique's preference was for a cream they went to Lia Obee for a Skye of this colour. A dog, Brilliant Brisk of the Isle of Skye (Int Ch Winter Whisper of the Isle of Skye ex Int Ch Cimmaron Czigana v d Litsberg), was chosen and named Wesley after the Janssens' first Skye. Wesley was shown consistently from ten months of age, winning many Best of Breed awards even at a very tender age, thus confirming to his owners that they had a very special dog with a great deal of potential. To date he holds Dutch, Belgian, Luxembourg, FCI Europe, World 1989, World 1991 and International Championships as well as several Groups and Best in Show at the Belgian Top Terrier Show in 1990.

Shortly after Wesley was purchased the Janssens went back to Lia Obee for a bitch. Zed Zingora of the Isle of Skye (Int Ch Olivia Wild West ex Int Ch Cimmaron Czigana v d Litsberg) joined the family, followed a few months later by Pemberley (Int Ch Winter Whisper of the Isle of Skye ex Pascale). In 1988 the Janssens bred their first litter, using Brilliant Brisk with Zed Zingora, which resulted in two puppies. A repeat mating in 1990 produced the outstanding young bitch, Brilliant Whispers Pillowtalk, who began her show career by taking Best Bitch at nine months of age. At one year old she took her second

CAC, Best of Breed and was placed fifth in the Terrier Group. At her fourth show, which was the World Show in Dortmund 1991, she won the Junior World Title. So far she has been awarded six CAC and three CACIB but is still too young to qualify for the title of Champion, though as soon as she reaches the necessary age will easily do so. A repeat of the mating which produced Pillowtalk produced yet another lovely bitch, Brilliant Whispers Gentle Gesture, who was exported to the Kishniga kennels in Canada.

From a litter by Brilliant Brisk ex Pemberley a bitch puppy, Brilliant Whispers Skye High, was kept for future campaigning and her litter brother, Brilliant Whispers Skye Lightening, won the Junior World Champion title in 1991. Yet another from this suc-

Brilliant Whispers Pillow talk.

cessful litter, Brilliant Whispers Skye Adventure, was sold as a pup on condition that the Janssens would be able to show him occasionally.

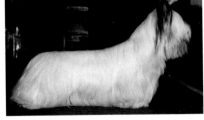

Int Ch Brilliant Whispers Skye Adventure.

Late in 1991 the owners were approached by the Janssens who wished to take the puppy to a show, but when they arrived to collect him they were told that they should not bring him back! Since then this remarkable young dog has been shown ten times, winning Best of Breed at each show, Best Terrier on seven occasions and Best in Show four times, including his very first show. His wins include taking the World Champion title at Valencia, Spain, in 1992, and the Terrier Group.

SKYEDREAM CANCANGUS

Skyedream Cancangus Lady Leika and puppies.

Mrs Inge Printz acquired her first Skye, a bitch named Cancan of Skye Devils Inn (Ch Top Secret of Skye Devils Inn ex Go Go Girl of Skye Devils Inn) when her original owner became seriously ill. In 1986 Cancan was bred to Int Ch Angus and a bitch, Skyedream Cancangus Canny Monika, was retained for exhibition. Monika was bred in 1989 to Ch Arline's Magic Mr Muzzle, which resulted in a litter of nine pups. From this litter Mrs Printz kept the lovely silver bitch, Skyedream Cancangus Lady Laika, who has done some nice winning for her owner. In 1991 Cancangus Canny Monika produced a litter to Arline's Quicksilver Quispel.

GLENBRITTLE HEIGHTS

A photograph of a Skye Terrier first drew Irma de Roo Strous to seek further information on the breed. She and her husband decided they must try and find a real live model so they went to several shows until at last they discovered their objective. Knowing this was the breed for them they bought Angus (Baramis v d Litsberg ex Larrikins Ofelia) in 1981. Angus began his show career at six months of age and went on to win his Dutch, German, VDH, German Junior Champion, KFT Club Jugend (sieger 82), Bundes Jugendsieger 1982, Junior Winner Amsterdam 1982 and International Championship.

Glenbrittle Heights Bright Breeze at five and a half months.

From 1983-85 the Roo Strous lived in the Caribbean, during which time Angus continued to be shown, adding the champion titles of Puerto Rica and Dominican Republic to his extensive list. He also went Group 2 three times, and Group 1 and Reserve Best in Show at the CAC/CACIB Show in the Dominican Republic on 23rd October, 1983. On their return to the Netherlands in 1985 Irma bought Silver Silhouette of Morningsky (Int Ch Amity Columbus ex Ch Jennifer of Morningsky) from Germany who went on to win German Junior Champion, Dutch, German and International Champion titles.

In February 1986 a four months old black puppy, Finnsky Kamee (Ch Finnsky Fabian ex Int Ch Finnsky Glacier), joined the kennel from Finland. Kamee was campaigned to Junior Warrant Amsterdam 1986, German Junior Champion, Europasieger 1987, Dutch, German VDH Ch and International Champion. She also took second place in the Terrier Group at a German Terrier show.

Glenbrittle Heights' first litter in June 1988 (Int Ch Brilliant Brisk of the Isle of Skye ex Ch Finnsky Kamee) produced two dogs and six bitches. One bitch puppy, Glenbrittle Heights Gillie Glass was retained. With three generations of World Champions behind her great things were expected of Gillie Glass and she did not let her owner down. In 1989 at her first championship show in Holland she went Best Bitch at sixteen months of age. Gillie Glass was a group winner at the International CAC/CACIB Show held in Germany in March 1991. To date she holds the following titles: German Junior Champion, KFT Klau Jugend Sieger, Dutch, German, Belgian and International Champion.

Glenbrittle Heighs Gillie Glass.

A repeat mating in 1989 produced eight pups, and this time there were six dogs and two bitches. From this litter Glenbrittle Heights Luxury Liner was exported to the Finnsky kennels in Finland where he gained his title and is the sire of two litters. Litter brother Glenbrittle Heights Lovemaker was kept to show and won the Open Class at his first attempt, went on to Best of Beed and was placed third in the group. He is currently a Luxembourg Junior Champion. In 1990 Ch Silver Silhouette of Morningsky was bred to Lovemaker, producing two pups, Glenbrittle Heights Extra Elegant and Glenbrittle Heights Ebony

Eyes, a dark grey male. He in turn was bred to Kamee in 1991, siring an enormous litter of eleven! Glenbrittle Heights Skyes can be found in the Netherlands, Belgium, Germany and Finland.

ISLE OF SKYE

The Isle of Skye kennels were established in 1976 with True Diamond of Skye Devils Inn (Ch Silhill Silver Secret ex Kirkleyditch Diamond) who went on to become a Dutch, Luxembourg, and International Champion for owner Lia Obee. Some years later, in 1981 to be exact, Lia bought the exceptional cream, Cimarron Czigana v d Litsberg (Ch Amarous Ofelia's Son v d Litsberg ex I'm A Lady of Skye Devils Inn). This beautiful bitch was shown successfully but took time out to produce her first litter in 1983 to Int Ch Amity Columbus. The theme for this litter was "Flair", with Ch Flair Fellow of the Isle of Skye gaining his title. Cimmaron returned to the show ring after her litter and gained her own title at twenty-seven months of age.

Miracle Minx of the Isle of Skye.

A trip to Scotland in the early 1980s resulted in Balquhatston Eilean Caileag being imported from the Balquhatston kennel to Holland. Cimmaron was next bred to Int Ch Olivia Wild West which resulted in the successful "Winter" litter. From this came four champions: Winter Wish of the Isle of Skye (a champion in Yugoslavia), Winter Whirl and Winter Witch and the outstanding Winter Whisper. All went on to gain their titles, Whisper becoming Dutch, German, Belgian, Luxembourg, Danish, World Champion 1985, Int Champion, Bundesieger 1986 and Top Terrier of the Year 1986. He also won several Groups in the Netherlands and Denmark: a great dog and a great career.

In 1984 the third litter bred at the Isle of Skye kennels by Winter Whisper out of Balquhatston Eilean Caileag produced the "Miracle" litter with Ch Miracle Minx of the Isle of Skye going on to win his title.

Sandwich Saint the Isle of Skye.

Cimmaron, having added more titles to her list, was bred to her son, Winter Whisper, producing the "Brisk" litter, considered to be her best yet. One of this litter, Brilliant Brisk of the Isle of Skye, went on to become one of the top winning Skyes of all time in Holland, only having to give way to his son in 1992.

For her last litter in 1987 Cimmaron was bred to Int Ch Olivia Wild West producing the "Zed" litter. Zed Zodiac in Germany, Zenith Zed in Denmark, and Zoe Zed in the Netherlands all hold their titles, with Zed Zingora holding CCs in the Netherlands.

During 1987 the English import, French, Belgian, World and Int Ch Littlecreek Reay (Ch Littlecreek Glengarry ex Littlecreek Gigha), joined the kennel, quickly adding the Dutch title to her impressive array. The imported dog, Littlecreek Argyle Lad, was bred with Ch Winter Witch of the Isle of Skye to produce the "Laughing" litter in 1987, Laughing Law of the Isle of Skye going on to become a Belgian and International Champion with a Terrier Group win in Brussels to his credit.

In 1988 Ch Littlecreek Reay was bred to Int Ch Brilliant Brisk of the Isle of Skye, from which mating came the "Saint" litter. Two bitches were kept, Saving Saint of the Isle of Skye who won her titles in the Netherlands and Denmark and is an International Champion, and Saint Sarabande of the Isle of Skye, who has won her championships in the Netherlands, Belgium, and Luxembourg, and who also holds the 1990 International and World Champion titles in Denmark.

In 1990 Int Ch Littlecreek Reay produced the "Never" litter to Int Ch Winter Whisper. A lovely cream dog, Never Say Never of the Isle of Skye, won the Terrier Group in Leeuwarden in the Netherlands at just seventeen months of age. A litter sister, Name her Never, is just starting out on her show career.

Int Ch Saint Sarabande was bred to Int Ch Winter Whisper in 1990 producing the "Dog" litter with Dodgy Dog of the Isle of Skye being retained to carry on the good fortunes of this kennel. That's Taboo of the Isle of Skye (Int Ch Brilliant Brisk of the Isle of Skye ex In Ch Saving Saint of the Isle of Skye) is from the most recent litter at the kennel and the word from Holland is that we can expect to hear a lot from this young bitch in the near future.

Glenbrittle Heights Ballock Buff.

Name her Never of the Isle of Skye.

NEW ZEALAND

A remarkable record of early Skye Terriers is to be found in the offices of the New Zealand Kennel Club. The Archives Skye Terrier book contains a list of dogs born between 1897 and 1926 with a couple of entries in the 1930s, though one is described as "black and fawn" so we might assume that not all were pure bred Skyes. During the latter half of the nineteenth century, until they were separated into their own individual breeds, all Scottish breeds of terrier were found under the heading "Skye Terrier", and this should be taken into account before becoming too excited over this interesting record of registrations.

The Reid brothers deserve special mention for introducing a variety of animals, including Skyes, to their island home in New Zealand. Twin brothers James and John and their elder brother William were born in Campsie, Stirlingshire, in Scotland and emigrated to Melbourne, Australia, in the early 1860s, where they farmed. In 1867 they joined together in a journey of discovery, first to Queensland and then to Auckland, New Zealand, which they reached in 1869. There they discovered Motutapu Island in the Hauraki Gulf, whose situation, fertile soil and pleasant climate were ideal for their farming aspirations. Negotiations were entered into for the purchase of the island, but their offer was turned down by the owner. Bitterly disappointed the brothers returned to Australia to farm. However, several months later they were given the chance to buy the island, as the owner was in financial difficulties. The Reids wasted no time in taking up the offer!

Returning to Motutapu (a Maori word meaning "sacred island") they began clearing the land of scrub and introduced exotic birds and animals, including pedigree sheep and cattle as well as many breeds of deer. Gardens were laid out with many plants and heathers being brought from Britain. Word quickly spread about this island paradise, visitors arriving from far and wide to view the stock and enjoy the Reids' hospitality.

According to the Archive the Reids registered eighteen Skyes, stud dogs Greenhead and Sandy Scot appearing in several pedigrees. No indication is given as to where the dogs came from. Perhaps the Reids brought them out from Scotland when they first emigrated, or maybe had them shipped over with the pedigree cattle and sheep.

Two other early Skye breeders in New Zealand are listed in the Archive: James Muir was one, and another, W Pike, bred several litters between 1907 and 1910 using the affix "Portree". Many decades passed before the next Skyes were registered in New Zealand.

NORTH ISLAND

Mr Donald Price of Auckland, a breeder of West Highland White and Scottish Terriers, decided to import a Skye after reading all the literature he could find on the breed. In 1969 he bought Danehill Freja (Ch Rhosneigr Blond Ever ex Rhosneigr Merrymount Wait Only), followed a year later by Danehill Kyleakin (Ch Rhosneigr Blond Ever ex Acheo Highland Wedding). These two were the foundation pair for the Radcliffe kennel.

Both Skyes went on to gain their New Zealand titles and produced their first litter of eight pups, five dogs and three bitches. On one occasion Mr Price took the entire litter, plus their sire and dam, to a show! Two further litters were bred, several of the progeny being shown in New Zealand and a few exported to Australia.

Mrs Carolyn Symmans, of Hawkes Bay, is famous for her Kiralee kennel of Australian Terriers. Her Skyes, imported from Australia, Skyeclan Bold Baron (Aust Ch Skyeclan Reo Speedwagon ex Aust Ch Santlin the Senterfold) and Skyeclan Blessn Indskyes are both New Zealand champions, with Skyeclan Fantasia (Skyeclan Nite Stalker ex Skyepara Seventh Heaven) a recent newcomer to the show ring, as is home-bred Kirralee His Lordship (Ch Skyeclan Bold Baron ex Skyeclan Blessn Indskyes).

Aus/NZ Ch Skyeclan Bold Baron.

Mrs Karen Harrison of Auckland, owner of the Folichon kennels of Pyrenean Mountain Dogs, decided to look for something smaller when her two elderly Pyreneans were past their best for the show ring and decided on Skye Terriers. Importing Gardony Maestro (Gardony Highland Lad ex Aust Ch Gildarre April Love) from Australia in 1988 she enjoyed some early successes, as he won Best Puppy in Group and Best Junior in Group at all breed shows before he gained his title at just over one year of age. Shortly after winning his title Maestro had to undergo surgery which resulted in his retirement from showing and breeding.

Down, but not out, Mrs Harrison imported from Australia Santlin Sitting Pretty (Santlin Sowin' Wild Oats ex Santlin Slightly Saucy) who repeated Maestro's wins and title at the same age. Santlin Speako The Devil, her litter brother, joined the kennel for a short stay and was campaigned to his title in just three months, winning a Best in Group in the process. On returning home he gained his Australian title.

In 1991 Australian Ch Santlin the Spycatcher (Ch Santlin Shotgun Wedding ex Santlin Shy Butsinful) joined the kennel to be campaigned, and also to be bred to Ch Santlin Sitting Pretty. This resulted in the first Folichon litter of Skyes, five dogs and a bitch.

The most recent kennel to be registered in New Zealand is the Skip a Skye affix owned by Debbie Coleman of Te Puke. Her first Skye Ch Ablie of Candilee (Remember the Eager Beava ex Ch Remember Chrismas Joy) was the result of a single litter bred by Mrs Newport in 1987. While being campaigned to his title Ablie won many groups from Puppy through to Open.

Ch Abile of Candilee.

Debbie Coleman's next Skye, a delightful puppy bitch, was imported from Australia. Named Woodrush Casino Capers (Wuruf Viva Las Vegas ex Wuruf Stormy Weather) she captured the heart of Debbie and her fiance, Tony Skipper, with her good looks and sound temperament. Casino Capers gained her title in April 1992. Now hooked on the breed they have recently imported Olivia Furiant (Ch Olivia American Dream ex Olivia Miss Universe) from America to introduce some new blood to the breed down under. After spending six months in Hawaii, four in quarantine and two in the home of a sponsor, Furiant made his arrival in New Zealand at the end of 1992 and settled in quickly. His owners hope to campaign him shortly.

Ch Woodrush Casino Capers.

Though not previously mentioned, the drop ear is also present in New Zealand. Judith Parks, an exhibitor on North Island, owns the beautiful drop ear, Skyeclan Bohemian Rhapsody.

During the 1980s several new fanciers took up the breed and there are now active breeders/exibitors on both islands for the first time in almost a century.

SOUTH ISLAND

Mrs Heather Wilson of South Otago on South Island bought Cumin of Radcliffe from Mr Price in 1972, campaigning her to her title in 1974. Having no available mate for her she turned to the Acheo kennel on the Isle of Skye for a suitable dog. Acheo Scottish Nationalist (Ch Acheo Olivia Whist ex Mo Cridhe Acheo) was imported by Mrs Wilson in 1974 and

Ch Skyeclan Bohemian Rhapsody.

quickly gained his title. The first litter for the Belvere affix, born in 1975, produced only two bitches; however, a second litter produced five pups, four dogs and one bitch.

In 1977 Mrs Jean Hartwell of Christchurch, South Island, imported Kirkleyditch Torrins Pride (Dracula's Luxy of Kirkleyditch ex Rhosneigr Silver Ronde) from Jill Bower in England. Pride gained her New Zealand championship and was joined by Gardony Skye Way (Ch Raldoris Milord Hamish ex Gardony Rebecca) from Australia in 1981, who also gained his New Zealand title. These two were the foundation pair for the Remember kennel and were later joined by Santlin Star Tremember, who also gained her title and produced Ch Remember Greyfrias Bobi and Ch Remember Honeybun by Ch Gardony Skye Way.

The Blackforth kennel belonging to Mrs Joan Stapleton of Canterbury is home to the Australian import, Ch Skyeclan Thunda Down Unda (Aust Ch Skyeclan Blu Suede Shu's ex Skyeclan Nite Moves) and Ch Remember Greyfrias Bobi.

Mrs Lyn Staig of Wakefield, well known for her Bel Ria Cairns, became equally famous with her Skyes. The imports Ch Skyeclan Great Pretender (Aust Ch Skyeclan Rio Speedwagon ex Aust Ch Santlin the Senterfold), Aust/NZ Ch Skyeclan Shake Discity (Aust/NZ Ch Santlin Stan N Deliva ex Aust Ch Santlin the Senterfold) and Skyeclan Lapo the Gods (Ch Skyeclan Great Pretender ex Skyepara Seventh Heaven) from Australia have all enjoyed some excellent placings.

Ch Skyeclan Shake Discity went Best in Group under the noted British Judge, Terry Thorn, at the National Show in 1989. Skyeclan Neva Endinstory (Skyeclan Nite Stalker ex Skyepara Seventh Heaven) and Ch Skyeclan Toucho Paradise (Aust Ch Skyeclan Blu Suede Shu's ex Aust Ch Skyeclan Standn Proud) complete this kennel of successful imports.

Mrs Staig was a great supporter of the breed and the Skye Terrier world in New Zealand was much saddened to hear of her death in August 1992. It is understood that her Skyes have gone back to the Skyeclan kennel in Australia.

Mrs D Lourie of Dunedin has enjoyed much success with her Ch Remember Honeybun.

With such a small population of Skyes split between two islands, show entries generally number less than ten. In 1989 thirteen Skyes appeared at the National Show, a record for New Zealand. Hopefully, given the present enthusiastic exhibitors, we will hear reports of higher entries in future.

Norway

The first Skye Terrier to be registered in Norway was imported from England by Mr Elias Kiær of Fredrikstad. Born in 1904, Skye was bred by Mr W Stechern, by Beau Lean out of Blacky. At the Norwegian Kennel Club Show in 1907 Skye won a first prize.

A few years later, in 1912, Punch was imported from Sweden, followed by Deborah from England. These two produced a litter of six puppies on 31 January 1915, the first recorded Skye litter in Norway. Deborah was shown and became a Norwegian Champion, as did one of her offspring, Whisky of Ulleberg, in 1918.

Many years passed before Skyes were seen again in Norway. Mrs Kristian Berg fell for the breed when she set eyes on one on a street in Berlin where she and her husband were living at the beginning of the 1930s. Mrs Berg discovered Frau Braunschweig, a breeder who was living in Berlin, and bought Jerry von Apenberg (Buster von Apenberg ex Gloria von Apenberg), who was born on 15 June 1932. "Ali Baba", as he was better known, was a great character.

When the Bergs returned to Norway in 1934 a Swedish diplomatic passport was procured for Ali Baba to travel to Sweden, where he was collected, as the laws regarding the import of dogs to Norway were very strict at that time. During the German occupation of Norway in the second World War Ali Baba showed his loyalty for his owners and adopted country by his dislike of the soldiers who patrolled outside the Bergs' house. If they hung their jackets over the gate he would pull them off, much to the annoyance of the troops.

Ali Baba enjoyed his freedom and disliked walking on the lead. Though he could walk perfectly well on a lead when no-one was about, the minute someone came into view he would sit and refuse to budge and had to be dragged along. This led to many rebukes from people who thought his owner was acting too harshly towards him. It is very sad to hear that in 1944 such a brave little dog, who had defended his house for so long, was run over and killed by the soldiers.

After the war Skyes were very hard to find but Mrs Lilli Arnesen managed to import two from Sweden, Tommy (Ch Boss of Merrymount ex Giggan) and Snorry (Mav av Tornø ex Mohva), who in 1947 produced a litter of six puppies. One of the pups, Peppy, was sold to Karin Scott whose Of Norskye affix is still very much to the fore today. A dog from the litter, Tomm, went to Mr Alfred Kristiansen of Oslo who, in 1949, imported Ego's Queen Bess (Ch Ego's Sonny Boy ex Ego's Jette) from Denmark.

Queen Bess gained her Norwegian title and in 1951 she and Tomm produced their first litter. Five years later another litter was bred, producing three bitches. One of these, whose name was Tusse, was bought by the Bergs. When Tusse died in 1986 the Bergs' daughter, Siri, bought Happyhill Joker (Ch Happyhill Hokey Cokey ex Happyhill Jemima Jane) from Miss Braham in England.

After Karin Scott lost Peppy she imported Maximillian (Ch Kirkby Mcmario ex Ch Witch) from Sweden, followed by Daisy of Skyeline (Nordic Ch Tarskavaig Royal Scot ex Nordic Ch Stella Jacqueline) from Mrs Westerholm in Finland. Both dog and bitch gained their Norwegian titles, Daisy going on to become an International and Nordic Champion. In December 1968 they produced a litter of four dogs and a bitch. Karin Scott kept the bitch, Peppy of Norskye, and campaigned her to her title.

Two dogs from the litter, Monty and Scotty of Norskye, were sold to Siri Berg. Scotty went on to gain his crown and to become the first Skye in Norway to win a Best in Show award, which he did at ten years of age under the British judge, Mary Blake. In 1974 Karin Scott imported Rosa Alba of Skyeline (Int and Nordic Ch Rhosneigr Silver Flash ex Int and Nordic Ch Merrymount Sun Myth) who became a Norwegian Champion.

Mr Eric Heckmann of Sarpsborg imported Bonnie of Skyeline (Int and Nordic Ch Rhosneigr Silver Flash ex Nordic Ch Forget Me Not of Skyeline) from Finland. In 1975 Bonnie was bred to Siri Berg's Scotty of Norskye, resulting in a litter of three.

Mr Fritz B Karlsson of Trondheim imported Amanda (Vagabond Scot of Skyeline ex Katinkullan Betty) and Ascot-Dream (Nordic Ch Zip of Skyeline ex White Rose of Skyeline) from Sweden in the early 1970s. They produced a litter of five in 1975, with one of the pups, Astra, going on to take Best Terrier at the Kennel Club's show in Mo i Rana on the Arctic Circle in 1976.

Ch Acheo Gavin Hastings.

At the beginning of the 1980s a number of Skyes were imported from Sweden. The bitch Apricot Brandy (Int Ch Silhill Silver Shadow ex Nordic Ch Skyelab Fiona) owned by the Hagens of Birkeland became a Norwegian champion, and Siri Berg imported Smarty (Skyelab Lord Nelson ex Amelie). Karin Scott imported Silverprint Cracklin Rose (Int Ch Pampas ex Nordic Ch Olivia Made in USA) from Mr Antonson's kennel in Sweden in 1985 and from Finland she imported Finnsky Kismet (Int and Nordic Ch Finnsky Fabian ex Int and Nordic Ch Finnsky Glacier). Both Skyes gained their Norwegian titles, Cracklin Rose going on to become an International Champion.

Acheo Gavin Hastings (Orasaidh an Gille Mor ex Ch Checkbar Jennifer Eccles) was imported from the Isle of Skye in 1986 by Siri Heyerdahl Jensen (formerly Berg) also gaining his title. A litter by Ch Gavin Hastings out of Cracklin Rose in 1989 resulted in two dogs and four bitches, with the two dogs doubling the Jensens' canine family to four, and the four bitches remaining with their breeder, Karin Scott. Evita and Sebastian of Norskye were shown first, quickly gaining their Norwegian crowns. At present Pia and Jonas of Norskye are being campaigned and have also added their titles with Pia winning some excellent Group placements. Ch Finnsky Ladystar, (Ch Finnsky Barracuda ex Finnsky Heartrose) was imported from Finland by Anita Stensheim of Svorkmo in 1987 and she, too, has her title.

Waiting for the boat: Skyes belonging to Sverre and Siri Hayerdahl Jensen.

Although the Skye has only a small Norwegian following compared to Sweden and Finland its admirers are very dedicated to the breed, and are doing their best to see that the Skye gets the recognition it deserves in the show ring in Norway.

POLAND

Waclaw Noskowski imported two Skyes in 1911, and bred a few litters until the outbreak of World War 2 when, as a result of the bombing, only two Skyes remained. The z Cieplic kennel belonging to Mrs Irena Zakubczyk began with a dog and a bitch, the survivors of Mr Noskowski's kennel. One was a cream male, Karamba, and the other was Tramp.

Ch Olivia Hermiona, Int Ch Orland z Cieplic, Ch Antares z Ceiplic and Acheo Mary Stuart.

In 1953 Bessy of Dirnhouse was imported from Austria, later producing the first litter for the kennel, sired by Tramp. From this litter Ali z Cieplic and Ali Baba z Cieplic were noted winners.

Ch Jukayama z Cieplic was the first champion for the kennel, followed in 1961 by the Czech import, Olivia Virginia (Olivia Superlativ ex Gaiety Girl de Luchar). A second Czech import, Olivia Hermiona (Ch Acheo Olivia Whist ex Int Ch Olivia Night Star) arrived in 1966 and gained her title quickly. In 1970 Acheo Mary Stuart (NZ Ch Acheo Scottish Nationalist ex Acheo Rosiebelle) was imported from the Isle of Skye. The kennel's best known Skye, Ch Antares z Cieplic (Ch Orland z Cieplic ex Pandora z Cieplic), a lovely cream, had a great show record.

Though little is known of current breeders in Poland, z Cieplic blood is in the pedigrees of most, if not all, including Ch Pegaz Night Star (Ch Orland z Cieplic ex Olivia Evergreen), a well known winner.

RUSSIA

The first Skyes imported into Russia came from Czechoslovakia in the late 1950s with Olivia Sonet (Elfe de Mandane ex Olivia Myosotis) and Olivia Tabu (Int Ch Olivia Jatagan ex Int Ch Olivia Night Star) imported by Dmitri Topcijev in Moscow; Olivia Triumph, bred the same way, was imported by a gentleman in Leningrad. Unfortunately this was an unsuccessful attempt to establish the breed in Russia as both these dogs became the victims of distemper.

The next attempt was, unfortunately, equally disappointing. The ballerina, Mrs Lepeshinskaya, imported a Merrymount Skye from England; this Skye also succumbed to this killer disease. However her next import, Olivia Undina (Int Ch Olivia Jatagan ex Ch Eike v Seehaus) from Czechoslovakia, and later, Guirey, a male from the Korosparti kennels in Hungary, fared better.

The Olivia kennels exported several good dogs to Russia: Olivia Antica, of the same parentage as Undina, and Olivia Bohem (Ch Acheo Oivia Whist ex Int Ch Olivia Night Star) went to Leningrad in 1964, Olivia Xix (Olivia Nonet ex Olivia Uracca) to Moscow in 1962, and the last of the Olivias from Czechoslovakia, Olivia Gemini (Int Ch Olivia Jatagan ex Gaiety Girl de Luchar), went to Mr Kurylev in Leningrad in 1966.

Mrs Chesnokova, a judge and a great Skye fancier, imported Olivia Encanta, a bitch of Jatagan and Night Star breeding, and Silver Atlas (Ch Olivia Rebel ex Olivia Allo) from Czechoslovakia in 1965, and this pair produced the first litter of Skyes to be born in Russia.

Tamesis Boston (imported from Czechoslovakia), Eta and Dr Nina Arsentyeva.

In 1967 Merrymount Sun Villa (Burmar Brig ex Merrymount Lovely Sunset) was imported from England by Mrs Kuzmina. Several more Skyes were imported from Czechoslovakia, Hungary, Poland and East Germany over the next few years to establish a small but enthusiastic band of devotees.

In 1988 Dr Nina Arsentieva imported Tamesis Boston (Fetisch v Silberblauen See ex Tamesis Apolena) from Dr Pavcik of Czechoslovakia. Dr Arsentieva is the owner of Eta, whose sire, John, and dam, Frezy, both go back to the Olivia strain. More recently a lovely puppy from the Arline kennel in Belgium, Arline's Sofia Briskova (Int Ch Brilliant Brisk of the Isle of Skye ex Arline's Cherokee Rose), joined Dr Arsentieva's home, but was another who fell victim to the scourge of distemper. However, she was replaced in 1992 by Arline's Yessica (Fine Fleur de Tanagra du Val de Saynons ex Arline's Fizgig

Flash) and it is hoped that the new blood will help to strengthen the breed. Mr Melknovitsky imported two bitches from East Germany, one of which, Bessy von Bobis Erbe, is out of Morningsky breeding.

During the years of communism several Skyes from East Germany were imported into Russia, including Cristina (from Siete Molinos and Canis Familiaris breeding) and Fredrika (Shadouk v Eisbach am Engl Garden ex Grazia v Silberblauen See).

Eta, owned by Dr Nina Arsentyeva.

At the World Show held in Brno, Czechoslovakia, in 1990 two Skyes from Russia were entered. At home in Russia sixteen Skyes appeared at the Moscow Spring Show in 1991. Records show a steady increase in the number of litters bred. In 1986 two litters were registered, one in 1987, four in 1989, and another four in 1991, which produced twenty-six puppies that year. Records also show that at present (ie 1993) there are seventeen Skyes in Moscow, seven in Irkutsk, six in Sverdlovsk, forty in St Petersburg, one in Saratov, one in Dnepropetrovski, two in Kiev and eight in the Baltic countries.

The top Skyes in Russia at present are Eney owned by Mr Ezov, Tamesis Boston owned by Dr Nina Arsentieva, Alisa-Ekka owned by Mrs Tatarenko, Bianita-Kris-Kros owned by Mrs Volkova, and Geraldina who was bred in Tallin, Estonia.

When the Russian Kennel Club is recognised by the FCI (Federation Cynologique Internationale) it will be possible for Russian breeders/exhibitors to show their dogs in Western countries such as Finland. There should also be the possibility of using stud dogs from other countries, thus opening a new chapter in the history of the Skye in Russia.

SOUTH AFRICA

In 1986 Dave and Pat McCann of the famous Whodeanie kennels in England emigrated to Natal in South Africa, taking with them several of their Skyes, including champions and well known winners.

Ch Whodeanie Fairisle, bred by Mr and Mrs D McCann and owned by Sarah Pringle.

They have continued their winning ways in South Africa, Ch Whodeanie Hopscotch and her brother Ch Whodeanie Sea Wolf (Int Ch Silhill Silver Shadow ex Ch Kirkleyditch Seanab of Whodeanie) both adding South African titles to their names, while Littlecreek Bridie (Ch Littlecreek Glengarry ex Littlecreek Gigha), well known in the British show ring, has gone on to win her South African title. It is understood that the McCanns, although they introduced the breed to South Africa, now only seldom breed or show.

One person who was particularly glad to hear of the McCanns arrival was Mrs Mel Hotz who years ago received a copy of *Skippy the Skye Terrier* as a school prize. After she had read the book it was Mel's wish to own a Skye one day, but no-one was breeding any in South Africa!

Twenty years later she bought Ch Whodeanie Kyleakin of Fairysaddle (Whodeanie Silver Sabre ex Ch Littlecreek Bridie of Whodeanie) from the McCanns, campaigning her to her title in Capetown. At the Terrier Club of Cape Town she was the first and only Skye ever shown! Mrs Hotz had her bitch spayed after gaining her title since, with only one other closely-related Skye in Cape Town, the prospect of finding a suitable mate was extremely remote.

SPAIN

Senor Sergi Montesinos' Sangonera kennel is best remembered for the lovely cream, Ch Noe de Sangonera (Ch Dracula's D'Artegnan ex Ch Dracula's Isolda), who was the winner of seventeen CACIBs, thirty-six CACs, four Best of Groups and thirty-six Best of Breed wins during the 1970s.

Senor Montesinos is a well respected judge who has judged the breed at championship Show level in Britain and officiated at the World Show held in Valencia, Spain in 1992.

Sweden

The first known Skye in Sweden was imported by Mr Karrberg who exhibited Jack, bred by Mr Christensen, at the Gothenburg Show in 1891. The same gentleman imported Micy from Scotland in 1897 and bred a number of good specimens. In 1911 Mr Karrberg imported Master of St Austell and Silver Rex, the former siring several champions, including Polly To Åre and Ch Bissi To Åre. The latter two were bred by Mr T Marcus of the To Åre affix before the first World War. In the mid 1920s Mrs D Lagerroth of the Lambda affix imported Ch The Cuttie (Para Handy ex Bannock Maid) and Ch Tommy (Chappie ex Mary) from Scotland.

Mrs Mary Stephens with some av Tornö Skyes.

Mrs Mary Stevens of the av Tornö kennel imported from England Ch Bob of Peacehaven (Ch Jonathan of Peacehaven ex Judykins) and Ch Mac of Merrymount (Lorne ex June), both of whom went on to win their titles. Mrs Stevens had a very impressive kennel of Skyes and produced many champions at her home during more than forty years of breeding and showing, up to the end of the 1970s. She also helped to save the true Swedish Lapphund from losing its identity during the 1940s, and was a great enthusiast of this native Spitz breed.

During the 1930s Mrs Mary Heilborn of the Miramar affix became involved with Skyes most successfully. One of her breeding, Ch Miramar Fluffy (Miramar Jimmy ex Ch Isadora Lambda), was owned by Princess Sibylla of Sweden. Not only was Fluffy a big winner at shows but her royal connection attracted a great deal of publicity for the breed.

By the 1950s interest in the Skye had waned somewhat though Mrs Stevens continued to keep the breed going. However in 1960 Mrs Annhild Düselius and her husband returned to Sweden from South Africa where they had spent the previous ten years. They brought with them two home bred Skyes, Basta and Baudouin (Patachou ex Sussi (Bambola). Their sire, Patachou, a black male, had been found by an American doctor amongst the rubble in Germany at the end of the war.

Mrs Düselius managed to register both her males with the Swedish Kennel Club. Basta, a born showman, easily gained his title and won Best in Show at the National Terrier Show in 1962. Mrs Düselius always kept two males who lived together without animosity and, in fact, were great ambassadors for the breed. Her last big winner, Int and Nordic Ch Brabant (Ch Prince of Skyeline ex Aniitta), was Reserve Best in Show at Falun International Show in 1974.

Several new exhibitors became involved with Skyes in the 1970s. Mrs Rose Envall of the Skyelab kennels attracted a lot of interest with the Skyes she imported from Finland from her close friend, Mrs Westerholm, of the famous Skyeline kennel. A few were co-owned with Mrs Westerholm and enjoyed great success in both countries. Mrs Envall's Int and Nordic Ch Zip of Skyeline (Int and Nordic Ch Captain Scot of Skyeline ex Ch Merrymount Sun Myth), Ch Marguerite of Skyeline (Int Ch Silhill Sea Breeze ex Ch Hällebergets Carmen Chic), Int Ch Silhill Sea Breeze (Ch Acheo Sea Sprite ex Coruisk Moonshee) and Ch Silhill Sparky of Zapangu (Ch Rhosneigr Silver Ravissant ex Marjayn Melissa) all had great careers.

Home bred Ch Skyelab Davy Crockett (Int Ch Zip of Skyeline ex Int Ch Yesterday of Skyeline), Ch Skyelab Ivory (Int Ch Zip of Skyeline ex Ch Marguerite of Skyeline), Ch Skyelab Countess Mary (Int Ch Zip of Skyeline ex White Rose of Skyeline) and the big winner, Int and Nordic Ch Skyelab Ginger Ale (Int Ch Silhill Sea Breeze ex White Rose of Skyeline) all ensured that the Skye had to be noticed in the show ring and attracted new exhibitors to the breed.

Mr and Mrs Swenson also began their association with the Skye with stock from the Skyeline kennel, acquiring Ch Zanta of Skyeline (Ch Rhosneigr Silver Flash ex Int Ch Heavenly of Skyeline) who gained her Swedish title and was later bred to Ch Brabant, producing nine champions in all. The Swensons then bought the outstanding Opulous of Skyeline (Ch Silhill Sea Breeze ex Ch Vogue of Skyeline) who quickly gained his Int and Nordic Champion titles.

This remarkable dog had a wonderful show career in Sweden with many group placings and a show record which is unrivalled. He was also an outstanding sire with many excellent offspring inheriting his quality. The Swensons' home bred champions include Ch Biskyea Kismet, Ch Bugatti Klaxon, Ch Bimbola Korina and Ch Bellman Kvick, all sired by Int and Nordic Ch Brabant ex Xanta of Skyeline.

Lennart Olanders' first Skye came from Mary Stevens' Av Törnö kennel, which contained some French blood from the Chamardière kennel. Mr Olander bred some very good Skyes, notably Ch Godsend Grace (Ch Merry Musketeer of Skyeline ex Ch Chinook), Ch Ivanhoe (Ch Merry Musketeer of Skyeline ex Chamsin) and the beautiful sisters, Ch Bizett Lee and Int and Nordic Ch Bonna Lucia (Int and Nordic Ch Brabant ex Godsend Grace) who were both big winners in the 1970s.

Peter and Barbro Rugerup of the Fairsky affix went to Rose Envall for their first Skye in 1973. They had great success in the 1970s with their drop ear, Ch Skyelab Bonaparte (Ch Jake ex Ch Forget Me Not of Skyeline), and then in 1975 they bought Rowers Lurifax (Ch Dackie ex Ch Hällebergets Clair), a black dog whose influence is behind all subsequent winners from the Fairsky kennels. From Finland they imported the black bitch, Ch Hällebergets Eliza (Ch Ficus of Skyeline ex Ch Hällebergets An Emy) who was successfully campaigned with Ch Bizett Lee.

In 1983 Ch Finnsky Galaxy (Ch Rowers Lurifax ex Ch Finnsky Dianah), who is co-owned with the Dahlboms, came to join the Rugerups and has been a consistent winner, including Best of Breed at the Swedish Kennel Club Centenary Show in Stockholm in 1989 among his credits.

The Rugerups also own the beautiful drop ear Int and Nordic Ch Locomotions Good Lollipop (Ch Rowers Lurifax ex Ch Disco Mayfair). Now a veteran, this lovely bitch continues to win well, with Best of Breed, Best Opposite Sex and placings in Veteran groups during 1992. Her three litters produced a total of twenty-seven pups, or which seven are champions, another four being Challenge Certificate winners though not yet old enough to qualify for their titles.

Ch Locomotions
Good Lollipop.

Ch Fairsky's Engel In My Heart and Fairsky's Evening Star.

Ch Fairsky's Famos Symphony (Int Ch Rannoch Skye Superstar ex Int Ch Locomotions Good Lollipop) has been a big winner, with ten Best of Breed awards, Best in Show once and Reserve Best in Show at the National Terrier Show in Eskiletuna. Also from this litter, Ch Fairsky's Follow Someone has two Group placements, and Ch Fairsky Flash of Summer and Ch Fairsky's Fantasy of Song have also gained their titles.

Mrs Gull Britt Frick's Rower kennel began with a bitch from Poland, Samantha z Cieplic (Antares z Cieplic ex Olivia Hermione). Samantha and her brother, Skald, were brought from Poland by their owners who left for political reasons. They found they could not afford to pay the quarantine fees and the dogs had to be sold by auction. Mrs Frick then bought from Finland Ch Hällebergets Flipper Japp (Ch Rhosneigr Silver Flash ex Ch Baby of Skyeline).

The Rower affix produced several champions including Ch Rowers Lurifax, Ch Rowers Superman and Ch Baby Scarlett, Ch Rowers Pilla and the well known bitch, Rowers True Love (Int and Nordic Ch Silverprint Pampas ex Ch Rowers Pilla), who would surely have gained her title but for a broken leg which ended her show career.

Anita Sperry bought her first Skyes from Mrs Frick and had great success with Ch Rowers Pilla (Rowers Martin ex Ch Hällebergets Clair). In 1980 she imported from Germany the beautiful Ch Florian of Morningsky (Int Ch Olivia Silver Solo ex Int Ch Alpha of Morningsky). This dog was a very big winner in Sweden with many Group placings. He won the Terrier Group at the Malmö International Show and continued to win right through to his veteran years when he was a consistent winner of veterans stakes and won the Champion of Champions title in the late 1980s, handled by his friend Svend Lövenkjaer.

In 1984 Anita Sperry looked to the Isle of Skye for a suitable mate for Florian, importing Ch Acheo Alice Springs (Acheo Bla Bheinn ex Acheo Inverie). Alice had been the top winning Skye bitch in Britain in 1984 and went on to win her International title in Sweden, winning Reserve Best in Show at Visby under noted judge, Ulla Segerström. From their first litter Alice and Florian produced Ch Fax, Int Ch Fantoman and Ch Flora Bell. Their second litter produced Ch Fleur de Lis and the drop ear Ch Floriando. In 1990 Anita Sperry went to live in America, and Alice Springs and Florian now live in Denmark.

Karl-Åke Antonson came into Skyes in 1974, though his involvement in dogs goes back many years, as he grew up with Hamiltonstovares and Fox Terriers, and always showed a lively interest in other breeds. In the 1960s he owned a Griffon Bruxellois which he used to show, then an Afghan Hound from the famous El Khyria kennel, though she was not to be a great star. In the early 1970s, while handling an Australian Silky Terrier, he met Mrs Düselius with her well known dogs, Ch Brabant and the cream drop ear, Ch Viceroy of Skyeline, and became enamoured of the breed.

He bought his first Skye in 1974, Ch Bimbola Korina (Int and Nordic Ch Brabant ex Xanta of Skyeline), who was joined the following year by Ch Koriander of Skyeline (Ch Zip of Skyeline ex Ch Tarskavaig Mary Morrison). Ch Koriander of Skyeling went on to gain his Swedish and Norwegian titles but was never used for breeding. Ch Bimbola Korina was bred first to Int Ch Florian of Morningsky, producing Ch Peppermint, who won her Swedish and Norwegian titles before being exported to America, where she took ten points towards her title. Korina was then bred to the great Ch Opulous of Skyeline, giving Mr Antonson the equally outstanding Int and Nordic Ch Pampas who was a huge winner in his day.

Ch Olivia Made in USA (Ch Olivia Nimrod ex Ch Skye Ark Princess Olga) joined the kennel in 1980 and gained her International and Nordic titles. She was twice bred to Pampas, producing, all told, Ch Silverprint Beetle, Ch Silverprint Boccaccio, Ch Silverprint Bittersweet, Ch Silverprint Crack the Sky and Ch Silverprint Cracklin Rose in Norway. In 1988 Mr Antonson moved to a larger property, so was able to expand his kennel to include the drop ear, Ch Floriando, his prick ear sister, Ch Fleur De Lis, and the silver bitch, Ch Skyeotts Clair Ice Crystal, all of whom have gone on to win their championships.

Ch Silverprint Beetle was first bred to Ch Silverprint Bocaccio, producing Ch Silverprint Dancing Shadow. She was then bred to Ch Floriando, producing Ch Silverprint Extra Edition, a drop ear, and his prick ear sister Ch Silverprint Easy Choice. A repeat mating in 1990 resulted in another drop ear, Silverprint Goodfellow at Esgia, who was exported to Scotland in 1991 to the Esgia kennels. After spending the mandatory six months in quarantine Goodfellow has begun his first year in the show ring and has already won two Reserve Challenge Certificates.

Ch Silverprint Beetle.

Acheo John Jeffrey (Ch Elissa's Alexander ex Acheo Houghmagandie) was imported from the Isle of Skye in 1991. The latest star of the Silverprint kennel is from the cream brother/sister mating, Skyedoor's Hot News at Silverprint (Fairsky's Fabel of Snowman ex Fairsky's Fergie Lady Sara), one of the most recent champions in the breed.

Fairsky's Fabel of Snowman.

Doris Eriksson began her involvement with the breed in 1979 with Ch Rowers Superman (Ch Otis Reding ex Ch Baby Scarlett) followed by Rowers True Love (Int and Nordic Ch Silverprint Pampas ex Ch Rowers Pilla), who both enjoyed success in the ring before a broken leg prematurely ended True Love's show career. The first litter born in the Skyeotts kennel in 1983 was from Superman and True Love. From three litters their seventeen offspring produced ten champions, including: Int and Nordic Ch Skyeotts Aisha and Ch Skyeotts Attila from the first litter; Int Ch Skyeotts Belladonna Morningstar and Ch Bellami Blue Sky from the second litter; and Ch Skyeotts Clair Ice Crystal, Ch Skyeotts Candy Sweet Caramel, Ch Skyeotts Cognac Ice Gold, Ch Skyeotts Felix Rex and Ch Skyeotts Countess Silver Cloud from the third litter.

Int and Nordic Ch Skyeotts Belladonna Morning Star, bred by Doris Eriksson and owned by Britt Westin.

Ch Blue Air Earl.

The next champion the kennel produced was the dog, Ch Skyeotts Diabol Deep Love, followed most recently by Ch Skyeotts Flake of Snowball. At the time of writing there are some promising puppies out of Ch Silverprint Dancing Shadow by Int and Nordic Ch Skyeotts Arroy.

Newest additions to the Skye fraternity are Frida Arnadottir with her Skyedoor kennels established with Fairsky stock. Her Skyedoor's Hot News at Silverprint, owned by Mr Antonson, is one of the latest champions in the breed.

Britt Westin owns Ch Skyeotts Belladonna Morningstar and recently imported from England Arym It's a Knockout (Ch Balquhatston Ghostbuster of Arym ex Acheo Flower of Scots at Arym). Mrs Westin's first litter of Superskyes by Norwegian Ch Acheo Gavin Hastings to Ch Skyeotts Belladonna Morningstar produced just two pups. A second litter by Arym It's a Knockout produced a bigger litter...three!

The latest registrations in Sweden show an increase in the breed. With only one registration in 1984, twenty-two in 1989 and thirty-three in 1990 the future of the breed in this lovely country looks quite encouraging.

Margaret Tainsh with Silverprint Fergus and Silverprint Great Scot.

S WITZERLAND

From 1910 Skyes have been found in Switzerland, Herr Mayer beginning a breeding kennel in 1911, followed by Frau Auer's successful Zurichberg line in 1919. Moritz v Zurichberg was one of the well known winners bred by Frau Auer.

In the 1940s, after many years in the breed, Frau Auer retired from active breeding and passed her line to Liselott Steinemann who, for a short period, continued to breed Zurichberg Skyes. One such, Anthony v Zurichberg, was owned by the Empress Soraya of Persia.

Frau Cardis' de la Chablière kennel, Frau Rambert's Rambert kennel, Frau Noetzli's Kyburg, Frau Thomas' Forest Hill and Frau Meyer-Gegauf's Von Neuen Schloss kennels were all noted for good stock, the last of these producing Ch Sambo v Neuen Schloss, winner of seven CACIBs, and Wilma v Neuen Schloss (by Sambo), another big winner. Frau Schreiber's Dimgod kennel was started in 1940 with Netti Dimgod (Uli v Neuen Schloss ex Cilla Dimgod) going to Olga Smidova in Czechoslovakia to help found the Olivia kennel.

The Orkney kennel owned by Frau Suter bred some excellent stock during the 1940s, and were well known in Europe. Frau Sylvia Kung's San Rocco kennel was established with imports from Germany and England. The German bitch, Utta v d Schnick (Furst v Orplid and Tilly v Juraland) with Merrymount Knight Errant (Merrymount Sunspot ex Merrymount Desire) and Merrymount Wot a Day (Ch Merrymount Wot No Sun ex Ch Bettina of the Mynd) were her foundation stock.

Frau Schlapfer established her Von Paradiesheim kennel on German and Czech bloodlines with Olivia Lyric (Int Ch Jack v Bary ex Ch Olivia Zinien) imported in 1968 at the time of the invasion of Czechoslovakia.

Frau Sylvia May's v Seehaus kennel imported the well known Ch Bettine of the Mynd (Punch of the Mynd ex Zerlina of the Mynd) in whelp to Ch Merrymount Wot No Sun from England in 1958. Two champions were produced from the litter, Edda and Eike v Seehaus. Bettine was campaigned after her litter and went on to become an International Champion. Later American import Int Ch Skyecrest Sir Dyce (Ch Agonistes Ashley v Skyecrest ex Skyecrest Lady Sheena) joined the kennel.

Merrymount Sweetheart and Merrymount High and Mighty were imported in 1965 by Frau Schmidheiny. They later produced a litter of which two, Fluffy and Kiltie of Garengo, were kept. During the 1980s Frau Elspeth Clerc of the famous Scottish and West Highland White Terrier kennels, having admired the Olivia Skyes for many years, decided to add the Skye breed to her clan. She imported from America Olivia Vamp (Ch Olivia Nimrod ex Ch Skye

Ark Princess Olga), a beautiful cream, who quickly won top honours all over Europe and gained her International Championship as well as many Group wins and Best in Show awards.

Vamp has turned out to be an excellent brood bitch with champion offspring from her litters to Ch Olivia American Dream. From her first litter she produced Ch Rannoch Skye Olivia, and Ch Rannoch Skye Surprise and Ch Rannoch Skye Superstar in Finland. Superstar is very aptly named as he has won top honours all over Europe, including World Champion in Brno in 1990, many Group wins and a Best in Show award in Finland where he also won the Contest of Champions.

Int Ch Rannoch Champagne, br by Mrs Elspeth C

From the second litter Vamp produced American Ch Rannoch Skye Chummie and Ch Rannoch Skye Champagne, who has been a consistent winner in Europe, including among her honours a Best in Show in Austria. In 1991 Champagne was bred with the Finnish dog, Int Ch Finnsky Manfred Man, producing some lovely puppies due to be campaigned in 1992. Ch Rannoch Skye Alison and Ch Rannoch Skye Agatha gained their titles quickly, emphasising the excellence one expects from this breeding. The latest young stars to shine are Olivia Instant W'Dream (Ch Silverspun Sundancer ex Ch Rannoch Skye Olivia) and Rannoch Skye Swiss Account (Int Ch Finnsky Manfred Man ex Ch Rannoch Skye Champagne).

Verena Stockli imported the bitch Olivia Windy Oklahoma (Ch Olivia Vino Veritas ex Ch Olivia Thanks for Memories) from America, and the dog Aye I'm First du Petit Tanagra (Int Ch Olivia Xplosion ex Tilleul Menthe du Petit Tanagra) and bitch Caramelita du Petit Tanagra (Int Ch Olivia Xplosion ex Upsilon du Petit Tanagra) from France in 1982.

She bred her first litter in 1986 by Aye I'm First out of Windy Oklahoma, producing Int Ch Adhara Alban's Loyce A'Lanna. A later litter in 1988 produced Int Ch Adhara Alban's Victor (Aye I'm First du Petit Tanagra ex Caramelita du Petit Tanagra), a consistent winner whose best win to date was Best of Breed under the famous Skye specialist, Walter Goodman, at the Belgian Terrier Show in 1991.

Ch Adhara Alban's Victor is owned by Anthoine Veillon. He also owns the bitch Forever Night du Val de Saynans (Aristocratique du Petit Tanagra ex A'Julie) who is currently doing well in the European shows.

In 1957 Adela Straubert of Zagreb imported some Olivia stock from Czechoslovakia, including Int Ch Olivia Mimosa (Merrymount Gold Digger ex Olivia Hallo) who was the winner of CACIBs in Yugoslavia, Italy and Austria.

Adelia Skyes were exported to Germany and Italy, and one, Adelia Sweetheart (Olivia Rigoletto ex Ch Olivia Mimosa), was exported to the Talisker kennels in Canada.

The Skyes from Adelia were not only prize winners in the show ring but also gained honours in their Hunting Examinations.

skye
207
terrier

Memorabilia

Once you own a Skye Terrier and perhaps become involved with showing, obedience work or agility competitions you realise that you own a rather special breed. There will be times when you are asked whether it is a draught excluder or what kind of crossbreed it is! Don't be disheartened as these people are clearly to be pitied for not having the good sense to own a dog as devoted and individual as yours. It becomes a habit when browsing in bookshops to look for references to the Skye Terrier. Sadly there are very few available books on the breed and the lack of reading material may lead you to browse through antique fairs where an occasional find will emerge. Should this happen you will suddenly find you have acquired a new hobby and the search will be on for cigarette cards, old prints or even oil paintings to satisfy your need for Skye memorabilia.

Skye Terrier models are more readily available and can be found at many of the championship shows. Antique models are eagerly sought and therefore are difficult to find, but occasionally bargains can be found at craft fairs so they are worth a visit. As you start collecting prints and paintings the need to search for a bigger house where you can display your treasures becomes a serious consideration! You will either have to devise a rota so all your collection spends some time on the wall or you will end up with a box full of prints waiting to be framed. Serious will power is needed when confronted with yet another new print or goes by the board if something painted by George Earl, Maud Earl, Arthur Wardle or Lilian Cheviot becomes available as these are greatly valued. In such cases you have acquired a sound investment and should take great care to insure your work of art.

To help you on your road to ruin, a list of books containing references to the Skye Terrier is given here. Some of these are available, and others may be found through the services of a book searcher.

1. The Skye Terrier Stud Book.
   Available from the Hon Secretary of The Skye Terrier Club. Some back copies are still available.

2. The Skye Terrier.
   Anna Katherine Nicholas, 1960.

3. The Complete Skye Terrier.
   Dr E S Montgomery, 1962.

4. How to Raise and Train a Skye Terrier.
   Seymour N Weiss, 1964.

5. This is the Skye Terrier.
   Joan McDonald Brearly and Anna Katherine Nicholas, 1975.

6. Our Friends the Dandie Dinmont and the Skye Terrier.
   Rowland Johns, 1938.

7. Greyfriars Bobby.
   Eleanor Atkinson, 1929.

8. The Story of Greyfriars Bobby.
   Forbes MacGregor, 1980.

9. Skippy, the Little Skye Terrier.
   Dorothy K L'Hommedieu, 1957.

10. Oscar, a Skye Terrier's Adventures.
    Lachlan MacLean Watt.

11. The Last of The Eccentrics: a life of Rosslyn Bruce.
    Verily Anderson, 1972.

12. Buffles, Story of a Dog.
    A L.

Books Of General Interest;

1. The Book of the Dog.
Vero Shaw.

2. The Dog Family.
Rev J G Wood, 1885.

3. The Dogs of the British Isles.
Stonehenge, 1886.

4. Our Friend the Dog.
Gordon Stables.

5. The Complete Book of the Dog.
Robert Leighton.

6. Dogs: their Points, Whims, Instincts and Peculiarities.
Henry Webb.

7. Hutchisons's Encyclopaedia.

8. Everyman's Book of the Dog.
A Croxton-Smith.

9. Memories and Portraits.
R L Stevenson 1917.

10. Wild Sports.
Charles St John, 1919.

11. The Scottish Dog.
Joyce and Maurice Lindsay, 1989.

12. Dog Tales.
Jean and Frank Jackson.

13. The Dog in Art .
Robert Rosenblum.

14. The Kennel Club's Illustrated Breed Standards.

Reference Books;

1. Doglopaedia.
(A Complete Guide To Dog Care)
J M Evans and Kay White.

2. Dog Problems (The Gentle Modern Cure)
Weston.

3. Book of the Bitch.
J M Evans and Kay White.

4. Dogs: Homoeopathic Remedies.
G MacLeod.

5. Natural Health for Dogs and Cats.
Richard and Susan Pitcairn.

6. Atlas of Dog Breeds of the World. 4th ed.
Bonnie Wilcox and Chris Walkowicz, 1993.

7. Canine Lexicon.
Andrew de Prisco and James B Johnson, 1993.

Clubs

The Kennel Club is the governing body on all matters pertaining to pedigree dogs in Britain. No dog can be exhibited unless it is registered at the Kennel Club, and all dogs which are to be exported need an export pedigree from the Kennel Club before registration can proceed in another country.

The Kennel Club may mete out disciplinary measures to anyone who breaks the rules regarding the care and showing of dogs by disqualification or a ban from breeding and exhibiting according to the severity of the case.

Each year the Kennel Club runs the famous Crufts Dog Show, the only show in the United Kingdom for which dogs have to qualify for entry by winning at other championship shows during the preceding year. All the dogs are competing for first prizes in their class, then for the best dog and best bitch, next for Best of Breed and ultimately for the triumphal Best in Show.

Information concerning the rules and regulations of dog shows, and for directions on where to find a breeder with puppies for sale the address is:

The Kennel Club
1-5 Clarges Street
Piccadilly
London W1Y 8AB

Very few countries have their own Skye Terrier Club but it is possible for anyone to join the parent club in Britain, provided the applicant is proposed and seconded by members and passed by the committee. The club welcomes overseas members who will receive a quarterly newsletter and can keep up to date with British exhibitors by having show results mailed to them. For further information please write to:

Mrs Mary Watts, Hon. Secretary
The Skye Terrier Club
Lilybank
Westfield
Ossett, Yorkshire

Tel: 01924 270386

In 1976 the Scottish branch of the Skye Terrier Club was formed. The Scottish branch holds several fund raising events each year to support Skye classes throughout Scotland. Their fund raising also helps to subsidise the Championship Show held on the Isle of Skye every five years. For further information please write to:

Mrs Margaret Macdonald-Cross, Hon Secretary
Scottish Branch of the
Skye Terrier Club
Fairways
Bankhead Road
Bellshill, Lanarkshire

Tel: 01698 745697

The Skye Terrier Club of Ireland which was started in 1976 is still in existence according to the Irish Kennel Club, but unfortunately it appears that interest in the breed in Ireland is very low at the present time.

The club in America is very well supported and publishes a quarterly Bulletin giving show results, notice of litters and details of champions. Many attractive advertisements are included, and also special features on health and breed rescue organisations making altogether an excellent quarterly magazine. For further information please contact:

Karen L Sanders, Hon Secretary
The Skye Terrier Club of America
11567 Sutters Mill Circle
Gold River
California 95670
USA

Tel: (916) 631-8716

The Skye Terrier Club of Finland was founded in 1970. Originally registered as The Skye Terrier Club of Scandinavia the club was supported by members in Norway, Sweden and Finland. In 1979 Sweden formed its own club and The Skye Terrier Club of Finland was established.

There are 300 members in the Finnish club, a remarkable achievement considering the small number of breeders in Finland. Breeders pay the membership fee of all new puppy owners for the first year. The club arranges matches, lectures and camps, and also publishes a newsletter four times a year which is full of information and pictures to encourage pet and show owners alike to participate in its production. For more information please write to:

Eija Kuusela
Ahveneva 4 C 26
02170 Espoo
Finland

Tel: 90 424 553

Canine Terms And Their Meaning

BRITAIN:

CC	Challenge Certificate
BOB	Best Of Breed
RCC	Reserve Challenge Certificate
BIG	Best In Group
BIS	Best In Show
JW	Junior Warrant
Ch	Champion
STC	Skye Terrier Club
KC	Kennel Club
SKC	Scottish Kennel Club
WKC	Welsh Kennel Club
IKC	Irish Kennel Club

EUROPE and SCANDINAVIA:

Fr Ch	French Champion
NL Ch	Netherlands Champion
It Ch	Italian Champion
SF Ch	Finnish Champion
S Ch	Swedish Champion
DK Ch	Danish Champion
Nord Ch	Nordic Champion (dog with CCs from Sweden, Norway, and/or Finland).
CAC	Challenge Certificate
CACIB	International Challenge Certificate
FCI	Federation Cynologique Internationale

UNITED STATES OF AMERICA

To own a champion in America the dog must win a total of fifteen points which must include two majors which start at three points, and go up to five at a Specialty, provided two of his majors were won under two different judges. As the breed is so widely scattered across the USA the usual entry at shows numbers less than ten, therefore the win at a Specialty (Breed Club Show) will greatly enhance the chances of winning the dog's title.

WD   Winners Dog

WB   Winners Bitch

BOW   Best of Winners

Group 1   Best of Group

STCA   Skye Terrier Club of America

AKC   American Kennel Club

CD   Companion Dog

CDX   Companion Dog Excellent

UD   Utility Dog

TD   Tracking Dog

UDT   Utility and Tracking Dog

Index

Key to abbreviations:

A:	Austria	AUS:	Australia	B:	Belgiium	CAN:	Canada
CZ:	Czechoslovakia	D:	Germany	DK:	Denmark	ENG:	England
GB:	Great Britain	H:	Hungary	HK:	Hongkong	I:	Italy
LUX:	Luxembourg	N:	Norway	NL:	Netherlands	NZ:	New Zealand
R:	Russia	RSA:	South Africa	S:	Sweden	STH AM:	South America
SF:	Finland	USA:	United States of America	YUG:	Yugoslavia		

CH: Switzerland
F: France
J: Japan
POL: Poland
SCO: Scotland